45560

JK
271    BUTLER
.B75    Is America worth saving?
1972

# IS AMERICA WORTH
# SAVING?

## ADDRESSES ON NATIONAL PROBLEMS
## AND PARTY POLICIES

# IS AMERICA WORTH SAVING?

## ADDRESSES ON NATIONAL PROBLEMS
### AND PARTY POLICIES

**BY**

NICHOLAS MURRAY BUTLER, 1862 - 1947.

*Essay Index Reprint Series*

## BOOKS FOR LIBRARIES PRESS
### FREEPORT, NEW YORK

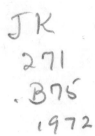
First Published 1920
Reprinted 1972

Library of Congress Cataloging in Publication Data

Butler, Nicholas Murray, 1862-1947.
    Is America worth saving? Addresses on national problems and
party politics, by Nicholas Murray Butler. ③ Freeport, N.Y., Books for Libraries Pr. ⤷ 1972 ⟶    xiii, 399 p.   22 cm. ③
    (Essay index reprint series)
    Reprint of the 1920 ed.
    CONTENTS:  Is America worth saving?--The founda-
tions of prosperity.--A programme of constructive
progress.
    1.  U. S.--Politics and government--Addresses,
essays, lectures.  2.  U. S.--Economic conditions
--1918-1945--Addresses, essays, lectures.  3.  Education, Higher--U. S.--Addresses, essays, lectures.
I.  Title.
JK271.B75  1972          309.1'73          76-37772
ISBN 0-8369-2583-1

PRINTED IN THE UNITED STATES OF AMERICA
BY
NEW WORLD BOOK MANUFACTURING CO., INC.
HALLANDALE, FLORIDA 33009

TO ALL THOSE AMERICANS WHO HAVE CLEAR
KNOWLEDGE OF THE PRINCIPLES ON WHICH
THE GOVERNMENT OF THE UNITED STATES IS
BUILT, AND WHO HAVE FAITH IN THOSE IDEALS
OF CIVIL AND POLITICAL LIBERTY WHICH
THE FATHERS CONCEIVED AND WHICH TRUE
AMERICANS AIM TO CHERISH AND TO FOLLOW

# CONTENTS

## ON PUBLIC OCCASIONS

## ON EDUCATION

# INTRODUCTION

These addresses have a common theme and a single purpose. That theme is an exposition and interpretation of the fundamental principles upon which the American government and American civil society are built. That purpose is to make these principles more familiar to a generation that is quite apt to overlook them, and to enlist in their support and defense those who may be tempted to listen to the invitations of some among us who are either openly or covertly waging war on American principles of government and of social and industrial life. The Fathers would have been amazed at the notion that within a century and a half there would arise in America those who would find it easy and convenient either to deny or to attempt to explain away the underlying moral and political principles upon which America is based. To the Fathers, as to those who understand these principles, they were quite as clear and as certain as the multiplication table itself. Their application will, of course, alter with the changing years; but the principles themselves do not and can not alter unless civilization is to revert to the chaos out of which it came.

Every American, young or old, should be familiar with the Declaration of Independence, and should learn by heart the preamble to the Constitution of the United States. He should also, so soon as his age and maturity will permit, study the *Federalist*, which is the very Bible of our American form of government. He should know accurately the contents of Washington's Farewell Address, and he should be able to recite from memory Lincoln's Address at Gettysburg and his Second Inaugural.

There have been many and familiar formulations of underlying American principles. Perhaps none is better or more compact than that contained in the first section of the Bill of Rights of the Constitution of the State of Ohio, which reads:

"All men are by nature free and independent, and have certain inalienable rights, among which are those of enjoying and defending life and liberty, acquiring, possessing, and protecting property, and seeking and obtaining happiness and safety."

It is to be observed that these rights are not derived from the consent of society and are not the grant of any government. They are natural and inalienable. Their roots are to be found in human personality, and their basis is therefore a moral one. What American civilization is striving to do is to give moral persons full opportunity for their own most complete development and expression. For this fundamental reason America cannot tolerate the notion of fixed or definite

economic classes, that have conflicting interests. To
that notion it opposes the ideal of one big union of
men and women whose groupings, however important
or however continuous, are wholly subordinate to
their equality in respect to opportunity and in obedience to law.

Moreover, it is American doctrine that property
is an essential element of liberty. The fruits of a man's
own labor whether manual or mental are his own, to
hold and to dispose of as he may see fit, subject only
to the equal right of every other man to do the same.
This is America's answer to all fantastic schemes of
communism that would limit or destroy private
property because of the inequalities that naturally
and necessarily exist between individuals. No form
of communism is consonant with American principles
or with an ethical system that recognizes personality
as its corner-stone.

It is American doctrine, sustained by uniform American experience, that the best results are obtained for
society as a whole when individuals are given large
opportunity for self-expression, for initiative, and
for inventiveness, and when they are trained and taught
to use their individual powers in the service of their
nation and of their kind. In other words, social service as a result of individual competence and individual
conviction is truly American, while social service as
a result of compulsion or of restraint upon individual
capacity is un-American.

American principles and their application present themselves from many points of view, and a number of these are discussed in the following pages. These principles may be illustrated by experience and by the facts of their practical application. They may be illuminated by history, and by reference to the conditions out of which they came. They may be urged, and their application in particular cases suggested, as the duty and the opportunity of a political party. They may be made familiar by reference to the life-history of some of their great exemplars, and they may be insisted upon as the special objects of education and instruction in the schools.

A very real difficulty in the way of the quick acceptance of these fundamental principles as the one key to the solution of our present-day political, economic and social problems, is their extreme simplicity. To some minds it seems quite impossible that the cure for the diseases from which we now suffer can possibly be so matter-of-fact and so near at hand. A generation that has been addicted to the use of political and economic patent-medicines of every kind, each of which was to be a panacea, finds it hard to accept the advice that all we need to protect our national health is to take regular exercise in the open air of sound and well-tested principle. Yet this is the fact.

The addresses here brought together were originally delivered in many different parts of the United States. If a reading and discussion of them shall advance in

any degree a more complete understanding of the
meaning of America, and a fuller devotion to its ideals,
they will have done their work.

NICHOLAS MURRAY BUTLER

COLUMBIA UNIVERSITY
   IN THE CITY OF NEW YORK
      February 22, 1920

# I

## IS AMERICA WORTH SAVING?

### A REPUBLIC OR A SOCIALIST AUTOCRACY?

An address delivered before the Commercial Club,
Cincinnati, Ohio, April 19, 1919

# IS AMERICA WORTH SAVING?

## A REPUBLIC OR A SOCIALIST AUTOCRACY?

We are living in the greatest days that the modern world has seen. Our customary habits of thought and our ordinary personal and local interests have been pushed into the background by great events that have justly absorbed the attention of the entire civilized world. Old forms of government that have existed for fifteen hundred years have tumbled down in ruins before our eyes. Ruling dynasties which traced back their origin to Charlemagne have been driven from the places of power and authority that they have occupied for centuries. New nations are being born in our very presence, and peoples who cannot remember the time when they have not been held in bondage by an alien military power are standing erect and making ready to march forward to take their independent place in the family of free nations. There is turbulence not only in the world of events, but in the world of ideas. Loud and angry voices are raised on every hand, urging the overthrow of the foundations of society and of the marvellous civilization which it has taken three thousand years to build. Destruction is the order of the day. Crude thinking accompanies unconsidered and hysterical action. Force, either military, economic, or political, and not reasonableness or justice, is everywhere appealed to as the arbiter of differences. It is probable that the world is now further removed from peace and order than it was on November 11 last when hostilities ceased. In this orgy of crooked thinking and false use of language, words are twisted from their accustomed meanings and are used to mislead the public through being given wrong significations. It is the fashion to describe a Doctrinaire as an Idealist; to call a Liberal a Tory; and to steal the splendid term Liberal to cover the nakedness of the Revolutionist. It is high time to attempt to dissipate the fog in which we are living and to get back to first principles and to straight thinking along the lines of hard and practical common sense and human experience.

Nothing in the whole history of these last momentous years can have made more direct and more touching appeal to the imagination of an American than what happened a few months ago at Independence Hall in Philadelphia. In that simple and dignified room where the Continental Congress met, where George Washington was chosen commander-in-chief of the Continental army, and where the Declaration of Independence and the Constitution were adopted, the accredited representatives of no fewer than twelve of the oppressed and submerged nationalities of the earth assembled to make their own solemn declaration of common aims. In the very room in which the American nation was born these new nations of to-

morrow made the public profession of faith which forever links their fortunes and their hopes with our own,
and which testifies that their nations and ours rest
upon one and the same indestructible foundation of
everlasting principle.  Where better than in the sono-
rous words of Thomas Jefferson can be found an interpretation of that happening:

> We hold these truths to be self-evident; that all men are created
> equal; that they are endowed by their Creator with certain in-
> alienable Rights; that among these are Life, Liberty, and the
> pursuit of Happiness.  That to secure these rights, Governments
> are instituted among Men, deriving their just powers from the
> consent of the governed.

Can we not imagine the spirits of Washington and
Franklin, of Hamilton and Jefferson, of Madison and
Adams, of Morris and Pinckney and the rest, hovering
over that company of men from distant parts of Europe
and of Asia who had come together to light their national fires at the altar of American liberty which our
fathers had so nobly builded?  Where in all history is
there a more significant or a more appealing picture
than that?

What is really happening round about us is the full
accomplishment of the American Revolution.  The
ideals which guided the building of the United States
and the making over of the older civilizations of Great
Britain and of France are the principles which we have
just now been defending in arms against the full force
and power of military autocracy and imperialism, and

which have given the breath of life to these new nations of the earth. There never has been a time when Americans could be so rightfully proud, not only of their accomplishment on the field of battle and in the organization of national effort, but of their example in the making of free government.

And yet it is at this very moment, when our pride and satisfaction in America and its history are at the highest, that destructive and reactionary forces are actively at work to turn our representative republic into a Socialist autocracy, to destroy liberty and equality of opportunity, and to paralyze the greatest force that the world has ever seen for the promotion of the happiness, the satisfaction, and the full development of free men and free women. What we have defended against German aggression and lust of conquest we must now band together to protect against those more insidious and no less powerful enemies who would undermine the foundations on which our American freedom rests. It would indeed be a cynical conclusion of this war if we who have helped so powerfully to defeat the German armies on the field of battle should surrender in any degree to the ideas that had taken possession of the German mind and that led the German nation into its mad war against the free world.

The corner-stone of American government and of American life is the civil liberty of the individual citizen. The essentials of that civil liberty are proclaimed in the Declaration of Independence and defined in the Constitution of the United States. Ours

is not a government of absolute or plenary power before whose exercise the individual must bow his head
in humble acquiescence. Our government is, on the
contrary, one of clearly defined and specifically designated powers, and the Constitution itself provides that
powers not delegated to the United States by the Constitution nor prohibited by it to the States are reserved to the States respectively or to the people.
This means that those powers which the people themselves have not seen fit definitely to grant either to
the national or to the State government are reserved
to the people to be exercised as they may individually
see fit. More than this, there are many things which
the government is specifically prevented from doing,
and the powers of the courts are sufficient to protect
even the humblest individual against the invasion of
his rights and liberties by any government, whether
of state or nation, however powerful or however popular. We do not derive our civil liberty or our right
to do business from government; we who were in possession of civil liberty and the right to do business
have instituted a government to protect and to defend
them.

It is on this civil liberty of the individual as a basis
that all American life, all American civilization, and
all American success have been built. We have offered
the individual an opportunity to make the most of
himself, to seek his fortune in what part of the country
he would, to enjoy the fruits of his own honest labor
and of his own just gains, and to hold whatever social

position his personality and his education might enable him to command. Under this system we have not only prospered mightily, but we have made a country that has drawn to itself the ambitious, the long-suffering, and the downtrodden from every part of the globe, in the hope and belief that here in America they would find the opportunity which conditions elsewhere denied them. In one hundred and fifty years we have not solved all the problems of mankind, and we have not been able to make every one prosperous and happy; but we have made immense progress toward those ends and thereby have become the envy and the admiration of a watching world. The millennium still remains ahead of us and all lasting improvement still takes time.

Where there is individual opportunity there will always be inequality. No two human beings have precisely the same ability, the same temperament, the same tastes, or the same physical power. Therefore it is that when individuals exert themselves freely some progress more rapidly than others, some secure larger rewards than others, and some gain greater enjoyment than others. The only way in which this inequality can be prevented is to substitute tyranny for liberty and to hold all men down to that level of accomplishment which is within the reach of the weakest and the least well-endowed. This, however, is false democracy, not true democracy. Such a policy would deprive men and women of liberty in order to gain a false and artificial equality. Democracy has begun to decay when it becomes a combination of the mediocre and the inferior to restrain and to punish the more able and the more progressive. The equality which true democracy seeks to protect and preserve is equality of opportunity, equality of rights, equality before the law. Any form of privilege is just as undemocratic as is any form of tyranny. Any exploitation of the body or soul of one individual by another is just as undemocratic as the Prussian military autocracy. If men and women are to be free, their bodies must be free as well as their souls and their spirits. This cannot be done if they are mere tools or instrumentalities in the hands of another, whether that other be an individual monarch or a despotic majority. How to bring about the protection of the individual from exploitation and how to prevent the growth of privilege without at the same time destroying civil liberty are the most difficult and the most persistent problems which human society has to face. Yet it is the price of progress to face them and to solve them. The one fact that is never to be forgotten is that pulling some men down raises no man up.

But we are now told that these inequalities due to liberty have become so very great and the disparity between individuals so marked that civil liberty and individual opportunity must be displaced by the organized power of the state. We hear it said that the conduct of our daily lives, what we eat and drink, the conduct of our business, what we do and gain, must all be under strict governmental supervision and control.

Men of Ohio, this is the first long and dangerous step on the path back toward autocracy and militarism. Once a state becomes all-powerful it easily thinks of itself as unable to do wrong, and so becomes the unmoral state of which Prussia and the German Empire have been the most perfect types. The all-powerful and unmoral state can see nothing higher than itself; it admits no principle of right or justice to which it must give heed; such a state is an end in itself and what it chooses to do is necessarily right.

The most pressing question that now confronts the American people, the question that underlies and conditions all problems of reconstruction and of advance as we pass from war conditions to the normal times of peace, is whether we shall go forward by preserving those American principles and American traditions that have already served us so well, or whether we shall abandon those principles and traditions and substitute for them a state built not upon the civil liberty of the individual but upon the plenary power of organized government.

Those whose eyes are turned toward a government of the latter type are designated in a general way as Socialists. The words Socialism and Socialist, though less than a century old, have lately become very common among us and are so loosely and so variously used as to make it difficult to think clearly regarding the ideas for which they stand. Socialism, in the large, general, and vague sense of the word, means simply social reform. In that sense every intelligent and forward-stepping man or woman is a socialist. All of us who are in our right minds are anxious to improve social conditions, to better the public health, to decrease the hours and the severity of labor, to increase the rewards and to add to the satisfactions of those who do the hard manual work of the world, to increase and make secure provision against illness, unemployment, and indigent old age, to use the power of public taxation to build roads, to multiply schoolhouses, to aid with information and guidance those who farm and those who mine, to bring together collections of books or objects of beauty and of art for the information and the pleasure of the great body of the people, to improve the conditions of housing in large cities, and to see to it that such essentials of life as water, light, and transportation are furnished of the best quality and at the lowest practicable cost. If by Socialism be meant that the individual must not live for himself alone, but must use his powers, his capacities, and his gains for the benefit of his community and his fellows, then every American and every Christian is a socialist, for these are fundamental to American life and to Christian teaching. All this, however, is social reform, not Socialism.

Socialism, in the strict and scientific sense of the word, is, however, something quite different from this. Socialism involves not social reform but political and social revolution. It is the name for a definite public policy which rests upon certain historical and economic assumptions, all of which have been proved to be false, and it proceeds to very drastic and far-reaching conclusions, all of which are in flat contradiction to American policy and American faith. The assumptions of Socialism are these:

*First*, that all of man's efforts, both past and present, are to be interpreted and explained in terms of his desire for wealth and of the processes which lead to the satisfaction of that desire. This assumption excludes at once all moral, religious, and unselfish considerations from history and from life and makes of man nothing but a gain-seeking animal preying upon his kind wherever he can lay hands upon him. There have been, and there doubtless are, many individuals of this type; but to suppose that the whole human race can be brought under such a description is an outrageous travesty on history, on morals, and on religion. This assumption would reduce all human history to the product of blind gain-seeking forces and would exclude from it both moral effort and moral purpose. Under such a theory, no man would make any sacrifice for liberty or for love, but only for gain. All human experience contradicts so cruel and so heartless an assumption.

*Second*, that in the struggle for wealth men are divided into permanent classes—those who employ and those who labor—and that between these classes there is and should be a class struggle or class war to be carried on to the bitter end until those who labor not only conquer those who employ but exclude them from any place in the community.

This doctrine of class struggle is the savage teaching of Karl Marx, a man whose consuming passion was hate. It has been well said of Marx that

He was without religion, having been conveyed from Judaism to Protestantism by his father at the age of six, and having abandoned Protestantism for aggressive Atheism when he grew to manhood. He was a man embittered by persecution, enraged by antagonism, soured by adversity, exasperated by suffering. . . . His inspiring and dominant passion was the passion of hate—hate in its virulent and peculiarly Germanic form. . . . It was hate that goaded him to his enormous literary labors; it was hate that determined his selection and rejection of historical facts for his distorted description of industrial England; it was hate that fixed his economic principles, that twisted all his arguments, that vitiated all his conclusions. . . . *Das Kapital* (1867) is the enduring testament of Marxian animosity. . . . It is a work of dogmatic mythology, the formula of a new religion of repulsion, the Koran of the class war.[1]

It is the extreme form of the doctrines of Karl Marx which Lenine and Trotzky have been applying in Russia for a year and a half past with such terrible results. In consequence, that once great country of boundless possibilities is now as helpless as a child, and it lies, for the moment, in social, economic, and moral ruin and is relapsing into barbarism. Its reorganized schools now devote part of each day to instruction in atheism and to removing any lingering traces of what used to be proudly called civilization. Russia had lost, happily, the cruel and tyrannous Tsar who ruled over it, but unhappily it has gained in his stead a

[1] Hearnshaw, *Democracy at the Crossways* (London, 1918), pp. 209–210.

small group of violent and equally cruel autocrats whose operations make those of the Tsar seem like child's play.   For the first time in history, on a stage which the whole world can witness, and on an immense scale, the doctrines and theories of Karl Marx are being put to the test of practical application.   No one not himself blinded by hate or by ignorance can be in any doubt as to the lesson which the world has quickly learned from the untold sufferings of Russia.

This doctrine of permanent economic classes and of a class struggle is the absolute contradiction of democracy.   It denies a common citizenship and an equality of rights and privileges in order to set up a privileged and an exploiting class by sheer force and terrorism. Here in America we know full well that there are no permanent and conflicting economic classes, for the wage-worker of to-day is the employer of a few years hence.   With us the son of the farmer may be the leader of a learned profession in a distant city, and he who begins self-support as signalman or telegraph-operator may easily find himself, in a few short years, the directing head of a great railway system.   Not long ago public attention was called to the fact that no fewer than nineteen of the men who then directed the great transportation systems of the United States had in every case begun their careers as wage-workers in the service of one or another of the railway companies.

We know, too, that the fundamental doctrine of American citizenship absolutely excludes the notion that men gain or lose anything by reason of their occupation. Here every man and woman stands on a level of political equality, and the vote of the man of wealth is no more potent than the vote of the man who at the moment may be seeking employment. In the socialistic state permanent economic classes with differing and opposing rights and privileges are fundamental. From the democratic state, on the other hand, they are excluded. Robert Burns was a true poet of democracy when he sang

"A man's a man for a' that."

*Third,* that in the course of economic development the rich are getting steadily richer and steadily fewer, while the poor are getting steadily poorer and steadily more numerous. This assumption is easily disposed of by the facts, which show that, as applied to America, these two statements are absolutely false.

Ours is a land in which more than twenty millions of men, women, and children have just now subscribed to Liberty Bonds.

It is a land with more than 18,000,000 dwellings occupied by about 21,000,000 families.

It is a land in which fully 6,000,000 families own their own homes without encumbrance, while 3,000,000 own their homes subject to mortgage.

It is a land in which more than 12,000,000 persons are depositors in mutual, stock, or postal-savings banks, with total deposits amounting to more than $6,500,000,000.

It is a land in which there are nearly 6,500,000 farms

having a value, including their buildings and equipment, of more than $41,000,000,000 and yielding an annual product of a value of more than $8,500,000,000.

It is a land with more than 266,000 miles of railway in operation, carrying in a year more than 1,000,000,000 individual passengers and more than 2,225,000,000 tons of freight.

It is a land in which schools for the people are maintained at a total expenditure of nearly $650,000,000, with an attendance of more than 20,000,000 children.

It is a land in which there are more than 3,000 public libraries having on their shelves more than 75,000,000 volumes for the instruction and inspiration of the people.

It is a land whose total wealth is now not less than $225,000,000,000 and in which the distribution of that wealth is steadily becoming more equitable and more satisfactory under the operation of the forces and principles that have guided American life so long and so well.

Who is it that has the temerity to wish to undermine the foundations of so noble and so inviting a political and social structure as this!

Forty years ago and more, when the doctrine of Socialism was systematically put forward by Karl Marx, it was quickly seized upon by those in Germany, and in every other European land who were discontented with existing forms of government and of social organization, and was converted by them into a political programme. That programme, which was to all intents and purposes made in Germany, although written in London, contradicts Americanism and democracy at every point. It calls, not for any programme of social reform in accordance with American principles and American ideals, but for a programme of collective control over the individual life, the individual occupation, and the individual reward that would destroy America absolutely. It would erect upon the ruins of our democracy an autocratic state in which the tyranny of a temporary or class majority would take the place once held by the tyranny of an hereditary monarch or an hereditary ruling class. Its most extreme exponents have not hesitated to announce themselves, as did Bakunin fifty years ago, as apostles of universal destruction.

As yet the number of formal adherents of the Socialist party in the United States is not large, but the theories and teachings of Socialism are being eagerly and systematically spread among us. Many schools and colleges and many pulpits are either unconscious or willing agents in this work. In the election of 1916 the Socialist party of the United States obtained almost exactly 3.3 per cent of the total vote. It is probable that by formally adopting the international policy of the Russian Bolshevists, the Socialist party has alienated enough of its former supporters to reduce its probable vote to-day to less than 2 per cent of the total. Small as this number is, it represents organization and activity out of all proportion to its size. There should be no mistake about its pro-

gramme. It openly calls our Constitution dishonest.
It denounces the fathers of our country as grafters, as
crooks, as men of mediocre intelligence, and as attor-
neys of the capitalist class.   In the making and building of America the Socialist can see nothing of idealism,
nothing of sacrifice, nothing of high principle, nothing
of love of liberty, nothing of aspiration for a finer and
a freer manhood.   The Socialist party platform of
1912 explicitly demanded not only the usual collectiv-
ist and communist policies, but also the abolition of
the United States Senate and of the veto power of the
President;  the abolition of all federal courts except
the United States Supreme Court and the election of
all judges for short terms;  the abolition of the power
of the Supreme Court of the United States to pass
upon the constitutionality of legislative acts;  and a
revision of the Constitution of the United States.

The Socialist party is in particular antagonism to
the courts, and the reason is easy to state.   Under our
American system the courts are established to protect
civil liberty from passion, from mob control, and from
improper assumption of power by public authorities
and public agents.   All this is most distasteful to the
orthodox Socialist.   He wishes to lay the hand of force
upon civil liberty and to destroy it for a despotism of
his own making.   The courts of justice are an obstacle in his way.

The sinister fact, never to be forgotten, about this
party and its programme is that they are in essence
and of necessity unpatriotic and un-American.   Re-

publicans and Democrats differ sharply as to public policy, but they both accept the principles of the Constitution and endeavor to apply and improve them, each in their own way. Neither Republicans nor Democrats would change the form of government under which we live. The Socialist party, on the other hand, openly declares its purpose to wreck the present form of government, to undo all the work that has been accomplished for a hundred and fifty years, and to bring to an end the greatest experiment in republicanism and the greatest achievement in social and political organization that the world has ever seen. Let there be no mistake about the definiteness of this issue. America's existence is challenged.

Orthodox Socialists are internationalists of a special kind. They are really not internationalists at all but rather antinationalists. They are not in favor of closer, more kindly, and more constructive international relations as a means toward justice and the security of the world, but they desire that sort of internationalism which shall extend class consciousness, class co-operation, and the class struggle beyond the boundaries of existing nations and so assist in breaking down those boundaries. This is why the logical orthodox Socialist is of necessity unpatriotic. He does not believe in patriotism, because he regards it as an obstacle to the further extension of the successful class struggle and of class rule. Happily, we have seen in our recent experience that men may be sincere believers in many of the tenets of Socialism and yet remain patriotic and loyal Americans. Such men as Russell, Walling, Spargo, and Montague have illustrated this fact. Unfortunately, these men have been but a small minority in the Socialist party or group, and they have seceded from it. Orthodox Socialists as a body cannot be loyal and devoted Americans, for the simple reason that American institutions and American ideals lie straight across the path which they would like to pursue.

This distinction between a true and a false internationalism is to be taken into account and clearly reckoned with in shaping the policies of the world. Just as the family relation enriches and strengthens the individual, and just as the community relation enriches and strengthens the family, and just as the State relation enriches and strengthens the community, and just as the national relation enriches and strengthens the State, so will a true international relationship enrich and strengthen every nation that enters into it. Any plan for a society of nations that would destroy national initiative, national responsibility, and national pride would be merely a strait-jacket upon human progress. The true and wise society of nations will be one built out of nations that are stronger, more resourceful, and more patriotic because of their new association and their new opportunities for world service.

Signs are not wanting that the advocates of Socialism think it will be easier and quicker to gain ground in the United States by the indirect method of involv-

ing us in a false international policy than by the direct
method of attempting to secure control of the machinery of government through the suffrage. This explains why Socialists and those who at heart sympathize
with them without openly assuming their name are so
anxious that Lenine and Trotzky shall be formally
recognized as heads of a government with which civilized and honorable men may have relations and that
the German people should, so far as possible, be saved
from the consequences of their public crime and their
military defeat. If Americans could only be led to
give up their historic patriotism for a sentimental hu-
manitarianism the battle of the Socialists would be
half won. This is why it behooves us to watch with
anxious care each step that our government proposes
to take in relation to international policy. If it is
proposed to build a world of strong, independent, self-
conscious nations with close and friendly international
relations for the preservation of the world's peace, well
and good. But if it is proposed to weaken or destroy
nations in order to build a world in which historic nations shall play but an insignificant part, and in which
patriotism and love of country shall disappear, then
Americans should oppose such a policy at every step
and with the utmost vigor.

That which the American of to-day opposes to Socialist autocracy is not the crude competitive individualism of the old-fashioned economist but co-operative
individualism with a moral purpose. It must not be
forgotten that on the existence of private capital,

which is only another name for private savings, depend the virtues of thrift, of liberality, and of sacrifice. The observation that liberality consists in the use which is made of property is as old as Aristotle. Under modern conditions private capital is much more highly and more freely co-operative than any system of Socialist organization could possibly be. The corporation, with its provision for the limited liability of the individual participant, is only a means of bringing about the co-operation of many individuals for a common cause and is one of the greatest and most beneficent developments of the past century. It links together in a common enterprise the joint labors or joint savings of hundreds, thousands, even tens of thousands, of men and women, who to that extent are organized as a single economic unit interested in promoting efficient production and entitled to divide among themselves the common product. Under the system of private capital all this individual co-operation is free. Under any Socialist system, whatever co-operation existed would be imposed by rule and enforced by the power of the majority or ruling group. Under the system of private capital the individual co-operating, whether investor or workman, comes and goes as he chooses. He is free to make what disposition he will of his own savings or of his own labor. Under any Socialist system all this would be regulated for him and directed by public authority. His freedom would be wholly gone.

America is worth saving, not only as a land in which

men and women may be free and increasingly prosperous, but as a land and a government under which character can be built, individual capacity given opportunity for free exercise, and co-operation on the widest scale promoted not only for private advantage but for the public good. As men become increasingly moral and increasingly intelligent, their personal activities will be increasingly impressed with a public interest. Their citizenship will not exhaust itself in the formal exercise of political rights or in merely political activity. It will show itself in ways that are economic, social, and ethical. Throughout this land there are thousands, hundreds of thousands, of men and women who illustrate this fact. Neither America nor mankind in general is likely to attain absolute perfection; but under the influence and guidance of those principles and ideals which are historically and truly American, there is every reason to believe that each succeeding generation will see new and increasing progress toward the goal of greater human happiness and greater human satisfaction.

The sure mark of the reactionary is unwillingness to make use of the teachings of past experience or to read the lessons of history and apply them to the problems of to-day. The real reactionary, who is always an egoist, insists that his own feelings, his own desires, his own ambitions take precedence over anything that all the rest of mankind may have said or done or recorded. He wishes to start life all over again in a Garden of Eden of his own, with a private serpent and a private apple. The true progressive, on the other hand, is he who carefully reads history and carefully examines the experience of mankind in order to see what lessons have already been learned, what mistakes need not be repeated, and what principles of organization and conduct have established themselves as sound and beneficent. Upon all this the progressive builds a new and consistent structure to meet the needs of to-day in the light of the experience of yesterday. He does not find it necessary to burn his own fingers in order to ascertain whether fire is hot.

America will be saved, not by those who have only contempt and despite for her founders and her history, but by those who look with respect and reverence upon the great series of happenings extending from the voyage of the *Mayflower* to the achievements of the American armies on the soil of France, and upon that long succession of statesmen, orators, men of letters, and men of affairs who have themselves been both the product and the highest promise of American life and American opportunity. The Declaration of Independence rings as true to-day as it did in 1776. The Constitution remains the surest and safest foundation for a free government that the wit of man has yet devised. Faithful adherence to these strong and enduring foundations, and a high purpose to apply the fundamental principles of American life with sympathy and open-mindedness to each new problem that presents itself, will give us a people increasingly prosperous, increasingly happy, and increasingly secure.

Just so soon as the American people, with their quick intelligence and alert apprehension, understand the difference between social reform and political Socialism, and the distinction between an internationalism that is false and destructive of patriotism and an internationalism that is true and full of appeal to every patriot, they will stamp political Socialism underfoot, together with all its subtle and half-conscious approximations and imitations, as something abhorrent to our free American life. They will prefer to save America.

# II

# THE FOUNDATIONS OF PROSPERITY

An address delivered before the Chamber of Commerce,
Utica, New York, May 16, 1919

# THE FOUNDATIONS OF PROSPERITY

The foundations of prosperity are public security, public order, and public satisfaction. Unless a nation feels itself secure from outside attack it cannot devote its energies undividedly to economic, social, and moral advance. It must maintain costly and burdensome armaments and it must live in constant dread of war. Unless a nation is conscious of its power to preserve order within its own boundaries and to enforce the laws, as well as in all such action to appeal successfully to the sober judgment of the people for support, it cannot hope to be prosperous. Unless a nation is successful in providing ways and means by which the normal and honorable hopes and ambitions of its people may be reasonably satisfied, it will be confronted by a constant unrest and a turbulence which hold prosperity in check. These are the reasons why international peace, industrial peace, and an improving social order are so eagerly desired by all those who would increase the happiness and multiply the satisfactions of mankind. No one of these three aims, however, is to be achieved through rhetorical formulas, international agreements, or national legislation alone. Behind any or all of these must be a convinced public opinion and a satisfied public conscience. What we must deal with is not so much formulas and treaties and laws as the hearts and minds of men.

The entire world has been for a long time past in a state of peculiarly unstable equilibrium. This has been due to the operation over the whole area of civilization of two sets of powerful forces, one political and one economic, which have been added to the ordinary and customary human strivings for improvement and for change. The world is always in process of development; but for at least three hundred years this development has taken the form of constant and wide-spread agitation for immediate results.

The political forces that have been and still are at work are those making for the building of independent and homogeneous nations and those making for increased and better-established civil and political liberty for the individual. In the former case these strivings have led to many international wars. In the latter case they have led to many domestic revolutions, some peaceful and some violent. The history of the making of Great Britain, of France, of Italy, and of the German Empire illustrates how peoples have had to fight their way to national unity through war. The history of the English, the American, the French, and the Russian Revolutions illustrates by what various methods men have struggled to achieve adequate and well-established civil and political liberty as well as what dangers and excesses may attend and accompany these struggles.

As a result of the great war whose issues are now in

process of settlement, the movement toward nation-building has received great impetus. Poland, Czecho-slovakia, Jugoslavia, and Armenia are taking their place as self-conscious and autonomous nationalities. Greece will certainly find her people reunited in one governmental system, including those who have so long lived under the Turkish yoke. The union of Italy will be completed and secured. It is probable that a great federal Russia will shortly rise on the site of the political and economic ruin which autocracy and Bolshevism have combined to produce. The peace and order of the world would be retarded, not advanced, if in this process any attempt were made to divide the German people among several sovereignties. The desire for nation-building is as strong among the Germans as among any other modern people, and Bismarck's great hold upon the German people was due to his being in their eyes the embodiment of the movement for national unity. To dismember and divide any modern people and to apportion them among several sovereignties is simply to invite new wars. The waters of national psychology cannot be made to flow up-hill.

When nation-building goes beyond its just limits and passes over into an ambition for world-domination, it invites, indeed it compels, war. This is precisely what happened in the case of the German Empire. The government of the Hohenzollerns was not content with a powerful and united Germany but conceived the ambition to dominate the world. What followed we all know.  This German ambition was an attempt to turn back the wheels of political progress and to emulate the Alexanders, the Cæsars, the Charlemagnes, the Charles Fifths, and the Napoleons of an old and outworn order.  The legitimate end of nation-building is not world-domination in any form but membership in an ordered society of nations.

The forces that have been making for the definition and establishment of civil and political liberty received most complete and most convincing recognition through the English, American, and French Revolutions and particularly through the framing and adoption of the Constitution of the United States. While those revolutions left many things yet to be done, some of them highly important, nevertheless, they did clearly establish the principles upon which civil and political liberty, as well as ordered government for their protection, must rest.  Sometimes, as in the case of the German Empire, the movement for civil and political liberty has been held in check until the movement for nation-building had run its full course.   In this way is to be explained the failure of the Revolution of 1848 in Germany, despite the strong and wide-spread support which that revolutionary movement possessed.  The quick success of the political revolution in Germany, following the defeat of German arms and German policy in this war, is the natural result of the free working of forces long pent up by the desire, first of all, to make Germany strong, prosperous, and world-dominating.

If we are to look for the foundations of prosperity we shall find them first in the satisfaction of these perfectly natural and very powerful human ambitions and political forces which make for nation-building and for the definition and establishment of civil and political liberty. Until these force have expressed themselves in achievement, and until the ambitions which they represent are reasonably well satisfied, there can be neither peace nor order between nations or within nations.

Until the process of nation-building is substantially complete, and until the ambition for world-domination has been given up by every nation, there can be no assurance of public security; and until that time one of the necessary foundations of prosperity will be lacking. Immense progress has been made toward the establishment of public security by the defeat of the imperialistic policies and ambitions of Germany and by the entry of Poland, Czechoslovakia, Jugoslavia, and Armenia into the family of independent nations. At the very moment when the forces that make for public security were rapidly gaining ground the forces that make for public order within a nation were being gravely weakened. This resulted primarily from the extreme and destructive course taken by the Russian Revolution. The disorderly, the lawless, and the irresponsible elements in other lands hailed the advent of Bolshevism in Russia as a signal to redouble their own energies as revolutionaries and as trouble-makers. If any nation is to be prosperous, and if the world is to be prosperous, these Bolshevist forces must not only be held in check but overthrown. They are active, persistent, and conscious enemies of any public order that is not based upon tyranny and of any prosperity that is not the exploitation of a people by a class. For lovers of civil and political liberty to strengthen the hands of the constructive forces that are working for the rebuilding of Russia is not an act of international interference but an act of national self-defense. Bolshevism seeks to conquer Russia only that it may have a starting-point from which to conquer France, Great Britain, and the United States. Public order, a necessary foundation of prosperity, will not be secure until civil and political liberty are finally and definitely protected against the assaults of Bolshevism.

The second great set of forces which have been operating, and with especial force for about a hundred years, are economic. These are the forces brought into being and let loose by the so-called industrial revolution, with its supplanting of the individual worker or guild of workmen by the factory system, with all its ramifications and results. What is called the industrial revolution is due to the introduction of steam and electricity as motive power and to the hundreds, indeed thousands, of mechanical inventions which have followed in their train and which have made industry and commerce the highly organized and very complex things which they now are. Under the much simpler and more individual system of manufacture which prevailed until a little more than a century ago, one and the same individual was capitalist and laborer. The factory system divided the capitalist from the laborer, the employer from the employed, and straightway there began to develop a more or less conscious diversity of interest between the two and a more or less conscious struggle as to the division of the product. There shortly developed a situation in which some employers at least came to look upon the employees as only so many cogs on a wheel, or so many parts of a machine, and not as human beings at all. On the other hand, there were employees who listened to the false teaching that all value is the product of labor and consequently felt themselves much aggrieved that their share in production seemed so small. Industry and commerce developed more or less rapidly into forms of conflict or war none the less real and none the less destructive because not carried on with rifles and with cannon. While very great progress has been made, particularly in the last few years, in giving just recognition to these economic forces and in changing industry and commerce from forms of conflict or war into forms of co-operation, very much yet remains to be done. It is true here, just as in the case of nation-building and of the struggle for civil and political liberty, that until these economic forces express themselves in achievement, and until the human ambitions which they represent are reasonably satisfied, there can be neither peace nor order in the industrial and commercial world.

Without that peace and order there can be no prosperity. Industrial war is quite as dangerous and quite as disastrous to a nation's prosperity as international war.

The time is now ripe to take up the industrial problem as part of the great human problem and to advance toward its solution in that spirit. So long as the industrial problem is conceived of in terms of profits alone, without regard to the effect of industrial processes and conditions upon human beings, just so long will it remain unsolved and be the source and the cause of constant and severe friction and unrest which will make permanent prosperity impossible. When the industrial problem is approached from the human point of view, one sees that its essential characteristic is the co-operation of human beings in the production of objects of value. Those who co-operate, whether with their savings, or with their brains, or with the work of their hands, are human beings and not machines or parts of a machine. They must be treated as human beings and given both the protection and the opportunity to which human beings are justly entitled under a free and republican form of government. No one of them must be consciously exploited by any other and no one of them must be consciously the beneficiary of law-made privilege. Each man and woman must be given not only a full chance but a free chance and a fair chance to make the most of himself. The object of this co-operation is the production of wealth, and it is from production, and from production alone, that both wages and profits are paid. The more production the greater the possibility of increased wages and the greater the possibility of increased profits. To restrict production artificially in the hope of increase either in wages or in profits is unsound in principle and disastrous in practice. A nation which distributes among its people more in wages and in so-called profits than its industrial system produces is living on its capital and must sooner or later come to grief. Prosperity requires large production under conditions that satisfy human needs and reasonable human aspirations.

Experience has taught us that under the unchecked and unregulated competitive system individuals and groups of individuals are often crushed to the wall without that full, free, and fair chance which is their due. It is to meet this situation that collective bargaining has been introduced and has so widely established itself, and it is to meet this same situation that the attempt has been made to organize industry in large co-operative units. Both these movements have been vigorously fought by those who pin their faith to the old purely competitive system, but the path of progress toward prosperity lies in the other direction. Co-operation between individuals and groups of individuals for a sound economic purpose is a constructive policy of almost limitless value and importance to the people. The danger that co-operating groups may establish undue control over public interests and so achieve privilege is to be met by public supervision and regulation. The experiences of the war have shown us that under pressure of a great emergency we must throw away the chains and shackles of our restrictive laws and allow the largest possible measure of economic co-operation under government control. What was found necessary in time of war will be found desirable and helpful in time of peace. The next step forward will be to enact constructive federal legislation that will not only permit but encourage the formation of large economic units for production and for commerce under such measure of government supervision as may be found necessary to prevent abuse. When this step is taken not only our export trade but our domestic trade will be mightily advanced and our power of national production will be vastly increased.

At the same time it is to be borne in mind that for the public satisfaction it is necessary to make increasingly sure that no American citizen is deprived of his opportunity to share in the nation's prosperity or is left to suffer from any cause but his own moral fault. For generations it has been the custom of civilized peoples to make the care of the impoverished aged or the impoverished disabled a charge upon the public. This has been done by way of relief and from motives of philanthropy. Would it not be better now to deal with this aspect of the problem by the use of modern methods of prevention and in a spirit not so much of philanthropy as of justice? No free government can permanently endure except upon the foundation of public satisfaction, and public satisfaction is impossible if large numbers of individuals or groups

of persons who are not perhaps as well equipped as
many of their fellows for success in the business of
life are allowed, while retaining the full rights of citizenship, to fall below that level of comfort and com-
petency which the common judgment indicates to be
necessary for a human being. In the United States
we have long undertaken, through compulsory education laws, to provide that minimum of formal instruction and training which we have felt it necessary for children to have in order that they might
grow into useful and intelligent citizens. Has not the
time come for our people, acting in the same spirit,
to study ways and means of providing a national
minimum for the health, comfort, and opportunity of
the individual as well as for his education? Such
policies of social advance as these, carried out by believers in a republican form of government, offer the
surest protection against the revolutionary threaten-
ings of international Socialism. A conviction that
justice, fair play, and broad human feeling animate a
nation will keep Bolshevism forever beyond its bor-
ders. Among a hundred millions of people there will
always be the degenerate, the psychopathic, and the
eager disturbers of the public peace and of the social
order; but they will all be powerless to overturn or
to undermine our form of government if it rests upon
public satisfaction.

Prosperity lies all about us and invites us to enter
into its broad field of opportunity. With the German

military power overthrown and broken forever, our national security is established beyond peradventure. If we insist upon a stalwart and patriotic Americanism as against the clamorous cries of those among us who are teaching and preaching international Socialism and Bolshevism, we shall have no trouble in establishing and maintaining public order. If, finally, we treat industry and commerce as undertakings in human co-operation for human ends, and build up the largest possible measure of co-operation between individuals and between groups under government supervision and control, taking care that a national minimum of health, of education, and of comfort be defined and provided, we shall have established that measure of public satisfaction which, combined with public security and public order, will make prosperity certain and long-continued.

# III

## A PROGRAMME OF CONSTRUCTIVE PROGRESS

An address delivered before the Commercial Club,
St. Louis, Missouri, February 16, 1918

# A PROGRAMME OF CONSTRUCTIVE
# PROGRESS

The record of the past four years shows that the free nations of the world have sadly lacked foresight. Autocracy knew what was coming, helped to bring it on, and systematically organized and prepared for it. The free peoples did not know what was coming, and they are now paying the heavy cost of failure to forecast the future and to be ready quickly and effectively to meet its problems.

One of the chief applications of scientific knowledge is in prediction. When one knows what has happened and why it happened he is in position to tell what is likely to happen next. Just so, one of the chief marks of civilization should be foresight. It is not a worthy use of liberty and opportunity merely to drift from day to day, to satisfy instant material and economic wants, with no thought of what is to follow. A truly civilized people will be a ready and a prepared people. So long as wars are inevitable, or even likely, the free peoples will hereafter be ready and prepared for war. But the demands of peace are even more insistent and more compelling than those of war. No civilized people is prepared for peace unless it takes account not only of yesterday and of to-day but of to-morrow and the day after to-morrow. The forces that are making for change and for progress, the ideas that are stimulating men to new undertakings and new aspirations are the driving forces to be taken into account by those who would guide and direct public opinion.

The novelty of an idea or a suggestion has an attractiveness out of all proportion to its value. Men like the new, the unfamiliar, the untried. Yet the fact that an idea or a suggestion is new sheds no light whatever upon its value or its truth. John Bright used to say that the first instinct of an English working man on hearing a new idea was to "'eave 'arf a brick at it." That is not a safe or a wise attitude for civilized peoples to take toward new ideas. It is better to welcome them, to examine them with sympathy, and to take from them whatever of value and helpfulness they offer. The important thing is not whether an idea is new, but whether it is true. Novelty and truth have absolutely no relation to each other.

The American people are going through a tremendous upheaval. This upheaval reaches and affects every part of their social, their industrial, and their political system. Habits of life and of business that have grown up over generations are rudely interrupted. Laws that have been hailed as great advances in the realm of government are wiped out by executive fiat. The distinction between the field of government and the field of free action, by means of which our whole American system has been built up, is practically swept away, at least for the moment. The nation finds that it was without proper governmental or economic organization to make the supreme effort necessary to win the war, and that such an organization must be improvised out of the materials that are at hand and without much regard to law, to tradition, or to past experience. Tremendous and unsettling as this revolution is, its effects are bound to be beneficial. The American people will not soon again be satisfied with old formulas or restrain themselves in patience while the slow forces of nature operate to mitigate conditions that directly affect human life and human happiness. The people as a whole will be more open-minded than they have been in a hundred years, and the country's business will be conducted by new methods and, it is to be hoped, upon lines of greater and more general satisfaction than ever before.

So long as we confine ourselves to generalities there is not likely to be disagreement as to these reflections. Difference and difficulty arise when we endeavor to state in terms of specific acts or policies how we should proceed better to prepare our government and our people, not alone for war, which is at best a passing phenomenon, but for that peace—and let us hope it will be a durable peace—which will be the outcome of the war.

Let me state as briefly as possible how I should like to see our nation prepare itself for its future tasks:

1. The American Government should as promptly as possible settle upon a definite and precise plan for the establishment of closer and better co-operation between nations in establishing and maintaining order

and justice throughout the world. The form of this co-operation would be built upon the conclusions of the Hague Conferences of 1899 and 1907. It would make international war increasingly unlikely and it might even make international war practically impossible. The materials for such a definite and precise plan are at hand in the state papers and public addresses of representative and responsible American statesmen, especially those who were charged with the conduct of the country's foreign policy from the time of the Spanish War to the outbreak of the present struggle. It would seem that some of the dreams of the seers of past centuries can shortly be realized. Out of the present alliance of free democratic peoples may readily be built the structure of a league or society of nations which shall not attempt too much but which shall at least put into effect the lessons taught by the present war.

A League to establish and to enforce the rules of international law and conduct is now in existence, with the United States as one of its most potent members. This League should be a permanent addition to the world's organization for order and for peace. Upon its firm establishment, three consequences will almost necessarily follow. First, there can be no separate alliances or ententes of a political or military character between nations included in the League, and this League must aim in time to include the whole civilized world. Second, there can be a speedy reduction of armaments both to lighten the burdens of taxation and to turn the minds of the nations away from international war, to prevent which will be such a League's chief aim. Third, the most-favored-nation clause must be made applicable to all members of the League whenever treaties of commerce are concluded between any two or more of the nations that are included in it. This will either greatly lessen or wholly remove one of the strongest economic temptations to international war.

The International Court of Justice urged by the American Delegation at the Second Hague Conference may surely now be called into being. This Court would have the same jurisdiction over questions affecting international relations and international law that the Supreme Court of the United States has over all cases in law and equity arising under the Constitution of the United States and treaties made under its authority. The enforcement, when necessary, of the findings of this Court should be a matter of joint international action in accordance with a definite plan to be determined upon when the Court is established. The principle upon which this action will rest has been stated with characteristic precision by Mr. Asquith when he said that the rule of the authority of an International Court "must be supported in case of need by the strength of all; that is, in the last resort, by armed force."

For the success of this Court it is imperative that secret international understandings be deprived of any validity whatever in international law. It would be well to provide that as a condition of the validity in international law of any treaty between two contracting Powers, a copy of it must be deposited, immediately upon its ratification, in the archives of the International Court of Justice at The Hague. There would then be at least one official public depository for every existing valid treaty. So far as the government of the United States is concerned secret treaties are not practicable, since every treaty must be ratified by the Senate. It has been quite customary in Europe, however, even in the case of some democratically governed countries, to keep from the knowledge of parliaments and of the people international understandings and agreements that are entered into from time to time.

It should be clearly understood that any such plan of international co-operation as is proposed involves giving up the absolute right of any government to deal finally, and without appeal except to war, with questions arising out of treaties or relations between itself and some other government. No serious progress can be made in getting rid of war unless the people of the United States, and the people of other countries as well, are ready to take this long step forward.

The war itself, however, has carried us far beyond even so advanced a programme as this. The war has taught its own lessons of international co-operation and international interdependence. It has brought about a new economic internationalism. The necessities of the conflict have broken down, one after another, many of the accustomed national barriers. Transpor-

tation on land and by sea, the manufacture and distribution of munitions and of the auxiliaries of war,
as well as financial resources, have all been removed
from the field of ordinary competition and reorganized
on a basis, first, of national and then of international
co-operation. Not all of these emergency undertakings are desirable to continue in times of peace; but
the lessons of economy, of avoidance of waste, and of
prompt effectiveness that they teach will not be lost.
Probably the attempt to enforce competition by law,
and similarly to punish co-operation, will now be everywhere abandoned in the light of these latest and most
convincing lessons of experience.

Unless the result of the war is not only to defeat
Germany and her allies, but to convince them that
they are defeated, there will be in the world for some
time to come two great international combinations,
the members of which will manifest their sympathies
in military, political, and economic co-operation.
Such a situation would not be a promising one from
the standpoint of those who hope that the present
may be the last of wars; but unless the war be resolutely pursued to victory by the Allies, at whatever
cost, such a situation is a possibility to be seriously
reckoned with.

A League of Nations that rests upon a moral foundation and that has for its aim the good order, the satisfaction, and the advancing happiness of the world,
cannot permanently exclude from its membership any
nation except one openly in arms against it.

2. The unpreparedness of America alike for war and for peace is now obvious to everybody. It calls upon us to establish without delay a well-ordered system of national training for national service. In no other way can the youth of the nation be instructed and disciplined for purposes of national defense, or imbued with a spirit of national devotion that will break down all limitations of race origin, of language, and of local patriotism, or given an adequate chance to fit themselves for useful and productive life work in truly democratic fashion. It has long been the policy of the several States to protect themselves and their citizens from the evils and the dangers that are characteristic of illiteracy, and that accompany lack of intellectual and moral discipline, by requiring attendance upon the elementary school for a definitely prescribed period. In this same spirit and on similar grounds, the nation should now say to each youth approaching manhood, that, for part of one year, or of two successive years, he must submit himself for a definite period to instruction and training under direct national supervision and control, in order that three distinct purposes may be accomplished—first, that he may, in association with youth of like age, get a new and vivid sense of the meaning and obligations of citizenship; second, that he may be physically and intellectually prepared to take part in his country's service or his country's defense should occasion ever arise; third, that specific direction may be given to his capacities and powers, so

that he may be better prepared than would otherwise
be the case for useful and productive citizenship.
If it be objected that this is too large a task, the answer is that it involves the training in any one year
of only about as many individuals as are now annually
enrolled in the public school systems of New York
and Chicago, and that the nation's security and well-
being depend upon its accomplishment.

The first of these aims involves the building of the
nation, strong and firm, out of the many divergent
elements that have now entered into its composition,
particularly in the large cities and on the Atlantic and
Pacific seaboards. A call to citizenship so direct and
so imperative would in most cases quite outweigh the
prejudices and prepossessions that alien birth or alien
sympathies may have created. The second of these
aims would, when accomplished, provide us with a
trained citizen soldiery similar to that of Switzerland,
without any large standing army, without any militaristic spirit or ambitions, and without interrupting,
save to its advantage, the ordinary course of a young
man's preparation and entrance upon the active duties
of life. The third of these aims would be a powerful
contribution to the world-wide problem of vocational
training. It would fit men to do better that for which
they have natural capacity, and it would multiply the
economic power of the nation.

It seems an entirely safe prediction that were this
system established, its advantages would be so obvious

and so direct that there would be a quick demand to make similar provision for the national training of young women as well.

The nation has just expended tens of millions of dollars in the building of cantonments in different parts of the country. These cantonments are now the homes of the hundreds of thousands of citizen soldiers who are being prepared to take their part in the war. Why should not these cantonments be made permanent? Why should not the money expended upon them be made continuously productive by using these camps for the training of the youth of the land for national service during a portion of each year?

When the war shall end the governments will be faced by the problems of demobilization. It has been estimated that there are now thirty-five million men under arms. The task of demobilizing these unprecedented armies and of returning their members to industrial, to commercial, and to professional life will be far more serious than has been the task of their mobilization, and fraught with even graver economic and political dangers and perils. Might it not be possible to have the American national army demobilized by a process just the reverse of that by which it has been brought together? Might not the returning armies be brought back to the national cantonments before being disbanded, in order that then and there those soldiers who were found to need assistance or further training might receive it before being cast as derelicts upon society? In these several cantonments it would be quite practicable to install the necessary equipment for training men in at least some of those numerous trades and occupations that are necessary to the support of armies. It has been estimated that there are nearly two hundred such trades and occupations. A few months, or even a few weeks, of instruction bestowed upon these men when the time of demobilization comes, might easily save them and the nation itself incalculable suffering and loss later on. The example of France shows what beneficent arrangements may be made, through an undertaking of this kind, to render self-supporting many of those who have been grievously wounded or maimed in the war.

The American people will be slow to accept a plan of national training for national service if it is presented solely from the military point of view, because, offered in that way, it runs counter to the deep convictions of many persons. If, on the other hand, it is presented from this larger, more constructive, and more catholic point of view, it will, perhaps, commend itself to those men and women of our land who long to see the nation still more completely unified in spirit, in purpose, and in loyalty, and who look with dismay upon the large number of youth who drift every year into the active work of life without either adequate or specific preparation, and with no notion of their national obligations. It may be questioned whether any single step in advance more helpful than this could be taken by our government at the present time.

3. Something must be done without much delay to

alter and to improve the relation of the population to the land. The steady drift toward the cities is unhealthy, and it is not merely an American phenomenon; it is manifesting itself in nearly every part of the world, and its causes are perhaps almost as much psychological as economic. The satisfactions of country life are reserved in too large part for the poets, the essayists, the writers for the agricultural papers, and the well-to-do. This problem of the land and of country life relates itself to the problem of demobilization in a way which should not be overlooked.

When at the close of the Civil War the Northern armies were disbanded there was wide-spread concern lest political and economic disturbance would follow. It happened, however, that the nation of fifty years ago absorbed the soldier-folk quickly and without much difficulty. In no inconsiderable degree this absorption was made possible by the provisions of the Homestead Act and other legislation which invited settlers to the public lands on easy terms. The result was the rapid development of a dozen new commonwealths that have long been an integral part of the nation's pride and of the nation's strength.

Having reference to what has been accomplished during the last generation in Denmark, Ireland, and elsewhere, it is worth consideration whether the nation could not, by the use of its credit and in co-operation with the several States, lead hundreds of thousands of Americans back to the land. The amount of public land available for entry is no longer significant, but scattered all over the country there are areas of land, very large indeed in total amount, that might be used for purchase, occupation, and development through the use of the nation's credit. An advance at a low rate of interest and payable in annual instalments extending over, say, twenty or twenty-five years, would enable great numbers of ambitious and intelligent Americans, many of them recently drawn from nations across the sea, to become owners and tillers of the soil and so added to the producers of the food supply of the nation and of the world. History seems to teach that nothing contributes more to social stability and satisfaction than widely distributed land ownership and land occupancy. We have recently seen the ill effects of an opposite policy in countries as widely separated and as different as Mexico and Russia. It seems likely that great good could be done just now by measures that would establish American families increasingly upon American soil. The success of such a policy would operate to diminish the congestion in city population, with its attendant evils of bad housing, industrial disease, and overtaxed educational facilities. It would have a continuing effect to diminish the high cost of living. Accompanied by good roads, multiplied telephone service, circulating libraries, and other similar enterprises, such a policy might well, before many years, put a very different face upon what is now discontent, unhappiness, and unrest in the great centres of population.

At the same time, we are not allowed to forget that

there are practical questions affecting the farmer himself which await a satisfactory answer. Probably the simplification and the cheapening of the farmer's access to his market and steadily improving methods of cultivation are what is chiefly required.

4. In order to punish offenses long since committed and to prevent their repetition, the people of the United States have for thirty years encouraged and given wide support to a governmental policy toward the railways which has now had its logical and its necessary result. Whatever could be said in support of the legislation of 1887, of 1890, and of 1906, when it was enacted, it is plain that the interest of the public, including both shippers and consumers, requires something different now. The transportation system of the country has been crippled at the moment of the country's greatest need, not because of anything that the railway companies themselves have done, but because of what they have been prevented by law from doing. The overlapping and the conflict of State and federal regulation, and the steady rise in the cost of labor and of materials without any corresponding increase in rates, have literally impoverished the greatest railway systems in the world. They have been unable to develop adequate terminal facilities or to keep their permanent way, their motive power, and their rolling stock in first-class condition and adequate to the country's business. Their credit has been injured to such an extent that as a war measure the country will find itself absolutely

compelled to expend hundreds of millions of dollars of money drawn from the taxpayers to do, when it is almost too late, what the railways themselves would gladly have done at their own cost and greatly to the public advantage, had not their credit been so seriously impaired by public action. Under the war powers of the President, much of the restrictive and harmful legislation relating to railways has been swept aside, at least temporarily. Let us hope that it will never again be allowed to work public injury.

Transportation within a State and throughout the United States has become so single a problem that the continued attempt to apply several sets of laws, State and federal, to its regulation can only produce conflict of authority, embarrassment in railway operation, and inconvenience and cost to the public. The entire transportation system of the country has, by force of events, become national. The time has come when it should be put under exclusive federal supervision and control and when its problems should be dealt with not in a spirit of antagonism and repression, but in one of constructive and sympathetic helpfulness toward what have been truly described as the arteries of the nation's economic life. National ownership and national operation of the railway systems, as have been proposed, would revolutionize our government to its grave disadvantage and overturn the basis on which our economic and business life rests. Such policies would soon reduce our railways to the level of those on the continent of Europe, and would constitute a policy not of progress but of reaction. Some of the largest human experience and some of the best human skill in the United States are to be found in the service of the great transportation systems. They should be fostered and developed by national co-operation and national oversight as one of the very greatest of the country's assets in peace and in war alike.

Transportation by sea, in which the United States has lagged far behind for two generations, and the problem of a mercantile marine, have taken on a wholly new aspect because of the war. The appalling destruction of the world's tonnage, coupled with the necessity of conveying huge amounts of supplies by water from one Allied nation to another, have stimulated shipbuilding to an unheard-of degree. At the close of the war the United States will probably be in possession of a great fleet of merchant vessels, and will so regain the prestige that was lost sixty years ago. The country stands in dire need, however, of schools of naval architecture and construction and of schools for the training of seamen and their officers to navigate these ships. The necessities of the situation will stimulate all these, but they should be regarded as arising to satisfy permanent, and not merely temporary, needs.

5. Quickened public intelligence and enlightened public conscience are moving steadily throughout the world toward a fuller appreciation of man's obligation to his fellow and of society's responsibility for the unfortunate, the dependent, and the unemployed.

These are not, as is often taught, problems of a class or for a class; they are problems of and for a true democracy inspired by human kindliness and human sympathy. The problem of production or work is not adequately stated in terms of capital and labor. The problem of production is a human problem, and the man who works with his hands, the man who works with his head, and the man who works with his just accumulations, are the three different elements that enter into it. They are so closely related that they often overlap each other. To regard any one of these co-operating elements as standing apart from the others and in antagonism to them is simply to fail to grasp the facts. All three co-operating factors in production have an economic, and each should have a human, interest in the product. The shortened hours of labor, the substantial increase in wages, the better sanitary and protective conditions that are everywhere being introduced to make labor safe and to guard against occupational disease, are long steps forward in the humanizing of production.

There is another step yet to be taken which it seems likely will be hastened by the war. The mental attitude of the man who works with his just accumulations must be changed so far as to put production for use or for enjoyment in the place of production for mere profit. Production for profit alone is plainly an inhuman undertaking; it can and does close its eyes to human exploitation, to human suffering, and to human want. Production for use and for enjoyment,

on the other hand, lays all possible stress upon human
satisfactions.

Perhaps no one could have predicted that the war
would have gone far toward putting this larger and
finer and more democratic view of production in the
place of that which has prevailed for more than a century; yet that is precisely what is happening. When
we think in terms of war, we at once think in terms of
human protection and of human satisfaction. We
make instant provision for illness and for dependent
old age. When we think in terms of peace, however,
we have been more than reluctant to face the fact that
in a state of peace the social waste and the social diseases due to illness, to unemployment, and to dependent
old age are both constant and very large. As a people
we have yet to begin to deal effectively and in a large
way with overwork, with under-pay, with bad housing,
and with industrial disease. What war is teaching
us in regard to all these matters must not be lost sight
of when war gives way to a durable peace.

We have in the United States an almost limitless
amount of individual efficiency, but in social efficiency
we have lagged far behind. This has not been due to
lack of ability or to lack of material, but to lack of an
impelling and dominating social ideal. Even this war
is a blessing in disguise if it brings us that ideal and
makes it permanent.

6. The business of national government has become
so huge and so complex that the sharp separation of the
executive and the legislative powers to which we have

been accustomed for one hundred and forty years is now distinctly disadvantageous. It brings in its train lack of coherence and of continuity in public policy; it conceals from the people much that they should know; and it prevents effective and quick co-operation between the Congress and the Executive Departments, both in times of emergency and in the conduct of the ordinary business of government. There is a way to overcome these embarrassments and difficulties without in any way altering the form of our government or breaking down the wise safeguards which the Constitution contains. That is to provide by law, as may be done very simply, that the members of the Cabinet shall be entitled to occupy seats on the floor of the Senate and House of Representatives, with the right to participate in debate on matters relating to the business of their several departments, under such rules as the Senate and House respectively may prescribe. Such an act should further provide that the members of the Cabinet *must* attend sessions of the Senate and House of Representatives at designated times, in order to give information asked by resolution or to reply to questions which may be propounded to them under the rules of the Senate and the House of Representatives.

Had such a provision been in force during the past generation the nation would have been spared many an unhappy and misleading controversy. What has sometimes been made public only after the labor and cost of an elaborate investigation by committee, might

have been had without delay through the medium
of questions put to a Cabinet officer on the floor of
the Senate or the House of Representatives. No
feature of British Parliamentary practice is more useful, or contributes more to a public understanding of
what the executive is doing, than the proceedings at
question-time in the House of Commons. A Cabinet
officer is in a much more dignified position if he is
permitted to answer questions as to his official conduct and business on the floor of a legislative body
and to make his reply part of the public record, than
if he is interrogated in a committee-room as an incident in some general inquiry. Perhaps no single step
would do as much as this to restore public interest in
Congressional debates, to promote administrative
efficiency, and to bring about a just and proper inti-
macy between the legislative representatives of the
people and the people's chief executive agents.

This is not a new question, or one unsupported by
high authority; but unfortunately it had never been
pressed to a successful issue. The classic document
on the subject is the report of a select committee submitted to the Senate of the United States on February
4, 1881. That report accompanied and discussed a
bill containing the provisions just mentioned, and also
outlined certain rules to be adopted by the Senate
and House of Representatives in order to make the
provisions of the proposed bill effective. This report
was a unanimous one and was signed by senators be-
longing to each of the two great political parties. They

are men whose names carry great weight. The signatures are those of Senators Pendleton of Ohio, Allison of Iowa, Voorhees of Indiana, Blaine of Maine, Butler of South Carolina, Ingalls of Kansas, Platt of Connecticut, and Farley of California.

The bill which those senators reported thirty-seven years ago should now be revived and enacted. Their report discussed in elaborate detail both the advantages of the proposed measure and the possible objections to it, including those which might be raised on Constitutional grounds. That representative committee argued with convincing force that if, by a line of precedents since the organization of the government, the Congress has established its power to require the heads of departments to report to it directly, and also its power to admit persons to the floor of either house to address it, it would seem to be perfectly clear that the Congress may require the report to be made or the information to be given by the heads of departments on the floor of the houses, publicly and orally.

Were such a custom to be established an almost certain result would be the selection as heads of the great executive departments of men of large ability and personal force, men able to explain and to defend their policies and measures before the Congress of the United States in the face of the whole country. It would also follow that the nation's legislature would be enabled to exercise a more intelligent and a more effective control over the executive departments than is now the case, as well as to render them more intelligent and more effective aid in the form both of appropriations and of positive law.

Nothing would appear to stand in the way of this most desirable advance except our national political inertia, which always serves as a powerful obstacle to proposed political reforms. At the present moment, when the nation is making an unprecedented effort and when Congress is providing for loans and for taxes that are colossal in amount, and when new problems of far-reaching importance are constantly arising, it would be an inestimable public advantage were such a relation between the heads of the executive departments and the two Houses of Congress already established and in force.

7. If there is to be better and closer co-operation between the executive and the legislative departments of the government, and if that co-operation is to result in the largest practicable public benefit, there should be no further delay in agreeing upon a national budget system. The arguments for a budget have been presented many times and they are as convincing as they are familiar. The platform of the Democratic party adopted at St. Louis in 1916 and the platform of the Republican party adopted at Chicago in the same year, both declare explicitly for a budget system. It is hard to see why there should be any time lost in introducing it into the operations of our national government in view of the great advantages that must certainly follow.

In our form of government the Congress is made

responsible for determining what work the government shall undertake, what form of executive organization shall be established to carry on this work, and what amount of public funds shall be provided in general and in detail for the operations of the government, as well as how those funds shall be raised. Since no money may be drawn from the treasury but in consequence of appropriations made by law, a proper budget becomes the instrument of legislative control over the public administration. It is for Congress to determine what shall and what shall not be done, what shall and what shall not be undertaken. All experience proves that if what is to be done is decided in haphazard and desultory fashion, or in response to the unco-ordinated recommendations of a hundred different administrative officers, there will be waste, duplication of effort, and ineffectiveness. To escape these and to enable the Congress and the country to hold the President and his administration directly and fairly accountable for public policies, alike of omission and of commission, the President should himself be called upon to present each year to the House of Representatives a definite and well-analyzed estimate of those proposed expenditures which the administration wishes to support and to make its own. It should be within the power of the Congress to reduce or to strike out any of the items of this proposed expenditure, but the Congress should voluntarily relinquish or hold in abeyance—as it might readily do by a joint rule—its constitutional power to increase or to add to these items.

Moreover, the President should explicitly recommend the ways in which the moneys necessary to meet the proposed appropriations are to be raised. If the Congress accepts these recommendations, it makes the policy of the administration its own; if it departs from them, then the Congress publicly and of record assumes the responsibility. This makes for publicity of action and for responsible democratic government.

Everything of importance relating to a national budget is to be found in the report of the Commission on Economy and Efficiency presented to the second session of the Sixty-second Congress, on June 27, 1912. Happenings since that time have only served to strengthen the arguments that were used in that report. If the Congress is really to understand what the President and his administration wish to do and how they wish to do it, and if the people are to be in a position to hold the President and the Congress responsible for their several acts and policies, there must be established a national budget prepared and recommended by the chief executive. Every year's delay in bringing this about increases governmental confusion, inefficiency, and extravagance, and postpones the possibility of a simpler, a better-balanced, and a more effective administration of the public business.

8. As the result of nearly a century and a half of development and of a civil war which absorbed the entire energies of the people through four long years, the governmental and the geographic unity of the United States are secure. It is not by any means

so clear that there is a corresponding unity of spirit, of purpose, and of ideals among the American people themselves. Those differences among men which separate them into political parties having different policies but a common point of departure and a common goal, are merely incidental and strengthen rather than weaken national unity. If, on the other hand, there are within the nation forces and tendencies making for conflicts and antagonisms as to the fundamental purposes for which the nation and its government exist, then there is something to be done and that right away.

The war has brought clearly to view the fact that national unity is endangered, not only by illiteracy, which fact has long been recognized, but by diversity of language with its resulting lack of complete understanding and co-operation. No country can have a homogeneous or a safe basis for its public opinion and its institutions unless these rest upon the foundation of a single language. To protect the national unity and security no American community should be permitted to substitute any other language for English as the basis or instrument of common school education. Wherever another language has been introduced into the common schools, whether for conscious propaganda or otherwise, it should be ruthlessly stamped out as a wrong against our national unity and our national integrity.

No time should be lost in making adequate provision to teach English to those adult immigrants who are beyond the reach of the elementary school and yet have cast in their lot with the people of the United States.  A knowledge of the English language and evidence of some real understanding of the history and meaning of our institutions, should be required before the privilege of suffrage is conferred upon one who has grown up in another civilization than ours and under another flag than the Stars and Stripes.  Public safety is the supreme law, and public safety requires that the safeguarding and the improvement of our institutions be not committed to those who have had no opportunity to gain knowledge of them or to gain sympathy with them.

A still more subtle enemy of the American democracy is the wide-spread teaching that there is and should be a class struggle between those who have little and those who have more, between those who work with their hands and those who work in other ways.  The notion of fixed economic classes that are at war with each other is in flat contradiction to the principles and ideals of democracy.  The doctrine of a class conflict was made in Germany, and it represents a notion of social and political organization wholly at variance with the principles and conditions of our American life.  In this country we have no fixed economic classes and we desire none.  The handworker for wages of to-day is the employer of to-morrow, and the door of opportunity is so wide open that he who begins in industrial, commercial, or financial service at the bottom of the ladder may by competence and character speedily climb to its very top. Those who teach the justice and the necessity of a class struggle are not believers in democracy. They do not wish to lift all men up; they are bent upon pulling some men down. Their programme is one of destruction not construction, of reaction not progress. They do not believe in the equality of men before the law and in the equality of opportunity for all men and all women; they believe in a cruel, relentless, exploiting class. In other words, they believe in privilege and not in free government. Class consciousness and democracy are mutually exclusive. Its logical and necessary result would be to tear up the Declaration of Independence, to destroy the Constitution of the United States, and to put in their stead a Charter of Bedlam under whose provisions might, and might alone, would make right. Every movement and every effort to this end should be challenged peremptorily in the name of the American people, their traditions, and their ideals. It is as vitally important to oppose autocracy in this form as when it comes clad in imperial robes and accompanied with all the instruments of militarism.

No scheme of government and no social order can abolish every human ill. Certain of these ills are hardships which accompany human life; they are part of the order of nature and for them we cannot blame our fellow men. All that we can hope to do is to alleviate them and to do what lies in our power to surmount them. There are certain other human ills that arise

directly from the imperfections or errors of our civil
and economic institutions. These ills we must labor
to remove by the remedy of those imperfections and
by the correction of those errors.

All these are problems which lie directly in front of
us and which we cannot escape. We may, if we are so
minded, drift on the tide of daily happenings and trust
that these grave problems will solve themselves. Or
we may, if we are wiser and feel heavier responsibility
for the conduct of our government, face these problems with resolute determination to have them speedily
discussed and satisfactorily solved. It is hard enough
to bring our vast population to the active consideration of even a single new political or economic question,
to say nothing of half a score of them. Yet these are
unusual times. Men are casting off some of their old
trammels and encumbrances. The people are better
informed and more keenly interested in the details of
public and economic life than they have been since
the Civil War. The opportunity invites the American
people to enter without delay upon a new and splendid
path of real progress. Will they accept it?

# IV

# THE REAL LABOR PROBLEM

An address delivered before the Institute of Arts and Sciences,
Columbia University, October 13, 1919

# THE REAL LABOR PROBLEM

A few weeks ago I stood in one of the geyser basins of the Yellowstone National Park, and watched scores of openings in the earth's surface through which gas and steam and bubbling waters were escaping. The setting was superb. Great mountains raised their seared and rugged peaks high toward heaven; thousands of acres of unharmed forest, and a beauty of sky and exhilaration of air only to be found at a great elevation remote from the haunts of men, gave to the scene a beauty and a grandeur all its own. Men and women were coming and going filled with the joy of life, each one intent upon refreshing himself by contact with nature at its best. The query came naturally to one's lips, Can all this beauty and satisfaction last? May it not be that some day the hidden and heated forces of destruction that lie under the earth's crust, and that here come so close to the surface, will burst forth with irresistible power and overwhelm both the works and the satisfactions of men and the beauties of nature?

A like query must find its way to the lips of every thoughtful ·man who takes serious note of what is going on in the world. At no earlier time since recorded history began have the pleasures and the satisfactions of life been so numerous, so easily obtained, or so widely distributed. At no earlier time have the high aims and the strivings of men been so generally accomplished or set so far on the road toward accomplishment. Yet from numberless openings in the crust of the political and economic world on which we live there are coming constant signs, explosions growing more numerous and louder, which mark the presence of hidden and heated forces of destruction that may one day burst forth and destroy civilization. So many and so manifest are the evidences of this possibility, so emphatic and so wide-spread are the warnings of the presence of powerful forces of destruction, so constant and so manifold are acts in contempt alike of law and of social obligation, that we can only wonder at the levity of those who go their daily way without stopping even to reflect whether they may have any daily way to go a short time hence.

The situation which confronts us, and which is perhaps even more marked in Great Britain and in Italy than in the United States, is roughly and generally, though inaccurately, described as the industrial or labor problem. There is much more to it than that. It includes questions which go to the very foundation of civil society and national existence.

Thanks to the harmful dominance of some settled formulas, this problem has usually been presented to us as a contest between Capital and Labor over the product and rewards of industrial organization and activity. Since the word Capital is held to signify those fortunate ones who have been able to save, and the word Labor is held to signify those less fortunate ones who have not yet been able to save, public sympathy has been, with substantial uniformity, on the side of Labor in every such contest. Sympathy with the plight of the under-dog is well-nigh universal. For a full half-century the successive steps that have been taken to organize hand-workers to gain for themselves the privilege and the advantage of collective bargaining, to secure less severe hours and more healthful conditions of employment, and generally to increase their opportunities and their satisfactions, have commanded the increasing support and approval of the great mass of civilized men.

This has often been true even when the steps taken to bring about these advances and improvements have been in themselves rude, selfish, and destructive alike of the public order and the public weal. As a consequence, the condition of hand-workers has greatly and steadily improved. At no point in the complicated social and industrial system of modern times has so great personal and group advantage been reaped from the changes of the past generation as among the hand-workers. The rewards of invested savings or capital have steadily declined, while the lot of that immense fraction of the population which receives salaries rather than wages has grown constantly more difficult. Of the present population of the United States perhaps one-sixth, almost certainly one-seventh, is made up of persons in receipt of salaries and those immediately dependent upon them. These persons may be in a small way capitalists, and in a very large way hand-workers, but they are not usually classed with either Capital or Labor, but are rather expected to remain acquiescent spectators of a struggle from whose outcome they cannot possibly reap anything but disadvantage.

Matters were at about this point when the storm of war broke over the world. More or less quickly, and in some cases even with considerable difficulty, old-time ideals such as love of liberty, patriotism, and zeal to defend the weak against attack by the strong, overrode the obstacles to national effort and international co-operation which the economic and industrial struggle would otherwise have created. Because of the free world's lack of preparation for the attack made upon it, the war had to be carried on at immense cost. This immense cost, together with the constant pressure of war emergencies, entailed not only waste but colossal extravagance. These in turn led to an unhealthy expansion of credit and an undue inflation of currency. Prices quickly rose and money, or tokens of money, became relatively more plentiful than either goods or services. When the storm of war ceased the outstanding facts throughout the world were the high cost of living and the inability of men to resume their old mode of life at the old compensations. Quickly unrest and dissatisfaction began to spread like a contagious disease, and spreading they prepared the soil in readiness to receive any unwholesome, mad, or destructive political seed which might be sown. Those enemies of order, of liberty, and of progress who are always present, and who seem able to secure an amount of public attention wholly out of proportion to either their ability or their importance, redoubled their activities and have been openly or covertly urging social and industrial revolution from platform, from pulpit, and from press.

The result of all these manifestations and developments is that what used to be called the labor question or the industrial problem has entirely changed its form. The real labor problem, as it now presents itself to the people of the United States, is this:

Can the nation's industries be so organized and administered as to bring to the service of industry the well-tested principles and ideals of political democracy, without overturning the foundations of the Republic and without destroying the only guarantees on which order, liberty, and progress can possibly rest?

The problem, therefore, is no longer purely industrial or wholly economic; the course of events has made it, in large part, political as well. Otherwise stated it is this: Must the American form of government commit suicide in order to give to industry better and more satisfactory organization? Of course the question so put answers itself. If the American form of government commits suicide, it will make no difference to any one whether industry is better organized and conducted or not. Chaos will have come again and the right to rule men will be fought for with the usual result.   Might will certainly dethrone right, and there will be only darkness where now there is light.

There is a close parallel between some recent international happenings and some recent industrial happenings.   The air is filled with ultimatums.   One voice asserts that unless something which it strongly desires takes place within twenty-four hours, society will be deprived of the effective use of one of its great industries.   Another voice cries out that unless something which it strongly desires takes place within so many days, the whole transportation system of a great city or a wide-spread district will be paralyzed.   The strike in the steel industry is an excellent illustration of what is meant.   It is a convincing example of how not to deal with the labor problem.   The steel industry in modern life is basic.   All transportation, most manufacturing, and a very large part of the nation's building depend upon the supply of steel.   Therefore, to stop the output of steel for any reason whatsoever is to strike a definite and dangerous blow at the whole industrial organization of the modern state.   It must result in compelling wide-spread unemployment and a noticeable increase in the already high cost of living. The history of the beginnings of the steel strike read strangely like the beginnings of the European war. The ultimatums of Mr. Fitzpatrick and of Mr. Foster might well have been written by Count Berchtold, Chancellor Bethmann-Hollweg, or Minister von Jagow. The published statements associated with the names of each of these gentlemen are alike in that they make no appeal whatsoever to right or to justice, but simply give notice of peremptory demands and announce that when a fixed limit of time expires force will be used to support the demands. When the Austrian Government presented its ultimatum to Serbia on July 25, 1914, the world was shocked. But the same world did not appear to realize that the ultimatums of Mr. Fitzpatrick and Mr. Foster had in them far more seeds of danger both to America and to Europe, to liberty and to the rights of the weak, as well as to the wage-workers themselves, than did the Austrian ultimatum to Serbia. The ultimatums issued by Mr. Fitzpatrick and Mr. Foster were not a sincere and necessary step toward improving the condition of wage-workers in the steel industry, but were part of a new, carefully thought-out, and thoroughly well-planned attack on the principles upon which the American people have rested their government, their civilization, and their life. They were a declaration of war for power and the beginning of an attempt to compel the people and the government to enter upon a strange and wholly un-American public policy without deliberation or debate and under threat of industrial war and economic destruction. The Austrians and the Germans fought their war with different weapons, but the war that has been organized by Mr. Fitzpatrick and Mr. Foster, and the similar wars that were organized in Great Britain by Mr. Smillie and Mr. Thomas, are many times more dangerous than the Austrian ultimatum to Serbia or the German invasion of Belgium. The very

principles for which we have been fighting on so huge
a scale with military weapons are now at stake in the
contest to be waged with economic forces and with
ideas.

The question inevitably suggests itself, Why are we
so much concerned with the prevention of future international wars or with decreasing their likelihood, and
why are we apparently so indifferent to the question
of preventing industrial wars? Industrial wars can do
quite as much damage as international wars, huge as is
the burden of destruction which the latter have to
carry. In the case of international war we are all
pretty much convinced that while the ultimate use of
force in extreme cases cannot be dispensed with, yet a
very large area heretofore occupied by force may be
given over to the control of reasonableness in the hope
that eventually the habit of being reasonable will displace the habit of appealing to force in order to settle
differences between nations. It is along this path that
progress has been making for some generations past,
and it is along this path that future progress will most
hopefully be made. Why should not the same general
attitude of mind that we have agreed to adopt regarding international war serve us as we approach the
question of preventing industrial war? In the field of
industry, as in the field of international ambition,
might can only be dispossessed if right be called in to
take its place. Unless justice can rule, force must
control. There is no alternative.

When we begin the application of the test of reasonableness to matters of industry, we come straightway upon the damage done by misleading words, phrases, and formulas. For this damage we rightly have a grudge against the writers on economics, both classical and socialist, most of whom have discussed the intimate and highly practical questions of modern industry without either the specific information or the personal experience which enabled them to know precisely what their words and phrases meant. They have usually begun with an analysis of wealth, whereas the primary economic fact is not wealth but work—work in its psychological and ethical as well as its economic aspects.

Perhaps the starting-point of the difficulty is to be found in the sharp antithesis that exists between Capital and Labor, not only in the mind of the general public but even in that of those who are actively engaged in productive industry. So long as we speak of Capital and Labor as mere abstractions, struggling in some invisible way over the division of the product of industry, we not only get nowhere but we assist actively in spreading wholly false economic views. We give ground for the notion, very wide-spread among wage-workers, but utterly false, that the less work they do in a given time or for a given wage the better for themselves and for their group. Under such a theory each increase in wages must directly increase the cost of living for every one, including those who get the increased wages. In this way there is quickly established an endless chain of economic fallacies that will in time bring disaster to any industry or any people.

On the other hand, if we abandon our fondness for abstractions and look at any industrial process just as it is, we quickly discover that it is an enterprise in human co-operation, and that in it there may be and usually are three different kinds or sorts of co-operating human beings—those who work with their hands, those who work with their brains, and those who work with their savings. These are all alike essential to productive industry, and production is the joint enterprise in which all are engaged in common. In the case of the steel industry, for instance, a skilled employee in a rolling-mill who has bought some of the stock of the United States Steel Corporation represents in his own person all three kinds of co-operating influence. He works alike with his hands, with his brains, and with his savings. This is an almost ideal condition and one which we should strive to make just as universal as possible. If industry, then, whether it be the mining of coal, or the transportation of freight, or the cutting and sawing and trimming of timber, or the packing of salmon, or the manufacture of paper from wood-pulp, or the spinning, dyeing, weaving, and printing of cotton, is truly an enterprise in co-operative production, it follows that every co-operating agency is directly interested both in the quantity and the quality of the product. The greater the product per unit of occupation, the less the overhead charge and so much more the amount available to pay a satisfactory wage, to meet the prevailing rate of interest, and to provide a reasonable margin of profit as well as to take care of normal depreciation and repairs. If the wage-earner can be led to understand that his wages are paid out of product and not out of capital or out of profits, he will speedily assist in increasing production, because he will understand that only in that way is it possible to provide for any permanent increase in wages. Again, just so soon as the wage-earner is led to see the truth of the fact that he and the man who works with his savings, the so-called capitalist, are alike interested in greater production, he will begin to comprehend what co-operation in industrial production really means. Persons otherwise intelligent go about the country telling us that it is mere hypocrisy to say that the interests of employer and employed are the same. On the contrary, it is mere ignorance to say they are not the same.

When this point has been made clear and industry is viewed as a co-operative enterprise in production, then it follows that those who work with their hands, like those who work with their brains and those who work with their savings, are entitled to take part in the organization and direction of the industry and to have a voice in determining the conditions under which their co-operation shall be given and continued. No matter how many or how few persons may have contributed of their savings to the organization and carrying on of a given industry, that industry does not, therefore, belong in the broad sense of the word to them alone; it belongs, also, to those human beings who co-operate with them by aiding in the production of goods either by the work of their hands or by the work of their brains. This principle can readily be applied without interfering with the effectiveness of skilled and responsible management.

The policy of reasonableness will carry us a step farther. The industry so conceived and so organized will have to sell its product at a price that will enable it to pay to those who work with their hands a thoroughly satisfactory wage, to those who work with their brains an appropriate salary, and to those who work with their savings a definite minimum return based upon the current value of money. As the wages and the salaries must be paid in any event, it is interest or dividends upon savings which must bear the brunt of any shortage in net income. The cost of depreciation and replacement is also to be met. When all these have been provided for, whatever remains is profit. Reasonableness indicates that this profit should not go to one group alone of the three who co-operate in production, but should be apportioned between all three groups in accordance with a plan drawn to meet the facts of a given industry. If, on the other hand, there be a loss instead of a profit, or a deficiency in the amount needed to meet all of the items just stated, the amount of that deficiency is met, as matters now stand, by those who work with their savings alone. There is merit in the suggestion that a given industry should, in years of prosperity, establish an undistributed reserve fund against which should be charged any losses that might subsequently be incurred. It is impossible, however, to cover all contingencies by one formula. It would appear to be a complete justification of the method of reasonableness if industry be viewed as an enterprise in co-operative production; if the three co-operating agencies be all recognized and treated as human beings and not as abstractions; if the reward of each of these agencies be seen to be derived from the product and from it alone; and if the joint and co-operative interest in a common product be maintained and increased by giving to representatives of each of these elements a direct share in the conduct and control of the industry and its policies. A system of industrial organization such as this is not only entirely compatible with our American principles of government and of life, but it is nothing more than a decent application of those principles to modern industry. There would be no "wage slavery" under such a plan.

The rule of reasonableness in the field of industry will probably no more certainly supplant entirely the rule of force than will be the case in the field of international relations; but, as in the case of international relations, the habit of reasonableness will more or less speedily supplant the habit of force. Until the millennium comes and until selfishness and greed disappear from the world, there will be no frictionless industrial machinery. All that can be hoped for is to apply the methods of reasonableness and to support those methods by good-will, by sympathy, and by kindly criticism of happenings as they occur. This way lie peace, progress, and the preservation of American institutions and ideals.

If, however, we are not to use or are not to be permitted to use the methods of reasonableness in dealing with these problems, then we must be prepared for the use of force. This alternative is shocking. It would mean nothing less than the substitution of anarchy for order, of physical power for justice, and of a perpetual struggle between changing and conflicting interests for the calm and temperate discussion of principles. It would almost certainly involve the destruction of the individual's moral right to own property, which right is itself an attribute of liberty and an essential condition of social and political progress.

It would seem that it is precisely to prevent such happenings as these that man's political organization, the state and its government, have been brought into being. The power of the state, we say, will prevent these self-seeking and violent attacks on civilization, and will protect alike the achievements and the acquisitions of the people. This assumption ought to be correct and will yet be justified if men think clearly, and fully appreciate the relation in which their political organization stands to organization and affiliation of every other kind. The fundamental purpose of the state is to preserve order, to defend liberty, and to keep open the door of opportunity. Without order there can be no liberty, and without liberty there can be no continuing progress. These are the reasons why that form of human association and organization which has to do with order and with liberty and, therefore, with progress, namely, the political form known as the state, differs from other forms of human association and takes precedence over every other such form. In the democratically organized state, particularly that established by the Constitution of the United States, there is frequent and direct opportunity to shape public policy in orderly fashion after debate in the presence of the whole citizenship of the nation, and at the hands of the chosen representatives of that citizenship. Such is the normal and the healthy process of political life and political change. In recent years, however, the highly complex organization of our economic and industrial life and the manifold interdependences by means of which we sustain life and carry on business have brought into view the possibility of quickly checking the whole machinery of our economic and industrial life by bringing to a stop the operation of some necessary element in it. At first the checking of the operation of a necessary element in our economic life was made the means of enforcing changed conditions of compensation or of employment on the part of individual or corporate employers. This method is known as the strike and is, of course, a manifestation of force. The strike is at best not a method of reasonableness but a weapon of industrial war, and it ought in time to become obsolete with the submarine and the Big Bertha. It will become obsolete when men come more clearly to understand what industrial co-operation really involves, on what basis it rests, and how entirely at one are the interests in production of every co-operating agency in any industry.

Recently the startling doctrine has been taught and practised that the strike may be used to enforce the views and wishes of a small minority of the population in matters relating not only to public transportation and to other public utilities, but to political and public acts of every sort. This is to call back the *Liberum Veto* of ancient Poland with a vengeance. According to this doctrine a group of individuals who do not approve of the tariff levied on wool may unite to make impossible the operation of a steamer which carries a cargo of wool from Argentina to the United States, or to prevent the unloading of such cargo when the steamer reaches the docks of New York. The government of the United States may deem it necessary to send troops and to ship munitions to Siberia, but under this doctrine stevedores and longshoremen at the ports of San Francisco and of Seattle would be entirely justified in refusing to load or to permit to be loaded the vessels which were to carry such troops and munitions in case they as individuals should happen to disapprove of the government's policy in this regard. Still others might say that they would refuse to assist in operating the railways of the United States, and would unite to prevent their being operated by others, unless a certain designated public policy in regard to railway ownership and operation were quickly adopted. It must be apparent from these illustrations that without complete loyalty to the democratic principle, without respect for law, without sincere devotion to American ideals of government, and without good-will on the part of all elements and groups of society, the economic and political life of the nation can no longer go forward, and that we are in imminent danger of national shipwreck and of incalculable disaster.

Were it not for the well-known irresponsibility of many of those who attempt to guide the public by teaching and by writing, it would be startling to learn that at so critical a time as this in the history of American civilization the doctrine is actually being formally and systematically taught that man's political organization, the state, is not any more fundamental than several other forms of human association, and that, therefore, the state has no necessarily superior claim upon the loyalty and devotion of the citizen. There are those who assert that the political state is only one among many forms of human association, and that it is not necessarily any more in harmony with what some writers are pleased to call "the end of society" than a church, or a trade-union, or a masonic lodge, or a college fraternity. What this means when brought down from the language of academic detachment from facts to the plane of hard common sense is that the American nation is not really a unit but a multiple object composed of men in political relationships, in church memberships, in trade-union memberships, in college fraternity memberships, and in half a hundred other co-ordinate memberships, each of which has its own claims upon our loyalty. It is held that the political relationship is but one of many, and that the individual must decide which of his relationships and which of his loyalties is at any given time to take precedence of the others. For example, a man might decide that his loyalty to his college fraternity overrode his loyalty to the state, in so far as the latter required him to abstain from assault and battery. Or he might decide that his loyalty to his church or to his trade-union required him to defy some act of Congress or some decision of the Supreme Court of the United States. This course of reasoning and of procedure would make of life one continual lynching. Individuals or groups of individuals, would in this way be brought into constant contempt and defiance of law, with the certain result that civilization must disappear in the smoke of armed conflict between different groups of selfish and self-seeking men.

This doctrine, which it is asserted is now being taught in American universities and even in American law schools, is given several high-sounding names, but it is correctly and bluntly described as the gospel of anarchy and disorder, as well as of the complete destruction of everything that mankind has accomplished during the past three thousand years.

It is because of more or less conscious adherence to this sort of teaching that the I. W. W. and other like-minded organizations propose to force political action by economic pressure or by economic war. Those who are in this state of mind not only decry but despise democracy, and those who are frank among them do not hesitate to say so. They do not believe in equality of opportunity or in liberty, but in class organization, class privilege, and class tyranny. The spokesmen for this doctrine are often persons who have never done a day's work in their lives but who, out of sheer zeal for destruction and mad passion for notoriety, associate themselves with various organizations of wage-workers and others and endeavor to bend these organizations to their own ends.

At present this doctrine is supported by an organized and apparently well-financed propaganda. We have hardly comprehended how completely the American people are at the mercy of skilful propaganda of this sort. The experience of the war taught us that propaganda can do almost anything with public opinion, at least for a time; and at this moment propaganda of all kinds is well under way all about us except as regards the one essential subject of the state's own preservation. The state is so busy doing things for particular interests and groups that it is neglecting the protection of its own life. It would be an odd by-product of social and industrial change if state suicide were to be one of its results.

The possibility of this has just now been brought home to observant Americans by the police strike in Boston, Massachusetts. Dangerous as this strike was, it had its origin, I am convinced, more in ignorance than in malice. The police force of Boston had apparently never been taught that the servants of the community are in nowise to be regarded as in the same relation as are employees to a private or corporate employer. If the police force or any other set of servants of the community of Boston find the terms of their service harsh or unsatisfactory, there are perfectly definite and legitimate ways of securing both a hearing and action upon any request they may make without deserting their posts, stripping the community of its power of self-protection, and opening the door to every crime both of violence and of cunning.

A strike by a public servant is a direct assault on the whole community and is nothing less than only a mild form of treason; and it may not always be mild. The line between employer and employee, on the one hand, and the community and its servants, on the other, must be clearly drawn and stoutly maintained, not only in the interest of the community and its order, but in the interest of the wage-earners themselves. Nothing more disastrous could happen to the movement for the improvement of working conditions, now going forward so happily, than to have the general public get the idea that those who desire improvement for themselves are willing to conspire against the peace, order, and public service of the whole community. If public servants were to be assimilated in practice to employees of private and corporate enterprise, and if they were to use the strike as a mode of enforcing their requests or demands, then the American form of government would have come to an end. Neither justice nor liberty would longer be possible, and in their stead we should have disturbed and hectic rule by quickly succeeding minority groups, the result of which would be anarchy, universal impoverishment, and nation-wide distress.

For similar reasons an attempt by any part of the community to force political action through with-holding their service in the complex economic and in-dustrial life of the people is absolutely indefensible. We are so closely interdependent that it is quite im-possible for any considerable group of individuals sud-denly to withdraw their services without producing far-reaching and disastrous effects in ways and of a kind wholly unforeseen. It is not true that our loyalty to any one of a dozen of our associations is the same in character and quality as our loyalty to the state. The state demands our primary loyalty because only through loyalty to it can our other loyalties have any mean-ing or importance. If the loyalty upon which depend order, liberty, and progress is only the same in kind as the loyalty upon which depend some personal or eco-nomic satisfactions, patriotism is dissolved in selfish-ness and the sort of democratic Republic that we flat-tered ourselves we were building becomes an impos-sibility.

To solve the real labor problem, then, we must think straight and clear regarding facts of industry, and think straight and clear regarding principles of political organization. Continued industrial progress and far-reaching industrial reform are easily possible, and indeed in my view are only possible if the principles and ideals on which, and for which, the American people have been building for a century and a half are maintained and strengthened. Moreover, we must shun and take active steps to limit the influence of those who foment unrest and organize industrial war and who thrive upon this process. These are public enemies and the hand-workers' meanest friends. From the very active company of those who would not hesitate to tear down or to overthrow the government of the United States in order to attain their immediate personal or group ends, there has not come a single suggestion which does not spell destruction. Not one of those who claim to represent these movements and tendencies has proposed to build up anything. They are all bent upon destruction in the wild hope that after their joy in tearing down has had full satisfaction, somewhere and somehow personal advantage may accrue to them. In the process they would not hesitate to destroy America.

V

THE HIGH COST OF LIVING

An address delivered before the Commercial Club,
San Francisco, California, August 22, 1919

# THE HIGH COST OF LIVING

A year ago we spoke together of the situation which then confronted us, of the movements of thought and of action which were bringing the war to its close, but our doubts were not wholly resolved. We could not then see with definiteness the time of the outcome, and although we were convinced that the cause of righteousness for which we were making every sacrifice was certain to prevail, and while we felt, in addition, that with the aid of our splendid American armies, those who were singing the battle-cry of freedom had really gone over the top of the hill of difficulty, we were not prepared to say that the war would end within any measurable number of weeks or months.

Suddenly, the effects of the great corroding forces that were at work in the German and Austrian Empires, bringing about economic and social and political collapse, destruction of military morale and military power, taken in connection with the irresistible force of the great armies of France and Britain and Italy and America, under the single presiding genius of Marshal Foch, brought the war to a sudden end by the armistice of November 11 last. It was as if a great curtain had fallen upon the most magnificent and appalling of dramas which history could anywhere present to human contemplation. In a twinkling of an eye the contest, in the military sense, was over. The killing of men, the marching of armies, the raiding by submarines, the convulsions of every sort that grew out of this great military conflict, ceased, and the world found itself, without an instant's warning, without chance for preparation, without any opportunity to study or rehearse the steps that were to be taken, face to face with the problem of creating out of the chaotic elements which were the result and the accompaniment of war, a new world, that should continue all that was best and finest and most splendid in the old, and that should add to it everything which could be said to be a direct and definite and convincing lesson of the war itself.

Do you wonder that the imagination of mankind was staggered by a task like that? Can you wonder that human capacity everywhere was appalled, almost to paralysis, not alone by the far-reaching character of the task but by its novelty and by its pressing importance? For the old world of armed forces and international rivalries and national exploitations and varied forms of compromise, running all through the industrial, social, and the political structure—that world had gone, and something must be created to take its place.

That topic is so large; it presents so many aspects; it opens up so many avenues of contemplation and discussion that it would require days for an intelligent body of Americans even to pass together over the high spots of its importance. Therefore, this morning, I am going to confine myself to expressing some opinions and asking some questions in reference to one aspect only of our present-day problems, the one which I conceive to be of most immediate importance, and to have in it the seeds of the greatest danger, if not handled with courage, with knowledge, with firmness, and with statesmanlike capacity and vision.

Following the war, men have attempted to return to their accustomed occupations, to reorganize the business of the world, and they find themselves everywhere confronted by an imperative struggle for existence in more stringent form than they have been accustomed to for generations past. In the language of every-day speech, they are confronted by the high cost of living. They are confronted, not alone as communities and states and nations, not alone as corporations, or as individual employers, or as workers for wage or for salary; they are confronted by the problem in their capacity as individual citizens, because so heavily does the high cost of living press upon every individual that, in order to seek relief from it, in order to find the solution for it, he is all too ready to accept formulas for facts, doctrinaire leadership for statesmanlike analysis and direction, and a false and destructive solution for one that is true and constructive in its applications and in its results.

This issue in its larger reference is of gravest importance. When men in large masses and in large numbers cannot live, there is no security for even the oldest, the best-established, and the most highly honored of political and social institutions. Men must be able to live; the world's business must be able to go on; commerce, trade, industry, finance are all the essential underlying foundations of what we call the richer and the riper civilization. Without these there is no art, there is no literature, there is no education, there is no poetry, there is no opportunity for the flowering and the enjoyment of the intellectual and the spiritual life.

First of all, men must live. There are those who, when they find themselves face to face with a problem of that kind, begin to dash about like a lion in a cage, showing great excitement, making violent expressions, calling for the blood of some individual or group, but making no contribution whatever to an understanding of the problem.

I should like, if I may, briefly to suggest what I believe to be the essential elements of this problem, and the only way in which we, as Americans, men of thought, of consideration, of loyal patriotism, and of generous impulse for service to our fellow men—the only way in which we can hope to solve this problem and to avert from civilization the dangers which the failure to solve it will certainly entail.

Let me point out, first, that the problem of the high cost of living is by no means entirely a result of the war. The war has multiplied the elements that entered into it; it has increased their significance; it has spread over wider areas their effect; it has, of course, added some new and highly important elements of its own, but the problem of the high cost of living was upon us before the war, and, while less acute, it would in due time have come to vex our statesmanship and our economic, our industrial, and our political capacity.

Moreover, this problem is in no sense one for the people of the United States alone. It is a world-wide problem. It has had world-wide manifestations for a number of years, and these manifestations have been substantially alike in all of the great industrial nations of the earth. Inasmuch as the whole world has been involved in the war, directly and indirectly, the problem has been increased and accentuated for the whole world. The causes that were operating here were operating elsewhere. The additional impetus that has been given to those causes by the war here has been given to the operation of those causes elsewhere.

If I were asked to venture an opinion as to what were the factors in bringing about the world-wide problem of the high cost of living, I should suggest these five:

First: The extraordinary expansion of credit, accompanied by currency inflation, due, primarily, to public and private waste, extravagance, and borrowing for non-productive purposes. That had been going on everywhere before the war. The war immensely increased both borrowing and waste and extravagance. It increased some of it naturally and normally, because we had to win the war, no matter what it cost. But, in addition, under the pressure of the war emergency, under the pressure of the war spirit, nations and individuals alike, finding new opportunities for credit expansion, entered upon a scale of expenditure the like of which is not recorded anywhere in economic history.

And you cannot borrow from the future without having to pay. You are now paying in part for waste, extravagance, and credit expansion before the war, and, in part, the cost of the war itself. You cannot have a great world war and not pay for it. It cannot go on for nearly five years and consume a large part of the industrial competence of the world and leave costs and prices where they were before. We are not the only people from whose history evidence of the correctness of these statements can be drawn. In France there had been a steady expansion of credit and a steady inflation of the currency for years.

In 1906 the circulating medium of France was seven and one half billion francs; in 1914 it was twelve billion francs; in 1919 it is forty billion francs; and the population of France has not altered in the interval, save, perhaps, it has been somewhat diminished by the losses due to the war.

Down to 1881 our per-capita circulation in the United States had never gone above twenty dollars. Twenty years later it was still below thirty dollars. When the war broke out it was about forty dollars. At the present time it is fifty dollars and seventy-five or eighty cents. If that credit expansion and currency inflation alone had been operative, the cost of everything would have risen, because money itself, the circulating medium, would have been so much cheaper.

What is the remedy? The remedy is public economy and private thrift. Save and invest in productive industry. Every individual and every government can contribute to a reduction of the high cost of living by economy, frugality, and thrift, and by investment in productive industry alone, in place of expenditure for extravagant or wasteful purposes.

Very homely counsel, you say. It sounds so like a leaf from old Benjamin Franklin that it is too old-fashioned, perhaps, to be of any use to-day. No, gentlemen, that counsel is the beginning of a reduction of the high cost of living.

You have eighteen States in the American Union that are, every year, spending more than they are raising by taxation. To borrow is excellent policy, when the money borrowed is invested in productive industry and pays a return larger than the cost of borrowing, but to borrow for ordinary governmental expenses, or for household living, means, first, increased cost and, next, bankruptcy. And there I find, in my analysis of the facts, the first of the world-wide causes operating to increase the cost of living. Do you realize that the public debts of the world have gone up from forty billions to two hundred and twenty billions; that the world now owes almost the entire value of the United States—its land, its industries, its capital, its possessions of every sort? The world has borrowed from its future pretty nearly the whole value of the United States of America, and on that it is paying interest, and that interest is a charge upon industry, upon livelihood, and that interest is at this moment increasing the cost of living. When governments economize and bring their expenditures within their income; when individuals economize and bring their expenditures within their incomes, and when the two begin to reduce their indebtedness, then we shall have taken the first great and long step toward restoring economic equilibrium and toward getting back to a real business basis in the conduct of the affairs of the world.

A second cause is to be found in the marked diminution of production. That diminution of production has been greatly accelerated by the war, because the war took in round numbers twenty-five million men from productive industry and turned them into consumers, and into an occupation which, from the standpoint of economics, was expenditure of a wasteful kind. You cannot take twenty-five million men from production and turn them into consumers without increasing the cost of living for everybody. That is a legitimate war cost, and that has to be paid for, and that is paid for in part by the increased prices of everything that we eat and wear and use.

There is another cause which has diminished production, which was operative before the war, and which is still operating, and will continue to operate until checked in a manner which I should like briefly to indicate. That is the diminished hours of labor throughout the world have not yet been compensated for by more effective industrial production. During the past generation, probably fifty million men and women in the industrial nations of the world have had their stated hours of labor reduced from twelve, eleven, and ten, to eight. I conceive that to have been a great social advantage and in the interest of public stability, public satisfaction, and public health. That reduction in the hours of labor is a thoroughly justifiable public and economic policy, but it is bound to decrease production unless, by new methods, by improved machinery, by better distribution, by more effective shop organization, there can be produced in eight hours as much or more goods and services as were formerly produced in longer hours.

Our problem here is to speed up production under the conditions of a shortened day, under the healthful surroundings which are now becoming, fortunately, common in modern industry of every kind. It is to speed up production, and to speed it up by the use of brains, by the use of skill, by the use of organizing and executive ability, and by better organization of production and distribution.

We have been specially lacking in this country in organizing our means of distribution of the food supply. We have done wonderfully well in providing for the distribution of individuals desiring to move about the country for one form of business or another. We have done very well in arranging for the distribution of large bulk of goods, but we are still in a very primitive stage in regard to the distribution of what may be called the food supply drawn from the neighborhood. An examination and an analysis of the food supply of the city of New York, for example, or of the city of Philadelphia, or the city of Boston, would show that there are a great many waste motions; there is a great deal of duplication and unnecessary cost, because we have not yet put our brains upon the question of effective and economical distribution of the food supply for a great mass of population.

Therefore, as a second remedy for the high cost of living, I say that we must speed up production by the use of brains, by the use of skill, and by the use of organizing ability.

A third cause of the high cost of living is the natural rise in the cost of raw material of the food supply of the world, due to the operation of causes operative everywhere, including the drift of the rural population to the cities, the using up of the better and more accessible land in every country, and the failure in some parts of the world to make use of the newest and most improved methods of intensive and productive agriculture.

In addition to that, we have withdrawn from the food supply of the world the immense areas in Russia, Rumania, and Hungary—the great grain-producing area of southern and eastern Europe. That has been practically taken away from the world's production, owing to the war. Even if the land has been cultivated, and we know that it has only been cultivated in part, and under very difficult conditions—even if it has been cultivated, it has been cut off from the rest of the world by the blockade, by the line of military operations across western Europe, and by the inability to procure transportation, either by land or by sea. In part, those causes were working before the war; in part, they are the result of the war. Relief is to be found, first, in speedily restoring to productive agriculture for the world's consumption the areas in Russia, Rumania, and Hungary that have been cut off; and, second, in doing everything we can to develop more productive and intensive agriculture in America, in Great Britain, in France, in Holland, in Spain, and in Italy, and in quickening and cheapening distribution.

A fourth cause operating to increase the cost of living is one which seems largely to have escaped attention, but which is highly operative in England and in this country. The systems of taxation adopted in Great Britain and in the United States to finance the war, including the form of the income and the excess profit taxes, have operated to increase directly and everywhere the cost of living. The reason is this: if you take a producer, a trader, or a distributer, who is doing a business of a certain volume, and who desires to increase his profit or his business by one dollar per unit, he must increase the price to the public perhaps five dollars per unit in order to pay four dollars per unit to the government, and have one dollar per unit left. If the enterprise is one in which there are a large number of contributing parts, if the enterprise is a chain of six or seven links, and if each link of the chain finds it necessary to get one dollar more profit in order to do business, then each of the six or seven links must increase its charge by five dollars in order to get one dollar; and seven times five is thirty-five, of which seven is profit, and twenty-eight is tax.

What that means is this: not that we should take steps to relieve wealth of its just burden of taxation, but that we should so readjust and restudy those taxes that, instead of necessarily increasing the cost of living, they should stimulate enterprise, quicken initiative, increase production, reduce unemployment, and decrease the cost of living. It is all a question between thinking out the form of that tax, and where its incidence is going to lie, before you impose it, or not thinking about it at all, and letting it fall where it will.

If there is to be no revision of the form of those taxes, then you must be confronted with the fact that there will be a restriction of initiative, a constant decrease in production, and a steady increase in the cost of living. In the attempt to tax wealth heavily, a form has been chosen which has done that, but, in addition, has increased the cost of living. We shall not escape from this until we revise that form. Continue to tax wealth, but do so in a way that will not so heavily and so directly increase the cost of living.

A very large industrial enterprise recently made a comparison of its costs, and of its payments out in 1918 and in 1913, and it found that the excess of payments in 1918 over 1913 was to be accounted for in this way: labor, 57 per cent; taxes, 40 per cent; capital, 3 per cent—and that case is probably typical.  In other words, the labor cost, which can only be brought down by better methods of production, and the cost in taxation, which can only be brought down by economy in government and more scientific levying of taxes, had consumed 97 per cent of the excess in those five years. That shows you exactly where the high cost of living comes from, and the road along which you must travel in order to reduce it.  It does not involve any jugglery, any magic, any metaphysical handling of our economic and political and social system.  It requires hard, plain business sense to look the facts in the face, to see precisely what they are, and to organize industrial and social and political policy in view of those facts.

Last of all comes profiteering.  That there has been profiteering, everybody knows.  Under such a condition as has existed in the world for the last five years it has been possible for profiteering to go on in many directions.  There are those who would like to shoot profiteers.  There are those who would wish to imprison profiteers.  All profiteers, where they are really taking advantage of an opportunity to oppress the public, should be punished.  That goes without saying.  But, gentlemen, if we had punished all the profiteers, you would not reduce the cost of living appreciably for anybody, because the other and far more important causes of expenditure are operating all over the world.  If you had them all shot, or all locked up,

and everything which they have hoarded distributed
to us, you would still have expansion of credit and
currency inflation; you would still have diminution
of production; you would still have increase in the
cost of agricultural products; you would still have
the incidence of an unscientifically levied system of
taxation.

So that, while we wish to get rid of profiteering, we
wish to punish profiteering, let us not deceive ourselves
by supposing that when that is done the cost of living
is going automatically to drop to the point where it
was in 1880 or 1890, or 1900, or 1910, or 1914. It is
not. It is not going to approach what it was at any
one of those dates until the operation of economic law
brings about the conditions which prevailed at some
one or other of those dates.

The resource of many of those in authority in a situation like this is to try to satisfy public demand by
immediate and drastic action of some sort. This looks
very well; it fills the newspapers; it tickles the ears of
the groundlings; it makes an impression of great activity; but, gentlemen, these inexorable economic laws
which are not subject to amendment and repeal by
congresses and parliaments and legislatures, these inexorable economic laws are going their way behind
the scenes while the demagogues howl and rage and
rant all over these various countries with their formulas
and their maxims and their methods of immediate
solution.

Our task, as intelligent, self-respecting, patriotic

Americans, is to ask for the facts. If these which I have suggested are not the causes, or proximate causes, of the high cost of living, what are they? What has been operating in these countries to bring about this condition? If these methods of action, public and private, which I have pointed out will not lead to relief, what are the methods which will do so? This is no time for bravado; this is no time for cynicism; this is no time for violence or revolution. This is a time for clear, sane, courageous thinking on the facts of business, industrial, and political life.

When you examine the operation of these laws and forces you find something like this: taking 1913, the year before the war, as normal, or par, you will find that the cost of living five years before that, in 1908, was represented in the United States by 84; Great Britain, 84; France, 85. In other words, in the five years from 1908 to 1913, the cost of living in those three countries had risen substantially a like amount, owing, of course, to the operation of similar causes. But if you take those figures to-day, 1913 remaining par, or 100, they are, for the United States, 197; for Great Britain, 217, and for France, 312. That represents what has happened during the war in so far as the cost of living is related to wages and incomes in the countries named.

Inasmuch as the United States has to pay its share of the cost of the war, but felt little of the destruction of the war, our figure is the lowest, 197. Inasmuch as Great Britain had to pay its cost of the war, but felt directly some of the loss of the war, its figure is 217. Since France had not only to pay its share of the cost of the war, but felt in immense degree the destruction of the war, its figure is 312.

Just so when you turn to production; what is the use of looking for a profiteer in the English coal industry—the key or basic industry of Great Britain on which everything else depends, including all its foreign trade—when in 1918 the production was 240,000,000 tons, while in 1913, for a like period, it was 287,000,000 tons? If you reduce production of a staple fifty million tons in a like number of weeks, you do not need to look for profiteers to explain the increase in the cost of coal in Great Britain, as the increase in the cost of living, or the increase in the cost of every industry.

I commend to you as citizens of the United States, as men dealing directly with our commerce, with our industry, with our finance, as men taking a wide and sympathetic view of public problems and public movements, I submit to you that every American owes it to his country to make every possible effort to understand the causes that are at work in bringing about this present situation, and by every act and counsel of his own contribute all that lies in his power toward relief from these conditions. Those upon whom they rest with the greatest heaviness, those whose emotions make it impossible for them to think calmly and clearly concerning them, like the lion in his cage, of which I spoke a moment ago, feel revolution in their hearts. They say: "Let us tear down; nothing could be worse than this. Let us see what destruction has to give, if construction be not quickly forthcoming."

That is the meaning of these ominous words to which the chairman has referred. That is the meaning of the ominous and significant happenings in the great political and industrial capitals of the world, from southeastern Europe clear over to these United States. It means that human feeling and human emotion must find some kind of expression in the hope of gaining relief, if human intelligence and human reason are not at our disposal as a people, to guide us to a solution that is constructive, that is wise, that is just to every individual, every group, and every interest in this land, and that will make this new America that we are building finer and more just and more splendid and more prosperous than ever before.

What would we not give, in an hour like this, for the sturdy Americanism, the public virtue, and the personal courage of Grover Cleveland and Theodore Roosevelt ?

# VI

# THE ROAD TO DURABLE PEACE

An address delivered before the Chamber of Commerce,
St. Louis, Missouri, February 16, 1918

# THE ROAD TO DURABLE PEACE

The war which now involves the whole world is, on the part of the Allies, avowedly a war not for conquest, for revenge, or for economic advantage, but a war to restore the rule of law and to establish durable peace. No other war has ever been fought for a like motive. This explains the fact that it has been entered upon by the several allied peoples, not with shouting, with excitement, or with wild demonstration, but with restraint, with firm conviction, and with stern resolve. The aim of the war is to stop war so far as this is humanly possible.

If, in the past, war has seemed to be a biological necessity, an essential part of the struggle for existence, it is only because the world had not risen to the plane of substituting moral co-operation for physical competition. A materialistic world, bent only on profits and on accumulation, is likely always to be a world that plans and invites war. On the other hand, a world that is built on a foundation of moral and spiritual insight and conviction will be a world from which war is excluded by every means that man can devise.

In order to tread the road to a durable peace, we must grasp not only the exact facts as they relate to the origin and prosecution of the war on the part of

the Central Empires, but also the underlying causes
which conspired to bring the war about.

To say that the war sprang from the desire of Austria-Hungary to oppress Serbia, or from the conflicting
ambitions of Russia and Germany in southeastern
Europe, or from commercial rivalry between Germany
and Great Britain, is simply to delude oneself with
superficial appearances.  It is a case of camouflage.
The cause of the war and the reason that the war was
inevitable (as we can now see) is a conflict of ideals in
the life of the world.  It is clear now that the old
notion of a world-dominating power was not dead.
This was the notion which sent Alexander the Great
and his army into Asia.  This was the notion which
built up the legions and inspired the policy of ancient
Rome.  This was the notion which took possession of
the mind of Charlemagne.  This was the notion which
harnessed to its service the dynamic energy and the
military genius of Napoleon Bonaparte.  This notion
was not, as men generally thought in 1914, dead and
gone and a matter for the historian alone.  It was first
slumbering and then taking active form in the minds
of the ruling caste of the German Empire.  With them
it was based upon a philosophy of history and of life
which made the German people, like the Hebrews of
old, the chosen partners of God himself in the subjection and civilization of the world.

When this notion took possession of so powerful, so
active-minded, and so highly disciplined a people as
the Germans, it became only a question of time when

it must find itself in a life-and-death struggle with the opposing principle. This is the dominating fact which stands out above and beyond all particular explanations of the origin of the war. The war is at bottom a final struggle between the principle of world-domination and the principle of a group of friendly, co-operating nations, all equal in sovereignty and in dignity in the eye of the world's law, however varied they may be in resources and in power.

That with which we are at war, therefore, is not a people or a race, but an idea. We should have had to be at war with that idea no matter what people or what race had acted as its agents. If this idea of world-domination had been adopted by Italy, and if Italy had attacked the world in its interest, we should be at war with Italy. If this idea of world-domination had been adopted by Japan, and if Japan had attacked the world in its interest, we should be at war with Japan. If this idea of world-domination had been adopted by Russia, and if Russia had attacked the world in its interest, we should be at war with Russia. But as a matter of fact this idea was adopted by Germany, and it was Germany which attacked the world in its interest; therefore we are at war with Germany.

The road to durable peace begins at the point where this false notion of world-domination is given up once for all. Commercial interpenetration, financial control, and military dominance are the three forms in which the lust for world-power manifests itself. A free world made up of independent, liberty-loving nations must combine to prevent any one of these. The liberty-loving nations have almost with unanimity now combined in this war for that very purpose.

A false idea is not really conquered until it is overthrown in the minds of those who have entertained it. What we must reach, therefore, is the mind, the conscience, and the heart of the German people. We must by military defeat compel them to leave off looking for new worlds to conquer and turn their thought inward to prepare the way for those same ideas of co-operation between nations, of the sacredness of treaty obligations, of the rights of small nations, and of the duties of great powers toward submerged nationalities which are now part of the mental furniture of liberal-minded men and women throughout the world. If in 1848 the aspirations of so large a portion of the German people had not been disappointed and crushed, the history of the past fifty years might have been written in letters of gold instead of in letters of so much blood.

It has been plain, since the battle of the Marne, that Germany and her allies could not win this war. The history of the conflict from September 6, 1914, has been one of varying fortunes, but, viewed in the largest possible way, it is a history of slow but sure German defeat. The amazing exhibition of military power made by France and by the citizen-soldiers of Great Britain has been adequate to hold in check the enormous and highly trained armies of the Central Empires. Distress, unhappiness, and grave doubt as to the outcome and issues of the war are now wide-spread in Germany and in Austria-Hungary. All these facts contribute to the breaking down of the zeal for world-domination and increase the chance of a durable peace to follow the war.

The terms of that peace have been stated at intervals for three and one-half years past by some of the leading responsible statesmen of the world. The early declarations of Mr. Asquith and of M. Briand could hardly be improved. The later ones of the Prime Minister of England and of the President of the United States have awakened resounding echoes throughout the world and have been listened to even by the peoples with whom we are at war. It is quite idle, however, to talk of a negotiated peace if by that we mean a peace that shall leave the vital issues of the war unsettled. The result would be not a peace but an armistice. This would last until our children, or our children's children, armed to the teeth and bearing meanwhile the crushing burden of huge military establishments, took up again the task that we laid down without having carried it to accomplishment. That would not be a fortunate or an honorable legacy for this generation to leave to its successors. We must persist with steadfastness and with all possible speed until the war is definitively won and until our enemies admit that they have lost in the combat which they forced upon the world.

When that end has been accomplished, the world will have travelled a long way on the road toward a durable peace. While it is true that the coming international organization and the coming international economic relationships will powerfully aid in establishing and in maintaining peace, yet, after all, the main thing is to remove from the world a notion and a purpose that compel armaments and that eventually force war. That notion and that purpose are those of world-domination. The cry *Weltmacht oder Niedergang* comes from a shallow mind and from a hardened heart. The alternative to *Weltmacht* is not *Niedergang*. It is rather membership in a family of nations, each one of which is possessed of what I have described as the international mind. This is nothing else than that habit of thinking of foreign relations and business, and that habit of dealing with them, which regard the several nations of the civilized world as friendly and co-operating equals in aiding the progress of civilization, in developing commerce and industry, and in spreading enlightenment and culture throughout the world.

Given this, and it will be easy to establish and maintain an international organization to keep the peace of the world, as well as to establish and maintain international economic relationships that shall promote human happiness and human satisfaction. Without this condition, all schemes for international organization and international co-operation are futile, and will not long ward off a disaster which takes its origin in wrong and false ideas planted in the hearts of men and nations.

# VII

# A LEAGUE OF NATIONS

Written for the London *Daily Chronicle*
Published July 27, 1918

# A LEAGUE OF NATIONS

The experiences of the war have carried far forward the time-old project to bring about closer and better co-operation between nations in establishing and maintaining order and justice throughout the world. The dreams of the seers of past centuries can shortly be realized. Out of the present alliance of free democratic peoples it will not be difficult to build the structure of a league or society of nations which, without attempting too much, will at least put into effect the lessons taught by the present war, and erect the stoutest sort of a barrier against the recurrence of so terrible a calamity.

A league to establish and to enforce the rules of international law and conduct is now in existence, with Great Britain, France, Italy, and the United States as its most potent members. These nations and those associated with them have already, in effect, united under a single command their fighting armies, brought into closest co-operation their navies, pooled their mercantile shipping, their financial resources, their food-supplies, and their munitions of war. What seemed quite impossible five years ago has now been easily and smoothly accomplished under the pressure of the supreme need of resisting the Teutonic attempt to reduce the free nations of the world to the position of serfs under the domination of the Imperial German Government.

This league should be a permanent addition to the world's organization for order and peaceable progress. Upon its firm and permanent establishment three consequences will necessarily follow: First, there can be no separate alliances or ententes of a political or military character between the nations included in the league. Second, there can be a speedy reduction of armaments, both to lighten the burdens of taxation and to turn the minds of the nations away from international war, to prevent which will be one of the chief aims of such a league. Third, the most favored nation clause must be made applicable to all members of the league, whenever treaties of commerce are concluded between any two or more of the nations that are included in it. This will either greatly lessen, or wholly remove, one of the strongest economic temptations to international war.

The International Court of Justice urged by the American delegation at the second Hague Conference should now be called into being. This court would have the same jurisdiction over questions affecting international relations and international law that the Supreme Court of the United States has over all cases in law and equity arising under the Constitution of the United States and treaties made under its authority. A somewhat similar jurisdiction already attaches within the British Empire to the Judicial Committee of the Privy Council. The enforcement, when necessary, of the findings of this court, should be a matter of joint international action in accordance with a definite plan to be determined upon when the court is established. The principle upon which this action will rest has been stated with characteristic precision by Mr. Asquith when he said that the rule of the authority of an international court "must be supported in case of need by the strength of all; that is, in the last resort, by armed force." For the success of this court it is imperative that secret international understandings be deprived of any validity whatever in international law. It should be provided that, as a condition of the validity in international law of any treaty between two contracting powers, a copy of it must be deposited immediately upon its ratification in the archives of the international court of justice at The Hague. There would then be at least one official public depositary for every existing valid treaty.

It should be clearly understood that any such plan of international co-operation as this league of nations would involve the giving up by each nation included in the league of the absolute right of its government to deal finally and without appeal except to war with questions arising out of treaties or relations between itself and some other government. Little serious progress can be made in getting rid of war and in better organizing the world until the free peoples are ready to have their several governments take this long step forward.

It is important that this league of nations should begin by not attempting too much. The line of least resistance, and therefore of greatest possible progress, is to lay stress upon the power and authority of a single international judicial authority, and to accustom the public opinion of the world to seek and to defer to the findings of such authority. All international agreements between members of the league would in effect be acts of international legislation, and in due time some formal international legislative body might be brought into existence. It would be much better, however, to give this body a chance to grow up naturally, rather than to attempt to bring it into existence as part of a logical and systematically worked-out plan.

Such a league of nations as is here outlined will rest upon a moral foundation. Its aim will be to advance the good order, the satisfaction, and the happiness of the world. It will not be, and should not be, merely a league to enforce peace. A league of that name might well rest solely upon force and entirely overlook both law and equity. Doubtless Germany and Austria-Hungary now feel that they are joint and several members of a highly meritorious league to enforce peace— peace upon their own terms and as they conceive it. A league of nations that aims to declare and to enforce principles of international law and justice will of necessity be a league to establish peace, because it will be a league to establish those foundations upon which alone permanent peace can rest.

There is no good reason why there should be any

further delay in bringing this league formally into existence. Even while military and naval operations are being pressed forward to that certain victory which will one day be theirs, this league should be formally established and international organs created by it to prepare systematically and scientifically for promptly dealing with the grave economic, social, and political problems that the cessation of hostilities, the demobilization of armies, and the new world conditions that are to be the result of the overthrow of Prussian militarism will certainly bring forward for quick solution.

It would be difficult to make a better statement of the rights and duties of nations than those adopted by the American Institute of International Law at Washington on January 6, 1916, and supplemented by the same body at Havana, Republic of Cuba, on January 23, 1917.

# VIII

# AMERICAN OPINION AND PROBLEMS OF
PEACE

A statement published in *Echo de Paris*, December 5, 1918, and in the London *Observer*, December 8, 1918

# AMERICAN OPINION AND PROBLEMS OF PEACE

The American people approach the Peace Conference in a very fine and broad-minded spirit but without understanding the specific policies which they should consider and support and without any commitments to such policies. The public statements of the President have been almost universally and perhaps purposely couched in vague and general terms, and the more specific policies outlined by Senator Lodge were, of course, not advanced on behalf of the Administration.

There are three general phrases that the American people have been hearing constantly. They are "self-determination," "a League of Nations," and "the freedom of the seas." The first relates to the thousand-year-old problem of nationality; the second to the two-thousand-year-old problem of a better world-order; and the third to a specific and highly important item in that world-order.

The American people believe in the self-determination of peoples and in the principle of nationality involving national consciousness, national organization, national tradition, and national economic life. For this reason they are ready to support with complete unanimity policies permitting the Czecho-Slovaks, the

Jugo-Slavs, and the Poles to organize their own independent governments and to take their places in
the family of nations. For this reason they have
applauded the return of Alsace-Lorraine to France,
they will support the return of northern Slesvig to
Denmark, the return of the Trentino to Italy, and of
sectors of Macedonia, Thrace, and Asia Minor, which
have largely dominating Greek populations, to either
the sovereignty or the jurisdiction of Greece.

American opinion overwhelmingly favors Home Rule
for Ireland, but the sober, judicious majority would
regard with dismay any attempted application to this
problem of the principle of self-determination which
would disrupt or even weaken the British Empire, since
in every case except as to the still unsolved problem
of Ireland the British Imperial system has been a
veritable nest for the hatching out of new, free, and
self-governing peoples.

So far as the principle of self-determination is concerned, therefore, American public opinion will be
neither timid on the one hand nor chauvinistic on the
other.

The possibility of a League of Nations has been
discussed for centuries, and probably Metternich and
Talleyrand thought just such a League was being
organized at the Congress of Vienna one hundred and
four years ago. The foundations of that structure
were insecure, however, for it was built on the shift-
ing sands of reaction, of imperialism, of international
rivalry, and of military power.

Thus far two general and very different notions as to the League of Nations have found currency: the one is that supported by orthodox socialists and has in mind the destruction of all the essential elements and characteristics of nationality in order to bring about what I have sometimes called a colloidal or jelly-like internationalism, without real nations. This is the notion of the Lenines and the Trotskys, of the Liebknechts and the I. W. W. sympathizers. The achievement of this ideal would bring civilization to an end, make order impossible, destroy liberty, and put mankind back at the foot of the ladder from which it began to mount when the Roman Empire fell to pieces.

The other notion of the League of Nations involves what I have called crystalline or true internationalism. In this each nation remains self-conscious, self-determined, and ambitious in its own right, and takes its place in a new international structure as an independent element—like a single crystal in an ordered group of crystals.

In this case the group or league becomes stronger or more powerful according as the nations that compose it become stronger and more powerful.

True internationalism must be built on the union of strong and self-respecting nations. False internationalism would weaken or destroy together those nations which accept it.

The American people will have nothing to do with the false internationalism of Lenine and Trotsky, Liebknecht and the I. W. W. They know perfectly well that these men are enemies of a democratic republic, whether in Russia, Germany, or the United States. On the other hand, the American people will support, not with unanimity, by any means, but by a substantial majority, a well-considered and thoroughly practical project for a League of Nations which shall be based upon the principles of true internationalism.

There are those who urge that the example of the Constitution of the United States should be followed in organizing this League, that precise and definitive articles of government should be adopted, that an international legislature, executive and judiciary, should be erected, and that the part of the nations in the new organization should be similar to that of the States in the United States.

There are two difficulties in the way of so ambitious a programme. The first is that the public opinion of the world is not ready to support it, and the second is that some of the necessary conditions of success which were present in the case of the United States would be lacking in the case of such a League of Nations. The United States met with a century of difficulties in spite of unity of language, unity of tradition, and unity of legal system. These three vitally important unities would be lacking in a League of Nations which should take the United States as its model.

The true analogy between the United States and a League of Nations lies not on the surface, but deeper. It is found in the principle of federation with its accompanying characteristics of legal and economic co-operation. American opinion is ready for this if it be guided by a policy of lofty patriotism, broad international service, and sincere democratic feeling.

What the American people are asking to-day is this: Given conditions as they now exist in the world, how shall we proceed to form an effective League of Nations? This question the head of the American Government has not yet attempted to answer. The most practical procedure appears to be the following: The Allied Powers which have won the war have been for the purposes of war, and at the present moment are, a League of Nations. They have unified their international policies. They have put their armies and their navies under single commands: they have pooled all their resources in shipping, food, munitions, and credit. Let these nations, assembled by their representatives at Versailles, declare themselves to be a League of Nations organized for the precise purposes for which the war was fought, and with which their several peoples are entirely familiar, namely, the definition and protection of standards of international right and justice, the sanctity of international obligations, and the right of the smaller and less numerous peoples to be free from attack or domination by their larger and more powerful neighbors.

As a beginning nothing more is needed. There is no necessity for an international constitution, no necessity for an elaborate international government machine, in order that the great enterprise may be launched. So far as these may be needed, they very well may come later.

The second step should be to invite those nations that have been neutral in the war to join the League on condition that they formally give adhesion to the three ends or purposes for which the League is organized.

The third step should be to invite the recently submerged and oppressed nationalities to present before the League their several cases for hearing and determination. When these have fully shown the basis of their geographical and political claims, and when the League of Nations has been satisfied as to the justice of these claims, then the petitioners should be invited to form their own governments; and when they have done so, they should be admitted to the League of Nations as independent units.

While this process is going on and so long afterward as may be necessary, Germany and Austria-Hungary should be kept outside the League. It is inconceivable that the governments and peoples which almost disrupted and overthrew the civilized world should be invited to confer as to the method of the world's reconstruction, or as to their own punishment for their own sins, or as to the form of government to be adopted by the peoples whom they have so long dominated or terrorized.

When the League of Nations shall be wholly satisfied that Germany and Austria-Hungary, and the Germans and Austro-Hungarians, have washed from their hands the blood of Belgium and Serbia, have really repented for such crimes as the *Lusitania* and *Sussex*, and have exorcised the evil spirits that have possessed them, then and then only should Germany and Austria-Hungary be taken back into the family which they jointly attempted to murder.

I see no practical way other than this by which any headway can be made with regard to the project for a League of Nations. If there be an attempt to build it on the foundations of sentimentality or artificiality or neglect of the obvious facts, the project will fail and one of the greatest opportunities growing out of the World War will be lost.

The resumption of the work of Hague Conferences and the building of an international judicial and economic structure would follow the foundation of such a League as I suggest as a matter of course and in due time.

The American public is wholly mystified as to what is meant by "freedom of the seas." That phrase had a pretty definite meaning as late as the time of the American Civil War, but subsequent events have deprived that meaning of much significance. In time of peace the seas are and long have been entirely free. In time of war they have always been commanded by the possessor of the strongest navy. If that condition had not prevailed in 1914 Germany would have won the war just ended within twelve months from the time of its beginning. With Germany's army in a position to do as it chose, and the naval hands of

Great Britain and France tied behind their backs, the issue raised by Germany on August 4, 1914, would not long have remained uncertain. The mastery of the seas by the British navy has proved to be the most powerful single element in bringing about the downfall of militarism.

The world realizes that fact, and will not support any proposal which would change this condition in essence, although it may do so in form. Unquestionably the Allies have good reason to approve those conditions on the sea which just now have prevailed. The cowardly and wicked use of the submarine by Germany was the greatest menace to the freedom of the sea that history records. The Barbary pirates and roving privateers were negligible when compared with the submarines.

If the phrase "freedom of the seas" has to do with access to navigable waters by landlocked people or with unprivileged use of international straits, waterways, and canals, well and good. American opinion will support "freedom of the seas" when used in such a sense.

The American heart has been touched by this war as never before. The sufferings and sorrows, the patience and endurance, the heroism and sacrifice of the Allies, particularly of France and Great Britain, have stirred America to the depths. The American people realize that the difficulties of peace are to be quite comparable to the dangers and disasters of war, and that where the ruling principles are to have so many and so important concrete illustrations, there naturally will arise differences of opinion more or less sharp, and conflicts of temperament more or less open. The American people well remember the similar difficulties and conflict that arose between wholly patriotic and high-minded men in their own country at the close of the American Revolution and again at the close of the Civil War. We of the United States shall be patient and endeavor to see beyond and behind these superficial conflicts, first, because our people now understand Europe as they never did before, and second, because we are bound to the victorious peoples of Europe by stronger and more affectionate ties than ever have existed in the past.

# IX

## ALOOFNESS IMPOSSIBLE

A statement printed in the New York *Tribune*,
February 27, 1919

## ALOOFNESS IMPOSSIBLE

A society of nations is wholly in accord with Republican traditions, Republican principles, and well-established Republican policy. The only formal declaration known to me to have been made on this subject by any party convention in the United States is that adopted by the Republican State Convention held at Saratoga on July 19, 1918. That declaration reads as follows:

We favor the immediate creation by the United States and its allies of a league of nations to establish, from time to time to modify, and to enforce, the rules of international law and conduct. The purpose of this league should be, not to displace patriotism or devotion and loyalty to national ideals and traditions, but rather to give to these new opportunities of expression in cooperation with the other liberty loving nations of the world. To membership in this league any nation might be admitted that possesses a responsible government which will abide by those rules of law and equity, and by those principles of international justice and morality which are accepted by civilized people.

It would be most unfortunate for this question to become a partisan one, or to fail of consideration of its merits regardless of any party declaration hitherto made. Nevertheless, it may be helpful for Republicans to ask whether the draft plan that has been submitted for discussion and amendment, as a result of the pre-

liminary work of the Peace Conference at Paris, is or
is not a league of the type described in the declaration
just quoted.  If it is a league of this type, it will be
a logical deduction from the foreign policies of the
McKinley, Roosevelt, and Taft administrations, illuminated by the lessons of the war.  If it is not a league
of this type, then we may well strive to shape it so that
it will become such while the plan is still open to discussion and amendment.  Blindly to oppose any better form of world-organization because we do not like
some of the details of the plan now proposed, is political madness, as well as in the highest degree reactionary.

The draft plan is so ill-drawn and so full of unnecessary difficulties that its critics will have an easy task
in making those facts plain to the people.  The constructive critic, however, will not content himself with
opposition to any plan whatsoever, because he does not
like some of the points of this plan, but will endeavor
to show how it may be transformed into a wiser and
a better plan.

It is probable that the difficulties in the way of
acceptance by the Senate and the American people
generally of any plan for a society of nations may be
summarized under two heads: First, agreement upon
the principles of international law and international
administration which are hereafter to prevail in the
world; and, second, agreement upon a method for their
enforcement that will not displace the Monroe Doctrine.

If the votes of the two Hague conferences of 1899

and 1907 be taken as a starting-point, it should not be difficult to put into the draft plan a succinct statement of principles of international law and conduct upon which the whole civilized world will agree. The question will then arise as to the enforcement of these principles. There are grave objections to any plan which will compel America to accept responsibility for matters of international administration in Europe, in Asia, or in Africa, and there are equally grave objections to any plan that will substitute for the Monroe Doctrine international control on the part of the nations of Europe and Asia of matters affecting the American continents alone. It might be worth while to consider whether, given a single code of principles of international law and international administration, the world might not then be divided into three administrative areas: First, Europe, Africa, and the parts of Asia immediately adjoining Europe and Africa; second, the American continents, and, third, the Orient, including Japan, China, and Siam.

Should these three administrative areas be created, all owing allegiance to a common code of law and principle, then the world would have, in effect, a Monroe Doctrine for each area, and the original Monroe Doctrine would be preserved unharmed and unamended. Should any exceptional breach of international law and order take place within a given administrative area, as when Germany invaded Belgium in 1914, which the forces of law and order within that area were unable to subdue, the similar forces in one or both of the other administrative areas could then be called upon to take part in upholding the principles to which all alike had given allegiance.

Americans, and especially Republicans, will recall two striking sentences in President McKinley's last speech, delivered at Buffalo, on September 5, 1901:

> No nation can longer be indifferent to any other. . . .
> The period of aloofness is past.

These declarations marked the beginning of a new world attitude on the part of the people of the United States. The proposals contained in Theodore Roosevelt's address before the Nobel Prize Committee, delivered at Christiania, Norway, on May 5, 1910, should not be overlooked at this time, since some of them go even beyond the provisions of the present draft plan. This, for example:

> It would be a master stroke if those great powers honestly bent on peace would form a league of peace, not only to keep the peace among themselves, but to prevent, by force if necessary, its being broken by others. The supreme difficulty in connection with developing the peace work of The Hague arises from the lack of any executive power, of any police power, to enforce the decrees of the courts.

For several generations the American Government has had a large part in the development and establishment of international law and order. On many occasions, through resolutions of the Congress, through executive declarations, through diplomatic correspondence, through special treaties, and through participation in numerous international conferences and conventions, the American people have exerted far-reaching influence in making international law and in developing an international public opinion. Republicans in particular must not allow their justifiable resentment at the President's methods and policies to drive them into an unstatesmanlike attitude, and one wholly out of harmony with their long tradition, on the greatest question now before the court of public opinion.

# X

# WHAT IS PROGRESS IN POLITICS?

An address delivered before the Commercial Club,
Chicago, Illinois, December 14, 1912

# WHAT IS PROGRESS IN POLITICS?

For some time past it has not been easy to discuss politics from the standpoint of principle in the United States. For nearly twenty years two powerful and interesting personalities have dominated the imagination of large elements of the American people. Since the generation passed from the stage to whose lot it fell to settle for good or for ill the issues growing out of the Civil War, Mr. Bryan and Mr. Roosevelt have been the centre points of American political discussion. These two powerful men have some characteristics in common, as well as many points of sharp difference. The important fact is that when either of them is before the electorate as a candidate for high office, it is almost impossible to secure discussion of any political proposal save with reference to his personality. The effect of this limitation upon our political life has not always been happy. Passionate feeling has been aroused at a time when cool reason was most necessary, and blind personal advocacy or blind personal antagonism has taken the place of statesmanlike examination of principles and of policies. At the moment we are at rest in a political eddy. The glamour of candidacies and the rapidly succeeding turmoil of primaries, conventions, and elections is over for the time being. There is given opportunity, therefore, to discuss some fundamental questions of politics apart from their relation to any party, to any candidate, or to any personality.

It is high time that the American people undertook this task without either passion or partisanship, and with sincerity. Conditions are not favorable to national safety and stability if we pursue a policy of drifting, or if we permit specific proposals, in themselves attractive, to lead us away from sound principle. The American people are by nature, by temperament, and by opportunity a people of constant and continuing progress. They have never stood still or gone backward in the past, and it is highly unlikely that they will so far change their nature as to stand still or go backward in the near future.

We are constantly called upon to make progress, to move forward, and to adopt policies and to support measures in the name of advance. Before taking an attitude toward such invitations and proposals, it is advisable to assure ourselves that we know the points of the political compass, and that we are certain of the direction in which we are moving. For whether a man is progressing or not depends not upon whether he is in motion and the label that he bears, but entirely upon the direction in which he is facing when he begins to move. One who is borne by an avalanche rushing down the side of a mountain in obedience to the law of gravitation is not moving upward simply because he carries with him a sign marked "Excelsior."

I should describe progress in politics as moving for-

ward to the consideration and solution of new problems
with intelligence and sympathy, and in the full light
of experience gained and principles established in the
past. Change, on the other hand, which many persons mistake for progress, is the mere restless and ill-
considered disturbance of condition with little or no
regard to the teachings of experience. Progress in
politics will aim to make government just, efficient,
and quickly responsive to the public will, and to insure, so far as may be, equality of opportunity, together with security in the possessions of the fruits
of one's own brain and hands.

For some time past political progress has been urged
upon us and illustrated—indeed, it has almost been
defined—in terms of attack upon two very fundamental and far-reaching political principles that are
said to be outworn and harmful. If those who so illustrate and exemplify progress are correct, then it is
clear that nothing short of a revolution is soon to be
effected in our American life, and through it in the
world at large. If, on the other hand, they are wrong,
as I am profoundly convinced is the case, then progress
will lie not in the direction toward which they point,
but rather in orderly, reasoned, and permanent advance along the familiar lines of political evolution
without disturbing the principles that they attack,
without tearing up anything by the roots, without
overturning any long-established and beneficent institution, and without sapping the well-springs of intellectual and moral independence and responsibility

by leading the individual to look to the community, rather than to his own efforts, for support.

The two fundamental and far-reaching principles to which I refer are, first, the limitations of a written constitution, and, second, the relation that has hitherto existed in America between the individual and the state. We have lately been told in no uncertain terms that political progress consists in throwing off the shackles of a written constitution and in wholly altering the relation that has hitherto existed between the individual and the state. These appeals are not unfamiliar in other parts of the world, but to large numbers of thoughtful Americans they have a strange and sombre sound. They are nothing short of a challenge to the justice and wisdom of the basis on which our entire civilization rests, whether those who make them realize this or not. We must look carefully into these two contentions, and, if we can, meet and refute them with rational argument and with historical illustration. If we cannot do this, then we must, as thinking men, accept these new policies, however revolutionary they may seem to us to be.

What is a written constitution? What are its limitations and its shackles? A written constitution is nothing more than a court of appeal to man's sober and historically justified reason from his quick acting and present impulses and passions. A written constitution simply marks out and defines what has already been accomplished in the progress toward free government, and drives a stake, as it were, in order that we may return to it for guidance when we need to take a new measurement.

Nevertheless, for some time past impatience of a written constitution has been marked in this country in many places and in many ways. We have been told that our written Constitution attempted to bind us fast to an eighteenth-century view of society, and that it could not possibly adapt itself or be adapted to present-day needs and problems. It is one manifestation of this impatience when judges, who have taken a solemn oath to obey and enforce the Constitution and its limitations, are told from the platform and in the press that they should read into it some new and strange interpretation which a portion of the population honestly believe is necessary to the satisfaction of their ethical ideals or their social impulses. The same tendency is manifested when it is proposed to recall judges from their high positions, not because of any personal offense justifying impeachment, but because of their failure in official act to harmonize with some strongly held present-day opinion. Precisely the same temper is shown when it is proposed that the people at large shall by a plenary and direct exercise of the police power overturn a judicial decision which puts a constitutional barrier to some much-desired policy or act.

There would be justification for even the most extreme of these proposals if our written Constitution were unamendable; if it were really a strait-jacket into which our national life was long ago forced, and which could only be worn in these later days with harm and constant pain. But the contrary is the case. The Constitution is readily amendable whenever a large body of opinion, widely distributed throughout the country, genuinely desires its amendment. We are witnessing at the moment two illustrations of this fact. The amendment authorizing the levying of a federal income tax is well on its way to adoption, and will almost certainly become the Sixteenth Amendment to the Constitution within a few weeks. The proposal for the direct election of United States senators has been adopted by the constitutional majority in both the House of Representatives and the Senate, and it is perfectly plain to every political observer that it will have no difficulty in securing ratification by the legislatures of the States. Here are two important amendments to our fundamental law, at least one of which may prove to be very far-reaching in its effects and to involve consequences not now foreseen; and yet, when public opinion has really and unmistakably asserted itself in their support, they go forward with but slight interruption or delay to take their place in the Constitution of the United States.

The whole history of the Constitution illustrates this. By far the greater part of the hundreds of amendments that have been proposed from time to time, some of which have received a considerable measure of support, have failed to secure incorporation in the fundamental law because the great mass of the American people were not interested in them or did not believe

them to be important. On the other hand, the first
ten amendments were speedily adopted in order to
set at rest certain doubts and difficulties that had arisen
in the public mind at the time of the ratification of
the Constitution itself. The Eleventh Amendment
was adopted—not, I think, wisely—to give effect to
an interpretation of the Constitution other than that
which had been held by the United States Supreme
Court in the well-known case of Chisholm *v.* Georgia.
This amendment is sometimes pointed to as an illustration of what is meant by the recall of a judicial
decision. This use of it, however, rests upon an entire
misconception of the facts. So far from being the
recall of a judicial decision, it was a formal amendment to the Constitution in order to meet a general
situation which a judicial decision had created. This
is something which constitutional government always
contemplates, and there is nothing extraordinary or
abnormal about it. It is, on the other hand, an orderly,
reasoned, and proper way in which to exercise the
sovereign power of the people. Despite the feeling
that this particular decision created, because it ran
counter to the extreme State rights doctrine of the
time, it took nearly four years to secure the adoption
of the Eleventh Amendment. The Twelfth Amendment, relating to the mode of electing the President
and Vice-President, was adopted practically by unanimous consent, to remove an obvious difficulty in
the working of the original provisions of the Constitution on this point. The history of the Thirteenth,

Fourteenth, and Fifteenth Amendments is well known, as is the history of those that seem destined to become the Sixteenth and Seventeenth. The sovereign people of the United States are, then, demonstrably in full possession of their government, and they have not deprived themselves of the power to alter or amend its fundamental law when they believe such alteration or amendment to be necessary or desirable.

There are two questions that must be carefully distinguished. The one relates to the desirability of amending the Constitution in any specified manner at a given time, and the other relates to the breaking down or overriding of constitutional limitations, whether by executive usurpation or by legislative act, because some considerable body of opinion is ready to applaud the result. In the former case the issue is this: Will the sovereign people consciously and willingly, after consideration and debate, alter their fundamental law? In the latter case the question is this: Will the people permit their government to be changed and its underlying principles modified by what is in effect and often in form as well a revolutionary act?

There are those who believe and teach that the path of progress lies in the direction of breaking down and overriding constitutional limitations. It is essential to progress that all such proposals be met with a determined opposition. These constitutional limitations on governmental power are in the interest of individual liberty. They themselves mark the history of progress in government. They represent what our ancestors

for scores of generations have won, first from the form-
lessness of anarchy, and later from the tyranny of an
individual or a class. The reason why this matter is
so important for us is that only in the United States
has individual liberty been really made a part of constitutional law. Everywhere else it has only a statutory basis. Germany alone of modern peoples has
made progress toward the position of the United States
in this fundamental matter; but in Germany the judiciary is dependent upon the political departments of
the government, and, therefore, it lacks authority to
protect the individual from encroachments by them.
In France and in Great Britain individual liberty depends wholly upon the passing mood of a majority in
the legislative assembly or in the House of Commons.

What is at stake in preserving a written constitution
and its limitations upon government is nothing less
than the sovereignty of the people themselves. In the
United States the people are sovereign. The Constitution as from time to time amended sets up the people's
form of government and defines the functions and limitations of its various officers and agencies. The government has no authority but that which the sovereign
people choose to intrust to it, and an independent
judiciary is established by the people in order to make
sure that the executive and the legislative departments
of the government do not overstep their respective limitations. If these limitations on government be removed or nullified, or if the independent judiciary be
deprived of its independence, the effect will be to

transfer sovereignty from the people of the United States to the governmental organs and agencies for the time being.  Without constitutional limitations, the Congress of the United States would be as sovereign as is the House of Commons, and all those precious privileges and immunities that are set out in the Constitution and its amendments, and as to which the individual citizen may appeal to the judiciary for protection, would be placed upon the same plane as a statute authorizing the appointment of an interstate commerce commission or one denouncing a monopoly or other act in restraint of trade.   It must not be forgotten that there is no such thing as an unconstitutional law in Great Britain.  The fact that the Parliament enacts a law makes it constitutional, no matter what its effect upon life, liberty, or property may be; for Parliament is sovereign.  To propose to import this condition into the United States is not progress, but reaction.

It may be asked, what difference does it make in every-day life whether the sovereignty remains with the people of the United States, and whether the Congress and the several legislatures are held to the performance of their tasks under those limitations and restrictions which the people have in their constitutions laid upon them, or whether those restrictions and limitations are removed and the sovereignty, as you say, passes to the legislative body itself.  The answer is this: Any majority, however small, however fleeting, however unreasonable, or however incoherent, would then have at its immediate disposal the life, liberty, and property of each individual citizen of the United States. This may be a good form of government, but it is certainly not the American form. It is not that republican form of government which the people of the United States have guaranteed to the several States. It is a return to tyranny, with a many-headed majority in the place of power once held by the single despot. This again is not progress, but reaction. It is a proposal to undo what history has so effectively done; to give back to the mass what has been so painfully conquered for the individual; to alter absolutely and for the worse our standards of judgment and of accomplishment in public affairs. The harassing of individuals and of minorities is sometimes unavoidable in the processes of government, but it is neither wise nor necessary to exalt it to the position of a controlling principle.

By a curious perversion of clear thinking, this issue is sometimes stated to be one between those who believe that the people are wise enough and strong enough to carry on a government of comprehensive powers, and those who believe that they are not. It is described as an issue between those who trust the people and those who distrust the people. Nothing could be further from the fact. Those who trust the people are the ones who believe in individual liberty, who have confidence that a man can work out his own fortune and build his own character better than any one else can work it out or build it for him. Those who distrust the people are the ones who wish to regulate their every act, to limit their gains and their accomplishments, and to force by the strong arm of government an artificial and superficial equality as a substitute for that equal opportunity which is liberty. There could be no greater evidence of hopelessly confused thinking than to suppose that a government of limited powers is so limited because the people distrust themselves. The fact is precisely the opposite. To trust the people is to leave them in fullest possible possession of their liberty and to call upon them to use that liberty and its fruits for the public good.

The second fundamental and far-reaching principle that is under attack in the mistaken name of progress is that which governs the relation of the individual to the community or state. This principle is closely bound up with a written constitution and its limitations on the power of government, and the two really stand or fall together.

There are three broadly distinguished ways in which the relation of the individual to the community may be viewed. We may, in the first place, look upon the individual as everything and the community as nothing. In that case each individual becomes an end unto himself, and what we call civilization is reduced to a predatory war in which the remainder of mankind are the enemies of each individual. More than once in the history of human thinking doctrinaires have expounded this view and have exalted it as desirable. They have not, fortunately, been able to secure enough support to put their doctrine into practice over a wide area or for any considerable time.

We may, in the second place, look upon the individual as nothing and the community as everything. In one form or another this is the doctrine which underlies the civilization of the Orient. In the East, either by ancestor worship, by caste feeling, or by religious doctrine, whole masses of population have been held in subjection for centuries; for the controlling principle of life forbade an individual to assert his independence of the thought of the community of which he was a part.

If anarchy be the result of the first of these views, stagnation is the result of the second. The Western peoples from the time of the Greeks have endeavored to avoid both anarchy and stagnation by adopting and acting upon a third point of view. This point of view, in contradistinction to individualism on the one hand and to communism on the other, I call institutionalism, for the reason that it looks upon the individual as finding his highest purpose not in antagonizing his interests to those of his fellows, but in using his freedom and his power of initiative to help them build and maintain the institutions that are civilization. This is a view that lays great stress upon individuality, upon personal liberty, and upon personal character, but that sees liberty and character perfected and manifested in the free and willing service of the community and in those civil institutions which exemplify this service and aid it. This view differs sharply from that first described in that, while it emphasizes the individual, it yet regards him as a member of a group, a community, a society, in which he has duties and owes service as well as possesses rights and privileges. It differs from the second view in that it calls upon the individual to serve his fellow men willingly and out of conscience and good judgment, instead of reducing him by an external force to a uniform level of action and of belief.

There is no progress in politics in breaking down this third view of the relation between the individual and the community in favor of either the first or the second. The road that leads to that individualism which is anarchy is not one of progress. The road that leads to that communism which is stagnation is not one of progress. We have been walking in the path of progress for two thousand five hundred years, and the characteristic of that path is that it leads every individual to exert himself to the utmost, not alone that he may profit, but that he may be the better able to serve. The American people will not be wise if they fail to test every proposal made in the name of progress by this standard. Does it tend to exalt the individual at the expense of the community in a way that makes for privilege, monopoly, anarchy? If so, reject it. Does it tend to exalt the community at the expense of the individual in the way that makes for artificial equality, denial of initiative, stagnation? If so, reject it. Does it tend to call out the individual constantly to improve himself for wider and more effective service and good citizenship? If so, adopt it. It makes for progress.

If this analysis of underlying principles is correct—and I submit it with confidence to the judgment of thoughtful and unprejudiced Americans of whatever party—then we must hold fast in any programme of advance to a written constitution, with definite and precise limitations on government in the interest of liberty, which constitution is not to be overridden and ignored, but which may be amended in orderly fashion when public opinion demands; and also to a political policy which both in general and in detail will offer new and increasing opportunities to the individual, not primarily for his own aggrandizement, but for the public and general good.

Before passing from these questions of fundamental principle to some matters of detail, let me say a word as to the influence of the two-party system in effecting political progress. The parliamentary history of Great Britain and of the United States demonstrates that free government will progress most rapidly and most equitably if it is conducted under a system in which two political parties, differing sharply on some fundamental principle of government, stand over against each other as opponents and as critics. The constructive power of the nation will at times be represented more strongly in the one party, and at times more strongly in the other. But their honest, sincere, and straightforward criticism of each other's principles and policies, and their division of the community into two parties, each of which includes representatives of every class and type of citizenship, has in it far more of hope, far more promise of advance, and far more of democracy than has a series of temporary legislative majorities made up by a combination of rival groups, each representing a class interest and struggling not for principle, but for advantage. There is no progress to be had by the multiplication of parties or by introducing here the system of political groups, which has made so difficult the advance of parliamentary institutions on the continent of Europe, and which has at times so paralyzed the arm of effective government. The Labor party in Great Britain has greatly complicated the problems of government without materially advancing the cause of its own members, for the reason that it represents not a principle, but an interest in politics. The triumph of a combination of interests is more to be feared and deplored than the victory of an unsound principle. The latter can often be undone; the former rarely, and only after long tribulation. We should strive to strengthen, rather than to weaken, the party system which divides society by a perpendicular line running through all classes alike, and we should resist the substitution for it of a number of special groups and class interests that divide society horizontally.

What, now, are some of the real problems that are pressing for solution and whose satisfactory handling, without departing from sound principle, would constitute genuine progress in our politics? They are very many, and it is impossible to do more than mention the most important of them.

1. It is plain that a large number of persons are dissatisfied with what may be called the stiffness of the framework of our government. They have been induced to believe that representative institutions are not adequate to a just expression of the popular will, and that it is desirable to modify them or to overturn them entirely by going back to the once abandoned methods of direct democracy. It is not difficult to prove that the substitution of direct democracy for representative institutions is and must necessarily be a long step backward. On the other hand, it will be a step in advance to seek out and to remove the causes of dissatisfaction with representative government and the distrust of it that now exist. There are two ways of accomplishing this: One is to make the framework of government somewhat more flexible than now, and the other to simplify and to improve the methods by which public officers are chosen as well as those by which governmental policies are declared and executed.

To provide a less difficult mode of amending the Constitution than that now in force would be to make progress. A quarter century ago it was pointed out[1] that artificially excessive majorities are required to bring about constitutional change. At that time fewer than 3,000,000 people could successfully resist more than 45,000,000 in the attempt to secure an amendment to the Constitution. A safeguard of this kind

[1] Burgess: *Political Science and Comparative Constitutional Law*, I, 151.

is extreme, and of itself invites to revolution and violence. So far as the State constitutions are concerned, the process of amendment is already quite easy enough, and if the bad habit of putting into the organic law what are really legislative details could be checked, the wish to amend the State constitutions would be far less frequent than at present. With the Constitution of the United States, however, the case is different. The modification of the amending article has been discussed at various times since it was first proposed by Senator Henderson, of Missouri, in connection with the projected Thirteenth Amendment, in 1864. Professor Burgess, of Columbia University, made an important suggestion on this subject[1] more than twenty years ago, and more recently his suggestion has been modified and presented[2] in a way that deserves careful consideration as a part of any programme of political advance.

The suggestion is that in future amendments to the Constitution shall be submitted to the States for ratification when passed by a majority vote of both Houses of Congress in two successive Congresses. When so submitted they shall be voted upon either by the legislatures of the several States or by conventions in each State, or directly by the voters in each of the States, as one or another of these methods of ratification may be proposed by Congress. When so voted upon they shall be ratified whenever accepted by a majority of

---

[1] Burgess: *Political Science and Comparative Constitutional Law*, I, 152-3.
[2] Munroe Smith: "Shall We Make Our Constitution Flexible?" in *North American Review*, November, 1911, pp. 657-673.

the States—whether acting through their legislatures or by conventions, or by direct vote of the people, as may have been provided—on condition that the ratifying States also contain a majority of the population of all the States according to the last preceding enumeration. The advantages of this plan for amending the Constitution over that at present in force would be that a minority of one-third in either House of Congress could not withhold indefinitely, as now, the submission of a new constitutional proposal to the States, and that population would be given a due and proper weight in deciding whether or not a particular proposal should be ratified. On the other hand, deliberation and caution would be secured by the provision that a proposal to amend the Constitution must command a majority of both Houses in each of two successive Congresses. This suggestion, which is the result of much careful study, will, I think, commend itself the more closely it is examined as a genuine step in advance through making the framework of the government more flexible and more responsive to popular opinion, without breaking down any existing safeguard and without violating any fundamental principle.

2. The people as a whole are not satisfied with the present methods of nominating and electing public officers. The wide-spread movement to dispense with conventions and other intermediate bodies and to nominate all candidates for office by the direct primary is evidence of popular discontent with the methods that have heretofore existed. It is my belief, however, that

the rapid development of legislation controlling political party organization and procedure is not a step forward, but, rather, backward—or perhaps sideways; and that real progress lies in a different direction. I cannot agree with those who are urging the State in the name of progress to extend statutory control over party organizations and methods. It would, I believe, be wiser for the State to withdraw entirely from all legislation affecting political parties and their methods other than that which also affects churches, Masonic lodges, chambers of commerce, and other voluntary bodies. The attention of the State government should be fixed on the election, and on the election alone. Of course, in that case there should be no discrimination in favor of political parties in making up the official ballot. Access to the ballot should be open on the same terms to any responsible body of citizens sufficiently numerous to command attention and willing to give some evidence of good faith. The way would then be open for an appeal to the people, on equal terms, by parties other than the two leading ones, and by those voters who, not associated with any political party, so often hold the balance of power between parties and exercise a healthy influence upon them. A political party, like a Masonic lodge or a branch of the Christian church or a chamber of commerce, should be left to its own devices and allowed to regulate itself and to manage its own internal affairs as it wills. If the contrary view, which is at present so popular, be taken, then it may be safely predicted that before many years we shall find ourselves confronting problems arising out of this legal relation between the State and the political parties that will rival in complexity and difficulty those that have already arisen in European countries between the State and the legally recognized churches. The result will be not progress, but reaction.

This is a large and difficult subject, full of points of contention. I must be satisfied for the moment with merely indicating that the course of action which has hitherto been hailed as a mark of progress seems to me to be something quite different.

If the spirit animating a political party is one of justice and wisdom, it will permit its members to give expression to their wishes and preferences in any way that a majority of them desire. The method of the direct primary is doubtless advantageous within relatively small and homogeneous communities, where men know each other and where candidates for office can be discussed with some degree of understanding and personal acquaintance. That it will be highly disadvantageous to substitute the direct primary for the method of the convention and conference when large areas are involved, such as a great State or the nation as a whole, I am entirely certain. It will, among other things, exalt the professional politician and the man who can provide or secure the great sums of money needed to carry on a campaign for several weeks or months before a large and widely distributed body of electors. True progress will consist in freeing the con-

vention system from abuses, not in abolishing it. To
supplement the State and national conventions by a
direct expression of the preference of the individual
voter is one thing; to do away with such conventions
and their great advantages is quite another.

3. Again, the government will be more quickly responsive to the will of the people if the necessary steps
be taken to improve our legislative methods and procedure. Many if not most of our laws are loosely drawn
and carelessly considered, and in a great number of
cases they fail absolutely to accomplish the object
desired by those who urge them. These facts of themselves lead to much unnecessary and vexatious litiga-
tion, and tend to give ground for the belief that in
some way or other the processes of government are
used not to carry out, but to defeat, the popular will.

We might with advantage imitate the procedure of
the House of Commons in this respect, as it is far
superior to our own. The fault in this country does
not lie in our system of government, nor does it lie
with members of the legislatures as individuals. It is
to be found rather in the fact that we have utterly
neglected to perfect our methods of legislation. We
give little or no attention to the art of bill drafting,
and hardly any checks have been provided against the
indiscriminate introduction of bills in legislative bodies.
When bills are introduced without previous careful revision, and are submitted by the thousand in a single
session, it is plain that it is out of the question to
secure satisfactory results for the public.

We need, both in connection with the Congress of the United States and in connection with the several State legislatures, commissions of experts to draft bills in accordance with the wishes of those who have a particular proposal to bring forward. It ought not to be possible for an individual member of a legislature to present bills at random and haphazard at the request of this constituent or that, badly phrased, crudely and verbosely drawn, and utterly unsuited in form and in content to find a place upon the statute-book.

4. We have now had a long experience with the sharp separation of the executive and the legislative powers, and that this separation has some disadvantages is certain. Our governmental policies too often lack continuity and coherence because of it. In many ways the effectiveness and economy of the national government suffer severely owing to the fact that so often the executive and the legislature act at cross purposes, or on insufficient and inaccurate information, or from a misunderstanding of the motives of each other. This difficulty could be in large measure removed if action were taken, as might easily and constitutionally be done, giving to the members of the President's Cabinet seats upon the floor of the Senate and House of Representatives, with the right to participate in debate upon matters relating to their several departments, and with the obligation to answer questions and to give information in response to requests from senators and representatives. This is not a new proposal. It is associated chiefly with the

name of George H. Pendleton, of Ohio, who brought
it forward as long ago as 1864, when he was a member
of the House of Representatives. He was vigorously
supported at that time by Mr. Garfield and by Mr.
Blaine. Fifteen years later, when Mr. Pendleton was
United States Senator from Ohio, he returned to the
subject and introduced a bill dealing with the matter,
which was referred to a select committee and soon reported favorably over the signature of Senator Pendleton himself, together with those of Senators Allison
of Iowa, Voorhees of Indiana, Blaine of Maine, Butler
of South Carolina, Ingalls of Kansas, Platt of Connecticut, and Farley of California. Even these important leaders, however, could not accomplish this
desirable reform, although they were united in its
support. The proposal was renewed again by John
D. Long, of Massachusetts, when a member of the
House of Representatives, in 1886. It has recently
received the indorsement of President Taft.

That this action would, if taken, greatly increase the
efficiency of our government and bring the executive
and the legislative branches into closer understanding
of each other's methods and purposes, without in the
least trenching upon the independence and authority
of either, seems to me quite certain. One of the most
valuable features in the business of the House of Commons is the asking by members of the House of specific
questions on matters concerning which the public
wishes information, or about which some criticism or
discussion has arisen. Many a long and useless speech

that now extends over pages of the *Congressional Record* would be saved if a responsible Cabinet officer were at hand to give immediate answer to a definite question, or to offer a statement of fact.

5. There is no reason, save the sheer force of custom, for adhering longer to the present plan of electing a new Congress in November and providing for its first regular session to begin thirteen months afterward. The Congress would be more closely in touch with popular sentiment and more responsive to it, as well as in better mood for constructive legislation, if it were statedly convened within sixty or ninety days of the time when its members are chosen. As matters are at present, a member of the House of Representatives is already concerned with the preliminaries of a campaign for re-election before he has really entered upon the discharge of the duties of his office.

6. In the nation we have the principle of the short ballot. It will be a step in advance when we extend this principle to all the States. The State of New Jersey has enjoyed it for many years, and in consequence has one of the best governments of any State in the Union. Where the short ballot is adopted, public interest and attention are centred upon the most important executive and legislative officers, and they are chosen and held responsible for the selection of their associates in the minor offices of government. A large part of the extravagance and maladministration in county government throughout the United States is due to the election by the people of a long list of

minor officials who have no common sense of responsibility and no common purpose. We need the short ballot in the State and in the county as we already have it in the nation, and are rapidly getting it in the municipalities.

Here, then, are six important steps forward waiting to be taken: A more flexible method of amending the Constitution of the United States; a more satisfactory way of nominating and electing public officers; improvement in legislative methods and procedure; giving to members of the President's Cabinet seats on the floor of both Houses of Congress, with the right to participate in debates concerning their several departments; beginning the regular session of Congress at a point much nearer to the election of its members than now, and the extension of the principle of the short ballot.

Some of these reforms relate to the national government alone, while others affect both the government of the nation and that of the States. It can hardly be doubted that the cumulative effect of the adoption of all six proposals would be greatly to improve the work of our governmental system as a whole, and to allay a large part of the dissatisfaction with it that now exists.

Given these improvements, then concrete problems of legislation and administration may be attacked with greater hope of success and satisfaction. We should not delay even a month in trying to secure a modern and scientific system of banking and currency without waiting for the lessons of another money panic. We

should labor to bring greater economy into the field of
public expenditure, and to weigh carefully the effect
upon the cost of living of governmental extravagance
and the constant creation of huge volumes of bonded
indebtedness.

We should support the businesslike recommendation
of President Taft for the formulation of an annual
national budget, that some semblance of order may be
brought into the present chaos of national appropria-
tion and expenditure.  We should follow the suggestions of the American Bar Association and other important authorities, to the end that undue delay in
judicial procedure may be avoided and that numerous
and costly appeals, particularly when based on technical points, may be reduced so far as is consistent
with strict justice.  We should consider with an open
mind whether the effect is good or ill of depending so
largely as we do upon indirect taxation, and whether
if more direct taxes are to be levied, they should not
be levied with the lowest possible limit of exemption,
in order to bring the cost of government home to substantially the entire electorate.  We should push forward along the road already travelled by the national
government and by many States toward the improvement of social conditions and the betterment of those
who are forced to live on the very margin of want.
We should plan vigorously and wisely for the prevention, and not alone for the cure, of the many difficulties and injustices now existing in society, and do so
in a spirit that will not lead the individual to lean more

heavily upon the community, but, rather, help him to stand yet more surely and confidently upon his own feet. We should aim not to bring the government into partnership with monopoly and privilege, but in all our legislation affecting these matters, whether in the State or in the nation, to keep open the channels both of competition and of useful combination by preventing monopoly on the one hand, and by punishing specifically unfair and dishonorable business practices on the other. We have, fortunately, learned as a people the meaning of the words "the conservation of our natural resources," and it is the policy of progress to go forward systematically and intelligently with the course that has already been adopted. We should refrain always and under whatever temptation from a policy of international bravado and swagger, and should yield nothing, whether by careless act or by considered policy, of the leadership that we have gained in promoting the cause of international peace and the judicial settlement of disputes between the civilized nations.

All these matters and a score more suggest themselves to the eager American mind bent on high achievement and securing the just working of government for noble ends. A government must first of all make certain its own security and stability. It must then labor to advance the national ideal and at the same time strive to take an honorable part in the life and aspirations of the world as a whole.

In such ways as these lies the path of true progress

in politics. That path is not to be found amid the morasses of discontent, of class feeling, of the grasping for privilege and monopoly, or by making the individual lean constantly more heavily upon the community for maintenance and support. It is to be found, rather, out on the clear and sunlit heights of individual opportunity, where a fair chance is given to every man to stand erect and to do a man's work in the world, knowing that thereby he is serving the state and helping to build civilization on a yet securer basis.

For my own part, I should like to be able to say of the political party in whose tenets I believe, and to which I am glad to belong, what Robert Lowe said of the Liberal party in Great Britain in the dark days of 1878, when its prestige seemed fatally broken and its long-time power trampled under foot by the triumphant opposition:

The ideal of the Liberal party, said Robert Lowe, consists in a view of things undisturbed and undistorted by the promptings of interest or prejudice, in a complete independence of all class interests, and in relying for its success on the better feelings and higher intelligence of mankind.

"Happier words," said Matthew Arnold of this passage, "could not well be found."

Two years later the Liberal party, pursuing this ideal, was returned to power under the leadership of William E. Gladstone.

# XI

# ELIHU ROOT, STATESMAN

Nominating speech before the Republican National
Convention, Chicago, Illinois, June 9, 1916

# ELIHU ROOT, STATESMAN

To be elected twenty-ninth President of the United States, I shall nominate him who, by common consent, stands with the foremost statesmen of his time in this or any other land.

This is no ordinary convention. These are no ordinary times. The world is in upheaval. Forces thought to be long since cribbed, cabined and confined are loose in the world, spreading havoc and destruction on every side. There is everywhere uncertainty, unrest, grave concern for the happenings of to-morrow. The American people find themselves in the midst of a great world storm. Round about them the tempest is raging, and the great heaving waves of passion, of prejudice and of hate are threatening the total destruction of the craft which bears those fruits of human accomplishment that we call civilization. There is need of vision; there is need of leadership; there is need of sound, well-tested principle and policy, if all that we hold most dear is to ride this storm in safety.

Problems abroad multiply problems at home. Problems at home intensify problems abroad. Where can this nation turn for guidance and for accomplishment at a crisis like this if not to the party which has given to American life one after another of the great group of leaders and constructive statesmen who have made so large a part of American history for the past sixty years? That party is possessed of a body of fundamental principles which rest upon the foundation of American character, American history and American hope. That party does not draw back from difficulty, because it has grown great by surmounting one severe difficulty after another. That party does not draw back from problems, because it has made its repute in the history of free government by successfully solving one hard problem after another. That party is confident of finding leaders with vision, with sagacity and with power, because for two generations of men it has furnished one such after another to the causes which it has made its own. The best guide for the future is the knowledge and the experience of the past.

Just now every difficulty, every problem merges into one. That is the difficulty, that is the problem, of finding the voice and of executing the will of real America.

Our America is the land where hate expires. It is the land where differences of race, of creed, of language, all melt away before the powerful and welding heat of devotion to civil liberty. We are composite as a people, but we are one in fundamental belief, one in controlling principle, one in confident hope for the future. It was the task of the Republican party, with the splendid aid of men of other political faith, to preserve the integrity of the nation in the

60's, and to keep its financial and commercial honor unsullied in the 90's.  Shall it not be the goal of the Republican party, as the twentieth century unfolds itself to be a stage for the thoughts and the deeds of men, to integrate and to express the spirit and the soul of the American people at home and abroad? May we not call to our side for the accomplishment of this task, as our grandfathers and our fathers did for theirs, all patriotic Americans, men and women alike, whose faith may at times be different from ours but who see the compelling power of the one great problem and the one great need of this moment?

Nineteen sixteen is no ordinary year.  The American people find themselves voiceless, disunited, broken, owing to what we cannot but regard as the incompetence of the administration and its inability either to understand or to confront the stupendous happenings of the past two years.  We are gathered here, in the presence of this great company and under the scrutiny of the whole American people, to take the first step in substituting for the administration now in power a Republican administration that shall bring to the people of the United States safety, prosperity, happiness, and increasing self-respect.  We are here to choose leaders who, in turn, are to give voice and effect to Republican principles and to Republican policies.  One State after another will, in friendly rivalry, present the name of him whom it prefers to have selected to become the next President of the United States.  For there is every prospect that the

nominee of this Convention will succeed to the office
of President on March 4, 1917.

It is my privilege to offer you the name not only of
a typical American, but of an American whose character, abilities and public service, now in the ripe full-
ness of their power, have brought to him fame and
distinction such as fall to the lot of but few men in a
century. Born among the hills of central New York,
on the campus of an American college which appro-
priately enough bears the great name of Hamilton, he
made his way with credit and every evidence of promise
through college and law school to the bar. Admitted
to the bar at the age of twenty-two, his industry, his
native ability, and his power of clear and persuasive
speech quickly brought him both clients and reputation. Young as he was, President Arthur found in
him a trusted adviser and a close friend. He first
held public office as United States District Attorney,
by President Arthur's appointment. So wide-spread
was his reputation and so high his character that in
1899, when the problems left by the Spanish War
were pressing heavily upon the administration and the
people, President McKinley turned to him for counsel
and for great public responsibility and service. When
the message of invitation reached him to become
Secretary of War, he replied: "I know nothing about
the army. Thank the President for me, but say it is
quite absurd. I know nothing about war." Shortly
the answer came back: "President McKinley directs
me to say he is not looking for any one who knows

about war or about the army. He is looking for a statesman to organize and to direct the government of the new possessions that the war has brought to the people of the United States. You are the man he wants." Such an invitation was a command. The high-minded and conscientious lawyer laid aside the ordinary practice of his profession to answer the call of the greatest of all clients, the people of the United States. For sixteen years they have been his only clients, and how faithfully and with what distinction he has served them are now matters of history.

He reorganized the army of the United States and brought it to the highest point of efficiency it has ever reached. The General Staff and the War College are the fruits of his policies. In Cuba, in Porto Rico, in the Philippine Islands, at Panama, his administrative skill and his vision have made his name one to be conjured with. The policies that were then formulated and executed brought happiness and contentment to those distant people and new honor and credit to the government of the United States. He was in large measure the founder of our American colonial policy, and no more enlightened, more humane, or more successful colonial policy has yet been seen in the world.

Let us not forget that among the problems that press in the immediate future are problems relating to the army. He of whom I speak was perhaps our greatest Secretary of War.

On the death of John Hay, he was recalled to the Cabinet of President Roosevelt as Secretary of State.

Four brilliant years of constructive statesmanship and of rapidly growing international influence were the result. Never was our foreign policy more definite, never was it more precisely stated, and never was it more kindly and more firmly executed. In the South American Republics his name is acclaimed as has been that of no other American since the silvery voice of Henry Clay was stilled. In China, because of the re-mission of the Boxer indemnity, he is hailed as the most generous and most enlightened of statesmen, and our country is held to be the most beneficent and large-minded of nations. In Japan, because of the joint agreement which bears his name, he is trusted as having been able to propose a working solution of a difficult and delicate question of international policy. He found many and serious outstanding matters of difference with our neighbors to the north, and he left them all settled or in process of settlement. In every chancellery of Europe his name is known and honored.

Let us not forget that the chief problems that now confront this nation are those relating to international policy and international influence. He of whom I speak has unrivalled knowledge of international law and practice, and his name is written on the roll of Secretaries of State with the highest.

From the great post of Secretary of State he passed for six years to the United States Senate. Here again his rare knowledge, his familiarity with American political and diplomatic history, his firm grasp of con-stitutional and legal principle, and his unrivalled power of exposition, gave him from the moment of his entrance a place in the first rank. Political friends and political foes alike deferred to his judgment and respected his opinion. As a direct result of a single speech, dangerous provisions making financial inflation possible were stricken from the Federal Reserve Act. He retired from this post of service of his own free will in order that he might now seek years of well-earned rest and repose.

But the people are not willing that this notable ability, this exceptional experience, and this quite unequalled reputation shall be beyond their reach at a time like this. The American people are searching for the best they have. They are everywhere asking whether it is possible that when England and France and Germany and Russia, and every other nation on the globe, are seeking their most experienced and ablest men to take posts of highest service, the American democracy is to be content with anything less than the very best it has. This is no time to pay compliments. The stern duty of to-day is to place in the Presidency of the United States that Republican who by native ability, by long public service, by large and full contribution to public policy, and by force of conviction and power of expression, is best fitted among us to wield the executive power and to guide the destinies of this nation for the four anxious years upon which we are about to enter.

There are critics of democracy who tell us that nothing is so unpopular as excellence, that the best is too good for recognition under popular government. Who are those who so slander democracy, who are those who so reflect upon popular appreciation and popular judgment, who are those who so underestimate the intelligence and the virtue of the American people? Is it possible that democracy has made no progress since Athens of old? Are we still in that stage of civilization where we ostracize Aristides because we are weary of hearing him called the Just? Shall we, in this twentieth century, only recognize excellence in order to proscribe it? I do not think so meanly of democracy or of the American people. They wish leadership; they wish guidance; they long for a voice that is powerful enough to express all that their heart feels, and a brain that is clear enough to state in terms of public policy those hopes and aspirations which are democracy's life.

It is my good fortune to enjoy the friendship of many of those whose names are now to be presented for the consideration of this convention. They are men of character, men of capacity, men of public experience, men of high patriotism. It would be a pleasure, were we able to have many Republican Presidents, to find a place for them all. But we are compelled to make a choice. It is our duty to choose him as our candidate who, in the year 1916 and in the presence of the issues of this moment, is in our judgment best fitted and most competent effectively to represent Republican principles and best able to guide the policies of the American people.

Let us take counsel of courage, not of fear. Let us seek to lift this coming campaign above all the smaller and the more sordid phases of politics. Let us give to the nation a President than whom no public man in the history of this country has possessed larger powers of mind, firmer or more consistent character, greater capacity for public service, or more finished skill in exposition and persuasion. Let us fortify ourselves at home and re-establish our repute abroad.

Beyond to-day's raging storm of war I see forming a rainbow of promise. The bright colors that fade one into another are the colors of the Saxon and the Celt, the Teuton and the Latin, the Slav and the Hun. Slowly these pass into the pure white light of the day of peace and progress, of happiness and friendship among men. This rainbow is the symbol of our dear America. Each separate color marks an element of race or creed that goes into its making; but when the white light of day absorbs them all into itself, they exist no longer as separate colors but only as indistinguishable parts of a single and sufficient brightness. So, under competent and compelling leadership, I see a single, united America—strong, firm, resolute, just—made out of all the different elements that have sought these shores of hope and promise as a sailor seeks a safe and sheltered port for refuge when the tempest roars. This America, the America of Washington and Jefferson, of Hamilton and Marshall, of Webster and Lincoln, will be a light to lighten the whole world and ages yet unborn. This America will know its mind and do its will because it shall have found a leader and a voice.

To be Republican candidate for President of the United States, I name Elihu Root of New York.

# XII

## PROBLEMS OF PEACE AND AFTER-PEACE

An address delivered at the Lincoln Day Banquet under the auspices of the Republican County Committee of Passaic County, Paterson, New Jersey, February 11, 1919

# PROBLEMS OF PEACE AND AFTER-PEACE

It is fitting that Republicans throughout the nation should mark their loyal celebration of the anniversary of Lincoln's birth by invoking his spirit, his statesmanship, and his lofty patriotism, to guide the Republican party in its relation toward the grave questions, both national and international, that are pressing for answer. The duty and the opportunity of the Republican party are of supreme importance, and the party is called upon again, as it was in 1860 and in 1896, to bend all its energies and to unite all its abilities in solving problems which involve the very fabric and honor of the government. It must not be forgotten that the Congressional elections of 1918 indicated with clear emphasis that a large plurality of American voters place their confidence and their hope in the policies and in the leadership of the Republican party. Indeed, a change of but a few hundred votes in an electorate of more than one million in the State of California at the presidential election of 1916 would have put a Republican instead of a Democrat in the White House during these momentous years; and a change of some eight hundred votes in not more than nine congressional districts at the same election, would have enabled the Republicans to organize the House of Representatives and to elect the Speaker.

Despite these facts, the President of the United States, in his capacity as a party leader, was rash enough in October last to demand of the American people a vote of confidence in his administration. He drew a dismal picture of what would happen to him and his influence if his demand were refused. In reply, the administration received a vote of lack of confidence, which, all things considered, is more emphatic than any similar vote since the Republican party lost control of the House of Representatives in 1874, immediately after having re-elected General Grant to the presidency by an overwhelming majority in 1872.

It must not be forgotten, moreover, that when the elections of 1918 were held, the Democrat administration had all the benefit of participation in a successful war; that it had been disbursing public moneys by the billion, with an extravagant recklessness that was without parallel in the history of any government; that it controlled, through the railways, the telegraphs and telephones, as well as through the supervision of the banking and business interests of the country, an amount of patronage which made the list of office-holders of ten years ago sink into insignificance. Despite all these sources of political aid and strength, a Republican minority in the House of Representatives was turned into a majority of forty-four. Passaic County, a veritable capital of American industry, spoke with no uncertain sound; so did Maine; so did West Virginia; so did Indiana; so did Missouri; so

did Kansas; and so did Washington. Indeed, in some
of the Western States that were carried for Democrat
electors in 1916, it would have been only courteous
on the part of the Democrat organizations to move
to make the vote for the Republican candidates unanimous. The handwriting is on the wall. The next
President of the United States will be a Republican,
and he will have behind him a united Republican party,
eager to solve the new questions in a spirit of justice
and of human sympathy, and determined to protect
the foundations of the American republic against all
enemies, whether they be the Central Powers and their
allies without, or the anarchists, Bolshevists, and
enemies of liberty and social order within.

The American people are tired of politics given over
to rhetoric and to phrase-making, to carrying water
on both shoulders, to stooping with ear to the ground
and trying to avoid taking a definite and specific position on the issues raised by the revolutionists who
are busy among us. The American people, and particularly the young Americans, both men and women,
where women are already exercising the suffrage, are
crying out for leadership, for courage, for vision and
for capacity to lead the thought of the nation, as well
as to formulate its public action. Plain speaking and
not fine words are what the people demand; definite
policies and not platitudes are what they wish to have
presented for their judgment.

Just see what the situation now is: The war has been
triumphantly won by the courage, the endurance and

the high purpose of the people and the armies of France, of Great Britain, of Belgium, and of Italy, with the powerful aid of the financial and economic resources, and of the splendid fighting forces of the United States. The decisive part played in the final stage of the war by the fighting forces of America on land and on sea, was directly due to the resourcefulness, the capacity, the intelligence and the patriotism of the American people, and was in spite of the shortcomings, the extravagance, the quarrels, and the incapacity of many of those who were in conspicuous posts of official power and responsibility. The war is won, and as a result, the people of the United States are bound to the splendid peoples who have been their allies by new ties of respect and affection, which no selfish interests and no enemy propaganda must ever be allowed to weaken, much less to break. The result of the war is a new world—new in many of its interests; new in many of its problems; new in many of its opportunities. What is to be the place of America in this new world, and how shall the Republican party do its full duty to the country which it was born to protect and to serve?

The answer is, after all, comparatively simple. America is ready to take her just place as a member of a society of like-minded and co-operating nations, to all of which she is bound, not only by the ties knit by the events of the war, but by strong personal and family bonds growing out of the fact that our twentieth-century population has been drawn from nearly every country in the world. The position of America should be that of brother and friend, not that of guardian or attempted ruler. We shall have quite enough to do in minding our own business and in taking care of the interests of our own immense population, and our own complex system of trade and of industry, without assuming any part of the duty of minding other peoples' business.

The Republican party is certain to insist that the new organization of the world shall be a society of nations, and not a society without nations. It will strive constantly to strengthen and to protect the integrity and the freedom of action of America in order that America, tied down by no vain and empty formulas, may have more to give in service to other peoples and in co-operation with them. The Republican party will insist that the fruits of the war be not lost or traded away; that insidious German propaganda be not listened to; and that the manifest attempts to create discord between America on the one hand, and France, Great Britain, and Italy, as well as with the new nations of the Czechoslovaks and the Poles, on the other, shall not be permitted to succeed. We do not propose that a war which has been won by arms shall be lost by words. We do not propose that the sufferings and sorrows of France, Great Britain, Belgium, Italy, and Serbia, or those of tens of thousands of our own American families, shall be left without the full results of victory in establishing and maintaining peace and good order in the world.

There is grave disappointment among Republicans that the American delegation to the Peace Conference was not made more representative of the international knowledge, the international experience, and the international statesmanship of our country. There is grave disappointment, too, that the terms of peace with the Central Powers were not quickly and speedily arrived at, announced and enforced, as they might easily have been, in accordance with the convincing formula uttered by the statesmen of France early in the war, namely: Reparation, Restitution, Security. Had this course been pursued, the Central Powers and their allies would have known by this time exactly where they stood, and the splendid unity and concord of the Allies, as these existed on November 11 last, would have been preserved without the present discussion of the myriad details of a new world-order, that are quite irrelevant to the making of peace, and as to which sufficient time for a complete understanding and agreement should and can be had. The great need of this moment is to establish peace, not only in form but in fact; to enable business, industry, and agriculture to resume their normal course; to restore the broken lines of trade and commerce, both at home and abroad; to give men and women assurance in their employment and in the conduct of their business; and then, with normal life resumed, to take up during as many months as may be needed, the study of questions of world organization. It is my belief this is and has been the substantially unanimous view of the

most competent and experienced statesmen in every
one of the Allied countries, and in the United States;
but a contrary course has been followed and its results
are already seen to be unhappy. We are wholly in
the dark as to what is really being said and done in
Paris. The fulsome adulation and flattery of the news-
paper dispatches, so repugnant to right-thinking Americans, reveal little and conceal much. These dispatches
contradict each other, not only on successive days,
but on the same day, and no one in America, despite
the loud protestations of open diplomacy, has any
clear or accurate idea of what the American delegation
is pressing upon the Peace Conference or how it is
being received. What we do know is that while peace
waits, the splendid unity and spirit of the Allies are
being destroyed by irrelevant and largely mysterious
debates.

The spokesmen of the Republican party, both in
and out of Congress, have met this deplorable and
unhappy situation with high patriotism, and with
almost superhuman patience. They have held that
since our country is engaged in a great international
discussion, we must do everything in our power to
support our official representatives, even though we
do not know what they are doing, but suspect they
are doing many things which we cannot approve.
An occasional speech has been delivered on the floor
of the Senate or the House by way of warning to the
people that sooner or later the spokesmen of the Republican party will deem it their duty to speak out

and to tell the truth as they see it. We cannot, however, afford to shirk our responsibility for the protection and defense of American independence and American institutions, and we must not, through silence, allow sinister influences that are antagonistic to American principles, and that will in time alter or overthrow our government, to enter unchallenged into our life.

Two events have taken place in quick succession, which call for frank and clear speech. Just as the autocratic and criminal government of the Bolsheviks in Russia seemed to be tottering to its fall, its leaders, with their hands still dripping with the blood of their victims, were actually invited to confer with representatives of free and liberty-loving peoples. This step is in effect that "entering into a compact with crime" which the French Minister of Foreign Affairs, M. Pichon, only a few weeks ago said should not be done. From a moral as well as from a political point of view, this action, no matter what its excuse, deserves only most vigorous denunciation. If, as has been suggested, it is the price paid for relieving from a dangerous position the tiny military forces landed on the north coast of Russia, then it deserves something worse; for neither American nor British soldiers would ever ask for compromise with criminals as a substitute for their own courage and their own noble patriotism.

The worst criminals produced by the war are the Russian Bolsheviks. Even the horrors perpetrated by the Austrians in Serbia, and the outrages committed by the Germans in Belgium, seem mere exhibitions of temper when compared with the systematic cruelty and crime practised by the Bolshevik régime against everything in Russia that represented law, order and liberty, or that was capable of building upon the ruins left by the overthrow of the Romanoff dynasty. To desert the people of Russia now is an act of astounding folly and ingratitude. To strain at gnats like Huerta and William of Hohenzollern, and to swallow camels like Lenine and Trotsky, is certainly a curious proceeding. If one were seeking for ways to aid our enemies to re-establish their strength and their menace, his first step would be to leave the Russian people to their tender mercies.

Formal conference with the Bolsheviks was bad enough, and we may well contrast with this action the message which the stout-hearted and fearless Mayor of Seattle sent a few days ago to American Bolsheviks who were organizing war on the peace and order of that splendid city. His upholding of law and order is the short and easy way to deal with Bolsheviks. But once a conference had been determined upon, surely there could have been found among the hundred millions of Americans some man or woman of honor, of untarnished reputation, and with a record for public service who could have borne the credentials of the government of the United States without soiling or discrediting them. The appointment actually made has affronted our decent citizenship and aggrieved the moral and religious sentiment of the country. No one, however blinded by partisanship, has been found to rise in defense of this act. It is truly an astonishing performance.

We saw one journalistic adulator sent, without official commission but with high authority, to muddle our affairs with Mexico, and we saw him later turn up among the most active friends and agents of our Teuton enemies. We were told in explanation that, although without previous training or public experience, he had received this important commission as a reward for having written in flattering terms of the President and his policies. It appears that this new appointee also has busied himself with his pen, and that apparently just because he has published a crude and fulsome eulogy of the President's personality and public conduct, he has been selected to represent the people of the United States. Not a fraction of one per cent of those who know his record would be willing to take his hand, and yet he is to represent America at a conference on the vitally important question of the future of the Russian people and their relation to the rest of the world.

We have become accustomed during these past six years to the President's fondness for surrounding himself with intellectual and political midgets, but we have hitherto been spared anything so shocking as this appointment. What are the clergy going to say about it ? What are the women of the country, now granted the vote in many States, going to say about it ? What are high-minded patriots and jealous lovers of our country's honor, regardless of section or party,

going to say about it ? I for one do not believe that
true patriotism and decent feeling are dead in the land.

While our eyes are turned to the Peace Conference
and our minds are filled with international problems,
we are drifting at home, without executive or legislative leadership, in waters filled with rocks and floating mines. These rocks and floating mines are the
domestic problems which become every day more insistent, and whose solution we must not postpone one
instant longer than is absolutely necessary. What is
needed is more action and less talk. The Constitution of the United States, by far the most important
single political document of modern times, was completely drafted between May 25 and September 17.
There is no reason, save mental and political laziness
and inertia, for dragging out over five years a solution
of the railway problem, or for allowing the industrial
situation to continue to develop domestic wars which
are already disastrous, and might easily become comparable in their effects with the international war
through which we have just passed.

In order to deal with these problems in an American
spirit and in the interest of all America, we must get
back quickly to our American form of government.
Under pressure of the necessities of war we turned our
government, for the time being, into an autocracy
and a bureaucracy which Russia of the Tsars might
well have envied. There was manifold interference
with individual liberty, with civil rights, with trade
and commerce, and with all other normal activities

of a free people. Congress became a rubber stamp, and public discussion of public policies practically disappeared. As war measures, all these were defensible. We had to help to win the war, to win it quickly, and to win it completely. This has been done and we have now to return our government to its proper functions and to restore freedom to the individual and to business.

Of course, there are those who believe in transforming our American republic into a socialistic democracy, and they would be glad to continue permanently the autocratic and bureaucratic system which the war developed; and it must not be forgotten that socialism is the twin brother of autocracy, and that like autocracy it is the deadly enemy of republicanism and of individual liberty.

The people are now everywhere asking questions of business and of the relation of government to business; questions of finance and of financial provision for an expanding foreign trade; questions of labor and of the workingman's ambition to have his full share of the rewards and the satisfactions of American life; questions of agricultural development and of the utilization of the nation's resources; and, above all, questions of the administration and control of the nation's great systems of transportation and communication. All these cry aloud for answer and the Democrat administration has no answer to give. So long as these questions are unanswered, and so long as there is wide-spread anxiety and uncertainty as to future policies, just so long we offer invitation to the activities of those desperate revolutionaries who would destroy liberty and order to set up a new tyranny of the mob, who would overthrow equality of citizenship in order to establish a privileged ruling class, and who would declare war on American institutions in the name of that mad and murderous Bolshevism which is just now reducing the people of Russia to impotence and slavery. The way of escape from all this is to press forward quickly to the solution of our domestic problems with wisdom, with human sympathy, with courage, and with constructive power.

The greatest and most far-reaching of these problems is that of labor. Here very great progress had been made until the I. W. W. movement and Bolshevism appeared in America. The hours of work in essential industries were no longer excessive and were being steadily shortened; wages had risen greatly, both in money value and in purchasing power; conditions attaching to land work had been improved in healthfulness and in attractiveness; collective bargaining was well established over an increasing area, both of territory and of industry. The path of progress lies not in returning to a state of industrial war, but rather in applying to industrial conflicts precisely the same principles of justice, of understanding and of sympathy, by which we hope hereafter to avoid international conflicts.

The labor problem, so-called, is not, I think, primarily a question of wages or of hours of work; it is

primarily a human problem.  Just so soon as we recognize that wages are paid, not out of savings, or capital, but out of products, and that the greater the
product the more there will be available for wages,
we shall have begun to get on the right track.  The
next step is to realize that product is the result of co-
operation, not of capital and labor, considered as dead,
abstract things whose names are spelled with large
letters, but of the co-operation of three elements, all
of which are human: the man who works with his
hands, the man who works with his head, and the man
who works with his savings.  In each case the essential
thing is not the hands, the head, or the savings; the
essential thing is the man.

Let us establish co-operation and conference between
these three types of producers, not alone when difficulties and disputes have arisen or are about to rise,
but as a steady policy in the daily conduct of the particular business.  By taking counsel together as a
means of prevention, these three types of men will
come, after a while, to need very little counsel together
as a means of cure.  Action such as this is sometimes
called industrial democracy.  That is not a very happy
or a very exact term, but if it assists in making clear
what I have in mind then I am willing to use it.  If
we can deal satisfactorily with the labor question, the
next few years will be years of the greatest prosperity
in the industrial history of the American people.

The reason why the government was obliged to
take over and to operate the railways of the country

as a war measure was because our uncertain and unwise policies of the last thirty years had put the railways in a position where they could not themselves
co-operate as the government wished without violating the law. The first thing that the government
railway administration did was to set all restrictive
laws aside and to operate the railways with a view to
meeting the necessities of the moment. This fact
alone conclusively demonstrates to every thoughtful
man the unwisdom of our policy or policies toward
the railways during the past generation. We had injured or ruined their credit so that they could not
get money for additional terminals, for needed rolling
stock, or for improvements that were imperatively demanded. We had prevented them from combining to
divide the business of a given territory to the best
advantage, and we had put them under forty-nine
different sets of masters—namely, an Interstate Commerce Commission and forty-eight separate state commissions or systems of railway control. It is important
to remember that we ourselves had done these things
and not the railways. There had been very grave
abuses in the organization and conduct of the railway
systems years ago, and just resentment at these abuses
had played a large part in bringing about the situation which existed in 1917. Perhaps now we have
learned our lesson and are ready to deal with the
transportation systems of the country as an important
national asset to be preserved and developed for national service. There is no good reason why we

should take either five years or two years to work out and adopt a sound policy toward the railways.

The ruling principles are simple, and may perhaps be stated in this way:

1. Government ownership and operation of railways have been ineffective and unfortunate in Europe, and while compatible with an autocratic or a socialistic state are incompatible with a republic unless that republic is to drift either toward autocracy or toward socialistic democracy. To establish government ownership and operation of railways would be to take a long step toward changing our American form of government.

2. Private ownership and operation of railways, despite abuses, particularly in the early days, have contributed enormously to the development of the United States. They have offered unexampled opportunities for initiative and organizing skill. They had developed a transportation system which was without an equal in the world for cheapness, comfort, speed, and public service.

3. Under government ownership and operation of railways all officials and employees of the railway systems would become part of a great ruling bureaucracy. They would lose their sense of initiative and independence, and they as well as passengers and shippers would be deprived of any disinterested government tribunal to which to appeal for redress of grievances.

4. The experience of government railway administration during the war has clearly demonstrated the futility of attempting to continue to apply the provisions of the Sherman Act to transportation systems: combination, co-operation, and the pooling of business are an absolute necessity if the railways are to continue to serve the public successfully. Such combination, co-operation, and pooling can, however, only be permitted under government supervision and control.

5. While private ownership and operation of railways are not only advantageous but probably necessary to the continuance of

the American system of government, the railways themselves are not private undertakings. They are charged with a public interest and are distinctly public service institutions. For this additional reason, and because of experience in this and other countries, government supervision and control are essential.

6. Government supervision and control of railways involve large powers over capital issues, service, rates, and wages. This means absolute ruin for the railway systems unless with the supervision and control there goes a just measure of financial responsibility. In other words, the government must co-operate with the railways in making it possible for them to serve the public as the government may either desire or compel. One way to do this is to establish rates at a point which will produce a return sufficient to pay interest on bonded debt and dividends of a fixed minimum amount upon capital stock, provided that earnings in excess of the amount necessary for these purposes shall be applied in equal parts to reward labor, to effect improvements in permanent way and rolling stock, and finally to reward investors.

7. Create a Federal Transportation Board to take the place of the Interstate Commerce Commission with supervision of all transportation whether by land or by water, and provide that membership in the federal transportation system shall carry with it such advantages that no existing railway, and none hereafter organized, could afford to remain outside of it. Pursue in this respect a policy similar to that which has been successful in building up the Federal Reserve banking system.

8. Remove railways that are members of the federal transportation system from the jurisdiction or control of state commissions, while providing that local and regional interest in and concern for railway systems be fully recognized. Treat all transportation in law, as it is in fact, as part of one great system of national transportation, regardless of whether a particular shipment crosses a state line or not. The Republican National Convention of 1916 emphatically supported this policy.

9. Settlement of the relation to exist between the railways and the government is not a matter for railway managers, owners of securities and government officials alone. It is a matter which interests every citizen not only as a potential passenger or shipper, but as an American concerned in the protection of those fundamental principles upon which the country's liberty, opportunity, and prosperity have been built.

Given these principles, it should not be difficult for a disinterested body of men to prepare in a short time a bill for the exclusive federal supervision of the railway systems of the country. Were it announced that this was to be done, the wheels of industry would begin to revolve and trade to expand without an hour's delay.

The relation of the Federal Government to the country's business ought to be settled upon the basis of the experience of the last thirty years, and by the application of principles similar to those that have been suggested for the treatment of the transportation problem. The attempt to enforce competition by law and to punish co-operation has been a dismal failure, and it was dropped by the government the moment we entered the war. A constructive policy toward business will provide for the largest amount of initiative and co-operation on the part of individuals and corporations, while assuring the same measure of effective federal supervision and control that now exists in the case of the banks, and that ought to exist in the case of the railways. We need by the side of the Federal Reserve Board and the Federal Transportation Board, a Federal Trade Board with analogous powers and duties in relation to the producing, manufacturing, and shipping industries of the country.

To be sure, these problems are vast and touch directly the life and interest of every American, and for that reason they are problems which Americans must solve for themselves. How better can they set out to solve them than in the patient, long-suffering, and deeply patriotic spirit of Abraham Lincoln? He was born one hundred and ten years ago into a world which men then thought as troubled and as difficult as we now think ours. The menace of Napoleon hung over Europe and the people of Great Britain had undertaken, with all their resourcefulness, their energy and their determination, the task of his overthrow in order that the newly-established liberties of the people might not be limited or lost. While Lincoln was yet a child on the frontier in southern Indiana, Napoleon was a prisoner at St. Helena and was no more to trouble Europe or the world. Then, as now, American questions went hand in hand with international questions, and as Lincoln grew up his mind was turned toward matters of domestic government, of the settlement and organization of new territories, of human freedom and human slavery, and finally of the preservation of the Union itself. No man can tell what might have happened to America had Abraham Lincoln not been elected to the presidency in 1860, but of one thing we may be sure: The history of the world from that day

to this would have been strangely different. With
that wonderful combination of qualities of heart and
head which enabled him to carry the country safely
through the crisis of four years of civil war, and which
then placed him in the Pantheon of the world's noblest
heroes and servants, he made possible the America
which we know and love, the America of almost un-
limited power, of lofty purpose, and of stern determination not to let liberty wither or die in its hands.
The question to be settled by the people in 1860 was
whether the Union should be preserved or permitted
to dissolve.  Abraham Lincoln said that it should be
preserved at all costs, and that under no circumstances should it be permitted to dissolve.  The question to be settled by the people in 1920 will be whether
the American nation shall remain upon its foundation of ordered liberty and free opportunity, or whether
it shall be so modified, or perhaps even so largely
overturned, that there will arise in its stead a social
democracy, autocracy's nearest and best friend, to
take over the management of each individual's life
and business, to order his comings and his goings, to
limit his occupations and his savings, and to say
that the great experiment of Washington and Hamilton, of Jefferson and Madison, of Marshall and Webster, of Adams and Clay, and of Lincoln and Roosevelt has come to an end, and gone to join the list of
failures in free government with the ancient republics
of Greece and Rome and their later followers of Venice
and Genoa.

Lincoln quoted Scripture to his purpose when he said at Springfield in 1858: "'A house divided against itself cannot stand.' I believe this government cannot endure permanently half slave and half free. I do not expect the Union to be dissolved—I do not expect the house to fall—but I do expect that it will cease to be divided. It will become all one thing, or all the other."

We may almost echo his exact words, and say that a house divided against itself cannot stand, a nation cannot endure half American and half Bolshevik. I do not expect the nation to continue divided, but I do expect and believe that under the leadership and guidance of the Republican party it will become all American.

# XIII

## THE REPUBLICAN PARTY
### ITS PRESENT DUTY AND OPPORTUNITY

An address delivered before the Union League of Philadelphia,
November 22, 1919

# THE REPUBLICAN PARTY

## ITS PRESENT DUTY AND OPPORTUNITY

These are significant and stirring days. The privilege of speaking before the Union League on public questions of high importance at such a time is one which I greatly appreciate and for which I desire to express my hearty thanks.

It was no less a personality than Abraham Lincoln who spoke of the Union League as prompted in its formation by motives of the highest patriotism. Then he added: "I have many a time heard of its doing good, and no one has charged it with doing any wrong." Surely, gentlemen, that was a precious tribute to those who heard it spoken, and it will remain a precious tribute in the memories of their children so long as this republic shall endure.

I said just now that these are significant and stirring days. They are significant because they are to record the making of choices and the formulation of policies that have not to do with the routine or the mere details of our daily life, but that reach down to the very foundations of government and of civil society. They are stirring because they make compelling appeal to every American patriot to rouse himself from lethargy, from indifference, and from overconfidence, in order that he may take his place in the great army of convinced believers in the republic who propose to do victorious battle to defend the faith of the fathers and to protect the achievements and accomplishments of their sons.

For some time past there has been throughout the country an unjust and an unworthy tendency to decry politics and to urge the youth of this generation to hold themselves aloof from its contamination. No teaching could be more false or more unpatriotic. Politics is not office-seeking; politics is not the use of the devious arts of the demagogue or the self-seeker to secure power over men. Politics is one of the noblest and finest words in our language. It is nothing but the doctrine of how to live together happily and helpfully in organized society. In an autocracy, whether imperialist or socialist, there will be no need for politics. In an autocracy our politics will be made for us by some one else. In a democratic republic we make our own politics. In a republic every good citizen is or should be an active politician, because free government will not take care of itself. American institutions will not preserve themselves. They need the care, they need the devotion, they need the protection of thoughtful, high-minded, and patriotic men and women who are deeply interested in politics and deeply concerned about politics. Especially should every effort be made to draw into persistent political activity and responsibility the youth of to-day who are to be the nation's leaders of to-morrow. If the people are not going to run this government, who is going to run it? If we are not ourselves to shape policies for our happiness, our comfort, and our protection, who is going to shape them? There are active, persistent, and well-organized minorities quite ready to take this job off the hands of the people of the United States if the people of the United States are not ready to maintain and conduct their own government.

A free government cannot be maintained except on the basis of political principle. There are only two great classes of motive which drive men in life, whether it be their individual life, their community life, or their relation to the state. One of those motives is principle and the other motive is interest. If you are not driven by principle, then you give way to interest. A government that is nothing but a conflict of interests, nothing but the grasping and grabbing for privilege and for power of this individual and that, of this group and that, will produce chaos, anarchy, and ruin just so soon as the conflict becomes sufficiently widespread and sufficiently general. Over against interest we put principle—sound, far-reaching, constructive political principle. A body of men and women who gather about a principle or a set of principles constitute a party. The reason why parties are necessary to free government is that principles are necessary to free government, and organized bodies of men and women, that is, parties, are needed to maintain, to enforce, and to apply principles. The spirit of party which Washington decried in his Farewell Address was the spirit of faction, self-seeking and turbulent. He was himself an earnest defender of those principles adherence to which distinguishes a true party from a faction.

See what has happened in the history of free government in Europe. There the division into parties has been for two hundred and fifty years between the conservative and the liberal. The conservative party reflects the natural feeling of men who do not wish to go ahead too fast, who wish to hold to the old forms that have come down from long ago, and to yield just as little as possible to the spirit of progress and of change, to what we call the modern spirit. On the other hand, the liberal party is made up of those who wish to share and to lead in the movement of opinion among men, who are anxious to shape old institutions to meet new conditions, and who wish to hold themselves open-minded and sympathetic toward each new demand and each new aspiration that arises among great masses of men. The history of European politics shows that for more than two hundred years the pendulum has swung now to the conservative, now to the liberal, side, and that free government in Great Britain, free government in France, free government in Switzerland, free government in Holland, free government in the Scandinavian countries, has been worked out by the play of these two sets of forces. But in the United States we are all liberals in the European sense. We have never had in the United States a conservative party as that term is known abroad, because every American has wished for progress, every American has wished for advance, every American has wished for improvement. So in this country we divided upon a quite different line. We divided in the very beginning of our nation's history into those who believed in the power, the force, and the ideals of a great nation that had been created by the Constitution of the United States, and those who would deny to that nation many attributes of nationhood, who feared the strength of its government, and who would put shackles upon its activities in the fear that otherwise civil liberty might be lost.

George Washington and Alexander Hamilton were the leaders of the party of construction and nationalism. Thomas Jefferson and his friends were the leaders of the party of negation and doubt. Americans passed naturally according to their temperament or their convictions into one or the other of these groups. There were those who believed with all their heart in the nation, in its calling, in its opportunity, and in its power. On the other hand, there were those who doubted and held back. Mr. President, the reason why the Democrat party has never pursued a logical and consistent policy from the day of its foundation until to-day, the reason why it could never pursue a consistent and persistent public policy, is that it could not continue to doubt the power and reality of the nation and still survive. That fact speedily converted the Democrat party from a party of negation to a party of opportunism. To save itself from ex-

tinction it had, from time to time, to use the weapons
of its opponents. So from the very beginning, from
the day when Thomas Jefferson made the Louisiana
Purchase in flat violation of his political principles and
urged that the Constitution be amended so as specifically to authorize his act, the party that he founded
became a party of opportunism. If to-day Thomas
Jefferson could rise from his grave and witness some
of the deeds done at Washington and hear some of
the words spoken at Washington and elsewhere by
those who bear his party name, he would be amazed
and bewildered beyond all expression.

On the other hand, the reason why the Republican
party has been, first under one name and then under
another, a logical and constructive party, the reason
why it has to its credit the extraordinary list of achievements that make so large a part of the history of our
nation, is that its fundamental principle is faith in the
republic and belief in the republic's power as a nation
to progress and to solve the problems of to-morrow
in the light of the experience of yesterday.

Into the making of the Republican party there have
gone four sets of influences:

*First*, the strong and constructive nationalism of
Washington, Hamilton, Jay, Marshall, and Webster—
the men who laid the foundations of this government.

*Second*, the passionate Americanism of Henry Clay,
of Kentucky, with his zeal for the upbuilding of American industry, for the development of American roads
and canals, for the settlement of the then unbroken

West, and his sincere sympathy with the down-trodden and oppressed all over the world.

*Third,* the moral and political idealism of Abraham Lincoln, the man who from the high seat of his lofty spirit presided with unruffled calm over the most disturbed and troubled years in the history of the republic.

Then, last, there was the broad human sympathy, the keen insight into modern industrial and social needs and problems, the unbounded vitality for service, and the unflinching Americanism of Theodore Roosevelt.

Out of those four elements of faith and of action the constructive, advancing Republican party of to-day has been built. If that great party shall be true to itself, to its principles, to its ideals, and shall exert itself to meet face to face the people of the United States who may be troubled or in doubt, the future of this country will be secure and the great problems that are awaiting our solution will be solved in the general interest and in a way to promote the progress of our nation and of the race.

The English historian Trevelyan was true to fact when he wrote of the Republican party as "a famous and high-principled party." This it has been from the very beginnings of this nation, under whatever name its adherents have assembled. The Republican party has made its full share of mistakes, and its fame, its authority, and its opportunity have attracted to its ranks some who were unworthy to bear its name.

But, on the whole, the history of free government records no equally important, continuing, and constructive political group, with the possible exception of the liberal party in Great Britain during the reigns of Queen Victoria and Edward VII.

We are already preparing for a great political contest, and the signs are all favorable to the return of the Republican party to full power in the government of the nation unless it shall flinch from its clear duty and fail in its high opportunity. Reputation is an excellent thing, but it is not enough. Record for great public service is a splendid thing, but it is not enough. The first voter of to-morrow and the newly enfranchised women voters in many States must be given something more than a share in the pride which the older Republican feels in the history of his party. These new voters are ready to respond to an appeal to their patriotism and to their intelligence. They wish to have reasons given for the faith that should be in them, and for the course which they should take in choosing a political party with which and through which effectively to exert the influence of their citizenship.

In the approaching contest the nation faces a crisis because the contest will be waged over fundamental principles. This is not the first crisis in the history of the republic, nor is it the first time that the principles for which the Republican party stands have been called upon to save the country from its conscious or unconscious enemies. There was a crisis under the old Articles of Confederation, and it was met under the leadership of George Washington, Alexander Hamilton, and James Madison, the latter being at that time an adherent to the principles of the Republican party. There was a crisis during the second administration of Washington, when disorder and anarchy were abroad in the land, and the newly made government was threatened with ruin. Again George Washington was the pilot who guided the ship of state through that tempestuous sea. There was a crisis when the judicial interpretation of the Constitution was at stake, and when both public opinion and the Supreme Court of the United States had to be convinced that the United States was a nation, with all the powers and attributes of a sovereign people. That crisis was met by the clear judicial reasoning of Chief Justice Marshall and by the eloquent and convincing advocacy of Daniel Webster. There was a crisis when the unity and integrity of the nation were challenged and when Fort Sumter was fired upon by those who conscientiously believed that they were at liberty to disrupt the Union. That crisis was met under the leadership of Abraham Lincoln, of whom Secretary Stanton so beautifully and so truly said, "Now he belongs to the ages."

In 1920 the American people are to face still another crisis in their history, and they will meet and surmount it as they have those that have gone before. This time the crisis is precipitated by the activity of elements in our population which hold and teach doctrines that sound strange to the American ear. This crisis is brought about by those who have lost faith in America, who no longer believe in or who do not understand the principles of the Declaration of Independence and of the Constitution of the United States; who would turn their backs upon a republican form of government in order to set up in its place a system of control by a privileged class, with a view to the exploitation of all other groups or classes in the community. Such men frankly proclaim their preference for the political philosophy of a Lenine and a Trotzky to that of a Washington, a Hamilton, a Webster, or a Lincoln. Once let the American people understand this issue and they will rise in their might to overwhelm the enemies of America, as the citizens of Massachusetts, regardless of party preference, sprang to the defense of law and order on November 4 last. The issue is the preservation of the American form of government, with its incomparable blessing of liberty under law, and its fundamental principles of equality of citizenship, equality of opportunity, and the right to hold and dispose of one's own just gains. The attack purports to be directed against property, but it is really directed against liberty, for property is but one of the expressions of liberty. No man could be free who had not the right, protected by law, to dispose of his own goods and services as he may choose and to apply his just gains as he will, subject only to the limitation of every other man's right to do the same thing.

We are called upon both to explain democracy and to fight for democracy. We are called upon to make it clear that class divisions, class struggles, class control, are not only undemocratic but antidemocratic, and that the only end which they can possibly achieve is anarchy and economic stagnation.

How does it happen that it becomes the duty and the opportunity of the Republican party to defend and to explain America in this sense? The answer is because the present Democrat administration has trifled with this great issue, has given posts of honor and authority to those who hold and teach doctrines in flat antagonism to the principles on which our government rests, and has even commissioned men of this type to carry on more or less authoritative negotiations with revolutionaries in other lands. If the present administration had, since March 4, 1913, stood for American principles of government and for the American social order with definiteness and emphasis against all attacks, we might not now be faced by the serious situation which confronts us. The administration's incessant harping upon a distinction between a people and their government, and the insidious suggestion that the governments do not represent their several peoples and should be either corrected or overthrown, has helped to spread the seeds of disorder throughout the world. In Western Europe substantially every government rests upon a democratic basis. The responsible spokesmen and rulers can at any moment be changed by the people in accordance with their several constitutional forms. It is a travesty on the facts of history and of politics to spread abroad the notion that some unusual and perhaps revolutionary act on the part of a people is necessary in order to bring their government into harmony with them. There was of course ground for this suggestion so long as the Romanoffs, the Hapsburgs, and the Hohenzollerns were able to withhold self-government from hundreds of millions of human beings. But there is no ground for it in respect of Great Britain, France, Italy, Switzerland, Belgium, Holland, or the Scandinavian countries. Each one of these governments rests upon a democratic basis and is immediately responsive to changing public opinion.

Moreover, the administration has permitted the industrial problem to take such a form as directly menaces our political institutions. When in September, 1916, the Adamson Law was placed upon the statute-book, in response to what the Democrat managers believed to be a political necessity, a false step was taken that has never been wholly retraced, and whose ill effects are seen in what is taking place in a dozen States to-day. The far wiser policies that have just now been followed came too late to repair all the damage that had been done.

So complex is our present-day economic organization, and so interdependent are the interests of our entire citizenship, that unless we hold fast to our fundamental principles we may easily do irreparable damage to America through trying to solve the industrial problem by false methods. When any particular group of citizens propose unitedly to withhold their co-operation in industry in order to gain or to force some political end or some change in public policy, they are pointing a pistol at the head of the republic. A man or a group of men may of course withhold co-operation in industry if they will, and frequently they are justified in so doing in order to bring about better, more healthful, and more American conditions of employment. But to strike against the people of the United States and their social order, against the proper protection of their lives and their property, is revolution. This fact must be driven home and made so familiar to the men and women of the United States that they will, in overwhelming majorities, insist that our industrial problem be met and solved on American lines and in accordance with American principles of government and of social organization, and not by the overthrow or violent modification of our government and our social order.

From the time when Alexander Hamilton pointed out that the political independence of the United States would be quite meaningless without economic independence, the party which is now the Republican party has held and has taught that the productive forces of the nation should be the object of government concern and encouragement. This was not in order that special privilege might be bestowed upon any individual or group of individuals, or that the

power of taxation should be used for the direct or indirect benefit of a favored few, but, on the contrary,
in order that the nation as a whole might be able to
sustain itself, to improve itself, to defend itself. The
events of the past five years have brought home to
the consciousness of every one the fact that any nation, however rich or however populous, is in constant
danger if it cannot command and control the essentials to self-support and self-defense. Such nations
as are not able for reasons of climate, of product, or
of natural resources, to become economically independent, must find their protection, in last resort,
through a society of nations in which, as in a society
of men, the strong will protect the weak through the
establishment and enforcement of law. This Republican attitude toward national self-support and
productive enterprise has been opposed with more or
less consistency by the Democrat party since the time
of Jefferson.

The wisdom of Republican policy in this respect
has been convincingly demonstrated by the rapid development of our natural resources, by the active
spirit of invention and of industrial and commercial
enterprise that has been one of the wonders of the
world, and by the steady improvement in the economic condition of the vast mass of a rapidly growing
population, due to the diversification of industry and
to the constantly wiser and fairer distribution of its
product. The phenomenal increase in the wealth and
prosperity of the United States between 1900 and 1910

was not due to accident, but to carefully considered and wisely executed policies during the presidencies of McKinley and Roosevelt and Taft. There are many and difficult problems still ahead of us, but the Republican party has amply demonstrated that it possesses the principles, the ability, the courage, and the constructive statesmanship to deal with them.

The Republican party, if given control of both the executive and the legislative departments of the government at the elections of 1920, will find itself confronted by an international problem of grave difficulty and of highest importance. It is not a pleasant thing to discuss international policies from the standpoint of party principle and party responsibility; for it is most desirable that in its international relations the nation should think and act as a unit. Unfortunately, however, this possibility has been destroyed by the conduct of the present administration. From its first dealings with distracted Mexico in 1913 down to the work of the Peace Conference at Versailles in 1919, one grave blunder has followed another, until to-day the United States is without anything that can truly be described as a foreign policy. Moreover, the administration's partisan and secretive method of conducting the negotiations at Paris destroyed the possibility of united action at home. What is American policy in respect to Mexico, in respect to Japan, in respect to China, in respect to Russia, in respect to the large problems raised in Europe and in Asia by the victorious ending of the war? What part do we really expect to play in the League of Nations? What responsibility are we to assume and what principles are we to endeavor to establish? It does not seem likely that any one of these questions will be clearly and satisfactorily answered before the term of the present administration comes to an end. If so, the international problem which the next administration will have to face is this: So to settle the results of the war as to insure, so far as is humanly possible, that nothing of the kind shall ever take place again, without sacrificing the independence of the United States or putting any of its national policies in commission.

The consistent Republican policy through the administrations of McKinley, Roosevelt, and Taft, under the administration of the State Department by Hay, Root, and Knox, has been to endeavor to provide against international war by setting up a great tribunal, by which law should be substituted for force in the settlement of international disputes. Many of us had hoped that the treaty framed at Versailles would have that provision as the corner-stone of the new structure that it was building. We were bitterly disappointed when it did not, and when we saw that instead of establishing the rule of law the treaty largely relied upon recourse to political and diplomatic discussion as a means of preventing international war. It will be the first duty of a Republican administration to press for the establishment of an International Court of Justice, to hear and decide controversies between nations, and as Theodore Roosevelt insisted at

Christiania more than nine years ago, to give that court power to enforce its decrees. It must press also for a continuing international conference, meeting at stated intervals, to declare and define the rules of international law and conduct by which civilized nations are to be bound and in accordance with which the International Court of Justice would make its findings. There is no alternative to the use of force save the rule of law. Discussion and debate may delay the appeal to force, or they may change the form of that appeal, but they will never prevent it being ultimately made. Until nations are ruled in their relations to each other by law, and until it is established that a law-breaker among nations is to be treated like a law-breaker among men, we shall only be playing with the problem of preventing the outbreak of international war.

The world is ready, too, for the working out of constructive policies based upon the principle that there shall be no more exploitation of backward peoples, or of the natural resources of the lands which they inhabit. The more advanced and more fortunate peoples must come to regard themselves as elder brothers of those who have still their place to find and to make in the world. The backward peoples should, through international co-operation, be taught the ways and means of improving their own condition, of profiting by their own labor and their own natural resources, and of gradually preparing themselves to play a positive part in the development of civilization in time to come. The application of this principle means that a civilized nation cannot permit anarchy, cruelty, rapine, and outrage in a neighboring part of the world to go unnoticed. We are our brother's keepers. For a civilized nation to permit a neighbor, rich in soil and in opportunity, to be given over to anarchy and turbulence, is as faithless and as wicked as it would be for an individual to fail to spring to the rescue of his fellow whose life was in danger through no fault of his own. It is absolutely necessary that the backward peoples should be aided to come forward in the ranks of civilization. Through appropriate international co-operation and by appropriate international agencies this can be accomplished without repeating any of the abuses that have so frequently attended colonization and the exploitation of the weak by the strong. The policy pursued by Presidents McKinley and Roosevelt and by Secretaries Hay and Root toward Cuba and San Domingo is an admirable illustration of how the Republican party would work out the solution of problems of this kind.

The general principles of a sound American foreign policy have been set forth by successive Presidents and secretaries of state from the foundation of the government. The path of safety in the immediate future will lead not to a departure from these traditional policies, but to new applications of their underlying principles as new conditions arise and as circumstances may demand. It is not true that American foreign policy has been one of isolation and de-

tachment. We have never been isolated or detached
from the interests of mankind or from the struggles
for liberty in other parts of the world. We have
been preoccupied with our own domestic problems
and with our own internal development, but never
isolated or indifferent. The time has now come when
these domestic interests lead directly to an increasing
amount of international co-operation, for the reason
that both political security and economic prosperity
depend upon the preservation of international peace
and order.

Americans will tolerate no supergovernment to supplant their own Constitution, whether its seat be in
some foreign city or in the council-chamber of some
highly organized economic group, representative either
of capital or of labor. They will insist upon going forward in co-operation with other civilized and liberty-
loving people to preserve and protect the peace and
good order of the world, in full command of their own
policies and unhampered by any engagements which
public opinion would not permit the administration
of the moment to keep. Americans have long urged,
and would beyond question gladly welcome, a true
society of nations, but it must be a society of *nations*
and not any attempted international substitute for
independent and self-governing, co-operating peoples.
Given an International Court of Justice, given a body
to formulate and to keep plastic the rules of international law and conduct, and given a society of co-
operating nations bent upon preserving peace and

order throughout the world, on assisting backward nations to advance as quickly as may be in the scale of civilization, and on doing even-handed justice at home—given all these, the prospect for the steadily increasing happiness and prosperity of mankind will be bright indeed. In that case we shall have reasserted the controlling proposition that international relations must be ruled by law. We shall have done everything possible to restore international confidence and good-will, and we shall have laid the basis for an increasingly large and profitable international trade that will greatly add to the prosperity of our people, as well as promote our international influence and authority while assisting nations wrecked and impoverished by war to regain their strength.

The domestic problems that confront the country are even more grave and more pressing than those which relate to international policy. Partly as the result of the ineptitude of the present administration, partly as the result of movements and tendencies long at work among us that have now culminated, and partly as the result of the abnormal and disturbed conditions that accompanied and followed the war, there probably never has been a time when the American people were more urgently called upon to set their own house in order.

First of all, we must get back our usual and constitutional form of government by stripping the executive department of the extraordinary powers assumed during the war, by trying to restore confidence and co-operation between the executive and legislative branches of the government, and by bringing to an end the veritable orgy of waste, extravagance, and administrative incompetence that has marked the course of the present administration.

We must also leave no stone unturned to restore among our people a compelling respect for law, and punish with becoming severity those who insist upon resisting or defying the law, whether as individuals or as mobs. It is the spirit of contempt for law that has made possible the shocking outrages against colored men and women that have only lately disgraced Washington, Chicago, and Omaha. It is idle for the leaders of American opinion to appeal to other peoples and their governments to give fair and decent treatment to all those who are subject to their sovereignty, while no effective steps are taken to protect here in the United States the twelve millions of our colored citizens, whose constitutional rights to life, liberty, and the pursuit of happiness are the same as those of every other American.

In the forefront of domestic problems, affecting and conditioning every other, is that which has to do with the high cost of living. It is the high cost of living which foments dissatisfaction and unrest, and which throws industry and commerce into constant confusion. This is not a new question. In 1912 the Republican National Convention pointed out that the steadily increasing cost of living had then become a matter not only of national but of world-wide concern. The fact that it was not due to the tariff, as the Democrat party charged, was evidenced by the existence of similar conditions in countries which had a tariff system different from our own, as well as by the fact that the cost of living had increased even where rates of duty had remained stationary or had been reduced. At that time the Republican party promised its support to a scientific inquiry into the causes which were operative both in the United States and elsewhere to increase the cost of living, and it promised that when the exact facts were known it would take the necessary steps to remove any abuses that might be found to exist in order that the cost of the food, clothing, and shelter of the people should in no way be unduly or artificially increased. The present administration has shown itself wholly incompetent, or unwilling, to grapple with this problem, and it has done nothing save to ask for additional appropriations amounting to millions of dollars with which to meet the cost of prosecuting an occasional profiteer. Whatever profiteering exists,—and there is certainly a good deal of it,—only touches the fringe of this question.

The high cost of living is now known to be the effect of greatly expanded credit with resulting currency inflation; of decreased production due to fewer working hours, to constant and continuing strikes, and to artificial limitations upon output; of our truly mediæval system of distribution, in which field we have made almost no progress for years past, although we have spent untold brains and energy upon more and better production; and of colossal governmental and personal extravagance. Some of these causes can be reached and remedied by government action and some cannot. The government must do its share by checking extravagance and stopping waste, by bringing the cost of the government's business within the income of the year, by stimulating production in all possible ways, and by lending its aid in the study of improved methods of distribution, particularly as related to all that enters into the nation's food-supply. The people themselves must co-operate to increase production in their several occupations and to assist in the improvement of distribution, as well as by the practice of economy and thrift. It will not do to ask the people to wait indefinitely until natural economic forces at some distant time reduce the present high cost of living, nor will it do to attempt to dispose of the question by a few rhetorical phrases. The government in its sphere, and the individual citizen in his, must attack the causes of the high cost of living, and by so doing lift with all possible speed the almost intolerable burden under which the great mass of the people are now suffering.

The introduction of a national budget system, which thanks to the initiative of a Republican House of Representatives is now well under way, will greatly assist in putting the government upon a business basis, and in enabling the people to fix responsibility both for extravagance and for excessive and unfair taxation.

It is greatly to be hoped that both the House of Representatives and the Senate will so amend their present rules as to put the consideration of the budget in the hands of a single committee in each House, large enough to be representative of the entire membership and yet compact enough to make it a business body upon which responsibility for a report upon the budget can be specifically fixed.

We cannot indefinitely continue, without disaster, the present state of industrial turmoil, which is due to attempts to improve industrial and economic conditions by the use of methods of force. Industrial war must, in the public interest, go the way of international war, and by similar processes. It is futile to attempt to set up any agency for the promotion of industrial peace in which what is called capital, what is called labor, and what is called the public are equally represented and meet upon equal terms. Such a course simply gives new strength to the movement for a class struggle and the promotion of class consciousness. What we call capital is nothing more or less than a group of men and women who hold savings, all of whom are a part of the public. What we call labor is nothing more or less than a group of men and women who work for wages, all of whom are also a part of the public. Capital and labor may face each other on equal terms, but they cannot be permitted to face the public on equal terms. The public is always and everywhere their superior and includes them both.

Perhaps a practicable method of advancing indus-

trial peace would be to establish, by authority of
Congress, an Industrial Relations Commission before
which any industrial difference or dispute might be
brought at the instance of any party thereto or at that
of the Attorney-General of the United States. This
commission, to be made up of judicially minded persons sworn to serve only the public interest, would then
examine into the merits of such differences or disputes
as might be brought before it, take testimony, hear
arguments, and reach a finding with recommendations
for action. Public opinion may be trusted to bring
about compliance with the findings and recommendations of such a commission if properly constituted.

This is a reasonable and an American method of
dealing with a question which is at the moment most
acute. The public cannot tolerate a constant succession of strikes with their interruption of production,
their effect to increase the cost of living, and their
wide-spread suffering and distress. On the other hand,
the public cannot compel any man to work against
his will. Therefore dispassionate, impartial inquiry
into the facts of any given industrial difference or dispute and a reliance upon public opinion to deal fairly
with the disputants when all the facts are known,
appear to offer the only practicable way out of what
at the moment seems to be an insoluble difficulty.
The strike is an instrument of force and will one day
be looked upon as a relic of mediævalism in thought and
in action. Yet it cannot be escaped until the public
is put in possession of the precise facts that precede

and accompany a given strike, and is thus enabled to bring its all-powerful pressure to bear in order to secure a just settlement.

In the next place, a way must quickly be found to apply the lessons that have been learned during the past thirty years, and especially those taught by the experiences of the war, as to what is wise and what is unwise in the relationship between government and the business activities of the people. The attempt to force competition by law and to prevent co-operation, when undertaken with a view to increasing production, reducing costs, and developing foreign trade, has failed. As we now look back we can see that this attempt was bound to fail, for it ran counter to natural and healthy economic tendencies. This movement was supported by the people in good faith as a means of bringing to an end intolerable abuses that affected not only the business but the politics of the nation. In striking at the abuses, however, we also struck at the foundations of our industrial prosperity and of our national economic development. Instead of longer preventing the organization of large business units we should now provide a way by which they may be legally organized, and kept under national supervision and control, in order that the good effects of co-operation may not bring in their train any of the ill effects of monopoly and privilege. Public opinion is now ready for this forward step. When taken it will render immense service to the people of the United States and to their abundant and continued prosperity.

The unhappy experiences of the past three years have practically extinguished the clamor for the government ownership and operation of the railways. A Republican Congress is at this moment studying with patient care the terms of a proposed act by which the railways, when returned to the control of their several owners, will be related to each other and to government supervision and control in wiser and more satisfactory ways than those hitherto prevailing. These great arteries of travel and of traffic are in the highest sense public utilities. A forward-looking public policy will include in its scope the study and development of all possible means of internal transportation, not only the railways and canals, but the electric railway systems, the highways, and also traffic by air. Thoroughgoing study of this entire problem might well prove that it has direct bearing upon the question of better and cheaper distribution and so upon the cost of living itself. In this way we might well be able to aid the farmer in reaching his market and in selling his product, and we might also be able to aid the dwellers in the great cities by reducing the cost of their food-supply.

It is important for members of a great political party to remember that it is constantly on trial. Whatever may be said of the unsatisfactory history and policies of the Democrat party, it is a watchful and doughty opponent, and it can quickly bring to its side large bodies of unattached voters if the Republican party wavers in patriotism or is associated with unworthy acts. In the several state legislatures as well as in county and in municipal government it is imperative, in the national interest, that those who bear the name of the Republican party should remember the measure of responsibility which rests upon them. An unfortunate attitude on the part of a Republican majority in a state legislature or the support by such a majority of a policy of obscurantism, and blind opposition to some local measure that is clearly in the public interest, may easily alienate enough support to affect the presidential, senatorial, and congressional elections.

Nor will it do to allow overconfidence to weaken our efforts or to lower our high principles. It is true that the congressional elections of 1918 and every election held since mark a strong tendency to turn toward the Republican party for relief. It must not be forgotten, however, that it is a fixed habit in American politics to vote *against* some party or some candidate rather than to vote *for* their opponents. The people just now are everywhere voting against the Democrat party and the representatives of the policies of the present administration. The Republican party and its candidates are the necessary beneficiaries.

If, however, we are permanently to attract and hold the great body of voters who have not hitherto been with us, or whose support has been intermittent or reluctant, we must make clear to them not only that our principles are sound and our patriotism unwavering, but that we propose to go forward to meet every new public question as it arises in a spirit of constructive progress with open-mindedness, with broad human sympathy, and with a determination to do exact and even-handed justice to every individual among our hundred millions and more.

I said a few moments ago that the reputation of an individual or a party is a great and splendid thing, but that it is not everything. I say now that the reputation of an individual or a party is the very best ground for confidence that what is to be done to-morrow will be accomplished in the spirit of the achievement of yesterday. That is why I like to recall the splendid acts, the stupendous achievements, that America has done and made under the leadership of its constructive forces, and the great names that are forever associated with those acts and achievements. Take the names that have interwoven their teachings and their lives with the name and the fame of our republic through the medium of the principles of the Republican party: strike them out and what becomes of American history? Take away Washington and your whole fabric falls. Take away Hamilton and your whole philosophy of government disappears. Take away Jay and the foundations of your foreign policy are swept away. Take away Marshall and the epoch-making judicial interpretation of the Constitution has gone. Take away Webster and you have stilled the great organ-voice that moved this nation to understand itself as one. Take away Henry Clay and there goes the great spirit of the West, young and eagerly facing to-morrow. Take away Abraham Lincoln and the most pathetic and appealing figure in all modern history goes from its pages.   Take away Theodore Roosevelt and you destroy a name and a life that signify and represent the youth and vitality,  he open-mindedness and the vigor of America, young and old. Oh, my friends, you cannot take out of the story of America these names.  You cannot take out of the story of America these achievements.  You cannot take out of the story of America this record.  All that we can do is, so far as lies within the capacity of each one of us, to strive to be worthy of their example, of their counsel, and of our opportunity.

# XIV

# MAGNA CARTA, 1215–1915

An address delivered before the Constitutional Convention
of the State of New York, in the Assembly Chamber,
Albany, New York, June 15, 1915

# MAGNA CARTA, 1215–1915

This day seven hundred years ago that monarch whom John Richard Green has called the ablest and most ruthless of the Angevins rode out from Windsor Castle, followed by a group of retainers and dependents, to meet the assembled barons of England. They gathered with their knights some two thousand strong, with Robert Fitzwalter as marshal at their head. The place chosen for the meeting was within easy eye-shot of Windsor Castle and had been for generations a favorite meeting-place of kings in council. Runnymede—which is Running-Mede, a meadow of council—was in 1215 already a memorable spot. Here under an ancient and venerated oak, whose boughs and branches had looked down upon the ceremonies of Druids, at a spot where the valley of the Thames widens out to tempt the traveller's eye with its quiet beauty, the Saxon kings had been wont to gather their people about them to discuss questions of more than usual importance. One likes to think that the assembly of wise men, the Witenagemot—the elder statesmen of that day—had more than once gathered at Runnymede under its spreading oak. There perhaps an Alfred, an Athelstan, or an Edgar had sat in royal state to take counsel for the people of Saxon England.

The meeting, which began on June 15, 1215, and which extended over four days of anxious counsel and debate, was no ordinary gathering. Feelings, hopes, ambitions that had long been forming; tendencies of whose end and significance those who represented and voiced them were but dimly conscious; aspirations that lie deep in the heart of man from the beginning of time, but come to the surface only with the passing of long ages of years, were all struggling for expression. The turbulence of a century and a half had left its mark everywhere. The invading Norman with his disciplined troops and vigorous administrative skill had overthrown the Saxon kings and mounted the throne of England in their stead. Meanwhile for five generations the new Norman and the old Anglo-Saxon nationalities had been gradually welding themselves into a new nation in which the ancient Saxon customs and traditions were to come once more to the post of honor and to share the rule. The administrative, the financial, and the judicial reforms of William the Conqueror and of the two Henrys had provided the skeleton for a nation's government; while the intermingling of the two bloods, the two temperaments, and the two traditions was providing the body for a nation. The Crusades had stirred the imagination of men, and had lifted them up out of absorption in their merely local and personal concerns. They had also greatly stimulated trade and commerce. As a result, the towns were taking on new importance and were growing in size. There was stirring everywhere, and it was no longer likely that the people of England would rest content with the rule of even so popular a king as Richard the Lion-hearted, who during more than ten years of nominal reign could find but two opportunities to set foot on his island realm. Nor was it in the least likely that his brother John could interpret and lead and satisfy the new ambitions and the new hopes which felt their opportunity and their security to lie in the preservation of those ancient Anglo-Saxon liberties that had been granted by no man, but that had been taken for granted at the very beginning of their history by a people intended to be free.

The English-speaking race was born free. It never had to extort freedom from a tyrant, although it has time and again been faced by the necessity of keeping a tyrant from invading its freedom. Such a tyrant was King John. Here is the pen-picture of his character as drawn by Bishop Stubbs: "He was the very worst of all our kings: a man whom no oaths could bind, no pressure of conscience, no consideration of policy restrain from evil; to his people a hated tyrant. Polluted with every crime that could disgrace a man, false to every obligation that should bind a king, he had lost half his inheritance by sloth, and ruined and desolated the rest. Not devoid of natural ability, craft, or energy, with his full share of the personal valor and accomplishments of his house, he yet failed in every design he undertook, and had to bear humiliations which, although not without parallel, never fell on one who deserved them more thoroughly or received less sympathy under them.  In the whole view there is no redeeming trait; John seems as incapable of receiving a good impression as of carrying into effect a wise resolution." [1]  This was the sort of man who had during his more than fifteen years of reign been in constant trouble and serious conflict.  His cruelty and treachery, manifested in the murder of his nephew, Arthur, had forfeited his French fiefs and had led to the separation of Normandy from England.  He had quarrelled with the church and with the Pope himself, and then brought the quarrel to an end with a submission which was as humiliating as the quarrel itself was reckless.  For years he had been at odds with the barons and for no small part of the time at war with them.  His greed and avarice, his selfishness and cruelty, his arbitrariness and lusts had led him to invade the ancient Anglo-Saxon liberties at every turn. The time had come when the feudal lords must make common cause with the merchants and dwellers in towns and with the freeholding tenants in order to put a curb upon the despotism of the King.  Historians differ as to whether, in extorting Magna Carta at Runnymede, the barons were acting only for their own class and were gaining privileges, or whether they were acting for the people of England and were establishing rights. Whatever they themselves may have thought they were doing, the fact is that they did act for the people of England; and it is the people of England as well

[1] *Constitutional History of England* (Oxford, 1887), II, 17.

as the people of the great independent and colonial offshoots of the parent stock who are the beneficiaries of the document to which on that memorable day King John and his barons put their hands, and he his royal seal.

It is to a contemporary French scholar, M. Bémont, that we owe the simplest and most accurate description of what Magna Carta is. Magna Carta, he tells us,[1] is the act by which King John of England in the seventeenth year of his reign conceded and solemnly confirmed on June 15, 1215, the liberties of the English people. Magna Carta reproduced with much more fulness of detail the Charter of Liberties of Henry I, which in turn revived those ancient customs of the people and recognized the lawful freedom of the nation as these had been symbolized by the laws of Edward the Confessor. In this way Magna Carta made formal legal connection between the institutions of Anglo-Norman England and those of the Anglo-Saxon England of the days before the Conquest. King John was not a man to take so momentous a step willingly. It is, therefore, a matter of just surprise, even after making allowance for all the known attendant circumstances, that the demands of the barons were granted so speedily, and that within four days Magna Carta was perfected and enough copies made to place one in every diocese in England. The explanation is offered by Edmund Burke, who shrewdly says of John that "without questioning in any part the

---

[1] *Chartes des Libertés Anglaises* (Paris, 1892), VII.

terms of a treaty which he intended to observe in none, he agreed to everything the barons thought fit to ask, hoping that the exorbitancy of their demands would justify in the eyes of the world the breach of his promises." [1]  As a matter of fact, John did not keep his pledges made in Magna Carta and never intended to do so. The moment the Charter was granted, those who had united to obtain it fell into conflicting groups, and some even took the side of the King. For two months following the granting of the Charter various steps were taken that looked toward peace and reconciliation between the King, the barons, and the people.  August 16 was fixed as the date when the reconciliation was to be complete.  The day came, but the King failed to appear to meet the bishops and the barons, he insisting that he dared not trust himself within reach of their armed forces.  The barons on their side claimed that the King had been false to his promises, and under the terms of the Charter itself, they declared war upon him.  Pope Innocent III formally annulled the Charter and excommunicated the King's enemies and all disturbers of the peace. While chaos reigned and the future seemed trembling in the balance, the struggle was brought to an end by the death of John one year and four months after Magna Carta had been signed.  A child succeeded to the throne, and the wise regents reissued the Great Charter with various changes, and stated that no permanent infraction of its provisions was in contempla-

[1] Abridgment of British History, in *Works* (Boston, 1884), VII, 460.

tion. It was in this way that Magna Carta took its place in the statutes of the realm. Its annulment by Pope Innocent III within two months after its execution, with the resulting release of King John from the obligations of his oath, has been forgotten and is now a curious bit of mediæval history. On the other hand, the charter of Henry III, confirmed on February 11, 1225, when the young King was pronounced to be of age, establishes definitively and for all time the text of Magna Carta as this now exists in substantive law. It was the text of this Charter of 1225 that was confirmed, after the establishment of Parliament, by Edward I in 1297 as the common law and which, after that day, takes its place at the head of the statutes of the realm preceding the Provisions of Merton.

The traditional conception of Magna Carta and its place in the history of English-speaking peoples have been stoutly challenged as a result of the studies and researches of the past generation. The statement of Stubbs that "the great charter is the first great public act of the nation, after it has realized its own identity: the consummation of the work for which unconsciously kings, prelates, and lawyers have been laboring for a century"[1] remains substantially true, however, despite the ingenious interpretations of its provisions offered by M. Petit-Dutaillis[2] and the destructive criticisms of Mr. Edward Jenks,[3] who regards

[1] *Constitutional History of England* (Oxford, 1887), I, 571.
[2] Studies and Notes supplementary to Stubbs' *Constitutional History* (Manchester, 1908), pp. 127-145.
[3] See "The Myth of Magna Charta," *Independent Review*, IV, pp. 260-273.

any such view of Magna Carta as imposed upon history and historians by the "ingenious but unsound historical doctrines" of Coke.

A most competent American historian has recently pointed out that it behooves us to be modest in our rejoicings over the discoveries that reverse long-cherished beliefs.[1] We must remember that these reversals cannot be made retroactive so as to affect the thoughts and deeds of the generations who knew not the reality as we now perceive it, but who built upon the foundation of their own interpretations. We must remember, in short, that for very much of history there is more importance in the ancient error, if it be error, than in the new-found truth, if it be truth, for it was the ancient error that moulded the beliefs and directed the conduct of men. Whether Magna Carta was a treaty between a feudal king and his barons, or a statute promulgated by the king with the assent and approval of his barons, or merely a royal declaration like the Charters of Liberties of Henry I and Henry II which preceded it, or an act declaring and amending the law in a great number of particulars, or an act for the amending of the law of real property and for the advancement of justice, makes little difference and is now a question for the curious only. The important fact is that it placed the king below the law, and that it bound him not so much to the granting of new liberties and privileges as

---

[1] Dunning, "Truth in History," in *American Historical Review*, January, 1914, pp. 217–229.

to the confirmation of those older liberties and privileges which he had flaunted and violated. It did this by laying legal limitations on the feudal military power, principally in respect to matters of finance; by laying legal limitations on the judicial power; by laying legal limitations on the financial power or the power to tax; and by providing legal sanction for the liberties assured the people and for the assurances themselves.

The Charter was followed or accompanied by Assizes, Assizes by Provisions, Provisions by Statutes. Still later it became the single rule that the king, lords, and commons must concur in the enactment of a statute, and that a rule laid down with their concurrence was a statute. Blackstone is certainly justified in saying that Magna Carta is the earliest of those texts whose very words are law. From that time to this the methods of enacting law and the succession of great exponents and expounders of the law are established and well known: Glanvill in the twelfth century and Bracton in the thirteenth were followed by Littleton in the fifteenth, by Coke in the seventeenth, by Blackstone in the eighteenth, and by Kent, Chancellor of the State of New York, in the nineteenth century.

Burke has defined slavery as living under will, not under law. Magna Carta was a bold and successful attempt to substitute law for will in a number of particulars that were vitally important to the men of that day and generation. It is idle to say, as some have

said, that the barons had no conception of what was
meant by law.  It may be true that the barons did
not know or fully realize what they were moving toward,
but they had a very clear and definite idea of what
they were trying to get away from; and that was
none other than the absolute and arbitrary royal will.
As a substitute for the royal will, they insisted upon
the establishment of certain rules, and these rules
were in effect law.  Professor Gneist is quite right in
saying that through Magna Carta English history
irrevocably took the direction of securing constitutional
liberty by administrative law.[1]  He quotes with approval Hallam's emphatic words: "The Magna Carta
is still the keystone of English liberty.  All that has
since been obtained is little more than a confirmation
or commentary; and if every subsequent law were to
be swept away, there would remain the bold features
that distinguish a free from a despotic monarchy."
So great was the importance attached to the Magna
Carta by the English people that before the close of
the Middle Ages its confirmation had been thirty-
eight times demanded and granted.

The Charter itself is a document written on parchment 10¾ inches broad and 21½ inches in length,
including the fold for receiving the label.  To this
label, which is also of parchment, is appended the great
seal of King John.  A sufficient number of originals
was made to deposit one in every county, or at least
one in every diocese.  So, doubtless, it happens that

[1] *History of the English Constitution* (New York, 1886), I, 311.

of the four original copies still remaining, one is preserved in the library of the cathedral at Lincoln, and another in the library of the cathedral at Salisbury. The remaining two original copies are to be found in the Cotton Collection at the British Museum. The Charter, as originally written by its framers, was without division into chapters or paragraphs, but as it deals with sixty-three separate topics, editors and commentators have divided it into sixty-three chapters. Of these, by far the major portion relate to matters which were of grave moment in the thirteenth century, but which have no significance whatever for the twentieth. The importance of Magna Carta in the constitutional history of the English-speaking race depends not so much upon its actual contents as upon the interpretation which subsequent generations put upon the document itself and upon the fact of its existence. Magna Carta could not be used, as can the Constitution of the United States, as a rule for the organization and conduct of a definite government; it establishes no government, but deals with habits and customs that were anciently known as liberties and assures them "to the freemen of England and their heirs forever."

Of the sixty-three topics dealt with by the Charter, fourteen relate to matters merely formal or temporary in character, or deal with the execution of the agreement. Of those that remain, twenty-four are purely feudal and aim to protect the barons against abuses by the king, their overlord; two concern only the clergy and the church; ten deal with the organization and administration of the royal justice, a matter of grave importance in the thirteenth century; while the remainder have to do with the dwellers in towns and villages, including the city of London, and with merchants and their privileges.

The student of historical jurisprudence whose mind is fixed largely on technical distinctions may continue to insist that it is quite false to claim that Magna Carta contributed to constitutional progress. The student and interpreter of history with broader view and with his eye fixed on the actions and beliefs of men will find himself accepting the opinion of Sir Frederick Pollock and Professor Maitland that "with all its faults, this document becomes, and rightly becomes, a sacred text, the nearest approach to an irrepealable fundamental statute that England has ever had. . . . For, in brief, it means this, that the king is and shall be below the law."[1] Through guaranteeing the ancient customs of the English people; through protecting merchants against arbitrary taxes and harsh measures; through limiting the royal power to tax, and through providing that no free man shall be taken or imprisoned, disseized, or outlawed, or exiled, or in any wise destroyed save by the lawful judgment of his peers or the law of the land (which last provision is reproduced in almost identical language in Article I of the Constitution of the State of New York), the Great Charter really did lay the

---

[1] *History of English Law* (Cambridge, 1895), I, 952.

foundation of modern English and American liberty. No doubt this was an accidental and unforeseen effect of the contests between kings, barons, and clergy, but the tendency toward liberty was too strong to hold the rights granted and defined behind the barriers of any class. Voltaire,[1] following Bolingbroke, educated the continent of Europe to believe that in point of liberty the condition of the people was much improved by Magna Carta; and so, in truth, it was.

There is such a thing as a geology of politics. The political thoughts and acts of men lie in strata and in layers as do the various and divers rocks that make up the crust of the earth. Each one of these strata and layers carries in its structure the fossil records of the political ideas and the political life which then moved to and fro in the world. By studying these fossil records we may learn how political structures and functions that are familiar to us had their origin; how political structures and functions that were familiar in an older day and generation have passed away or have been transformed and adapted to other and newer needs and conditions, and what the relationship is that binds the political and social life of to-day to those far-off beginnings which we so attentively note and so gladly celebrate. As the student of geology must trace by patient steps the passage of one form of earth's structure and the life that accompanied it into another, so the student of politics must bring to bear all the resources of historical knowledge and of critical skill

---

[1] *Lettres philosophiques sur les Anglais* (Paris, 1909), I, 101-107.

in order to be able to follow down from its ancient sources the stream of modern political tendency and action. The appearance among men, and the evolution, of those forms of political organization that have marked the age-long struggle for liberty and for justice are fit subject-matter for the learning of an Aristotle, for the literary skill of a Plato, for the stirring eloquence of a Burke or a Webster, and for the masterful power of exposition and persuasion of a Hamilton.

Nothing in all the recorded passage of time so stirs the modern man as the story of the groping efforts to establish liberty and justice, to develop nationality, to open the way to opportunity, and to crown personal effort with personal reward. On his way to the guillotine, Danton, the great French revolutionary, is reported to have said that if he were able to live his life over again he would have nothing to do with the government of men. But where else, save in dealing with the government of men, in studying it, in promoting it, in taking part in it, is to be found higher and finer exercise for the best faculties of man? The individual, taken by himself, cannot develop institutions. His power and his skill must pass with his passing, and if he is to enforce his personality and his thought upon his fellows he must do so either through political institutions or through that barbaric struggle in which might makes right. True politics is the enemy of war, whether between individuals or between nations. It is the aim of true politics so to establish the foundations of justice and so to lay

open the road to liberty that man may build upon
the one and set his feet upon the other with the assurance that his personal effort will not be in vain and
that he will be rewarded with the product of his own
successful activity.

The individual man, therefore, must live as a member of a group, a family, a tribe, a society, a nation.
In these he must act and interact with others and so
co-operate with them that by joint and mutually
helpful effort they may bring into existence habits
and ways of doing things that must be done for the
common weal, and establish rules and laws for the
doing of these things. These habits and ways of
doing things and the laws and rules for their conduct are institutions—social institutions, political institutions, religious institutions. In this way arise
the family, the state, the church, private property,
freedom of speech, freedom of assembly, representative
government, and the manifold structures which the
foundations deep-laid in these institutions are suited
to bear.

It is easy for men of our day, and particularly for
Americans, to understand all this. For two hundred years this process has been going on before the
eyes of ourselves, our fathers, and our fathers' fathers;
but neither King John nor the opposing barons could
possibly have understood the meaning of much of the
language that we now use so familiarly. Yet across
this great gap of time, filled with achievements and
events that appall the imagination by their manifold-

ness and their importance, we can trace the chain
which binds Magna Carta to the work of this Convention. The people of the State of New York inherited
and brought across the sea the political and social
institutions of the seventeenth and eighteenth century England. The Constitution of England was their
constitution, and into the rights and benefits of Magna
Carta they entered as the lineal descendants of those
free men of England to whom those rights and benefits
had been assured forever. When New York was still
a colony, Chatham, replying in the House of Lords
to the Marquis of Rockingham's speech on the State
of the Nation (January 22, 1770), said: "The Constitution has its political Bible, by which, if it be fairly
consulted, every political question may and ought to
be determined. Magna Carta, the Petition of Right,
and the Bill of Rights form that code which I call the
Bible of the English Constitution." [1] These three
great documents mark the progress of the struggle
between the barons and the people of England with
the Plantagenet, the Tudor, and the Stuart kings,
through which struggles the government of England
was gradually transformed from a feudal monarchy
into a democracy in fact, with an elective kingship
and an aristocratic social system. Through the Declaration of Independence and the successful war which
followed, the American people assured to themselves
the benefits of democracy but revolted forever against

[1] Thackeray, *A History of the Right Honorable William Pitt, Earl of
Chatham* (London, 1827), II, 156.

the kingship and a social system based on caste. The chain, therefore, between Magna Carta and the Constitution of the State of New York, now undergoing scrutiny and revision at your hands, as elected representatives of the people, is clear and complete.

The government of men and the guarantees of justice and liberty have strangely lagged behind the other evidences and instrumentalities of civilization. When one reflects upon the learning, the art, the architecture, and the literature of the thirteenth century it seems hardly conceivable that the King of England and his barons should have been back at that elementary stage in the development of liberty which the execution of the Great Charter indicates; for the thirteenth century is one of the greatest and most striking epochs in the whole history of mankind. It is the century when thousands and tens of thousands of earnest and mature students were assembled at Bologna, at Paris, and at Oxford, to make the beginnings of those great universities which are at once the glory and a chief mark of the progress of the modern world. The architecture called Gothic was at the height of its excellence, and some of those fine and splendid monuments, which the freer men of the twentieth century are battering down and crumbling into dust, were being built by the patient and skilful toil of lord-ridden artists and builders. Roger Bacon was performing a marvellous service in mapping out the field of knowledge and even in suggesting, by what must have been intuition, some of the most modern

of our scientific inventions.   The great cathedrals of
Lincoln, of York, of Chartres, and of Bourges were
rising in all their rich and compelling beauty.   The
stories of the Cid, of the Holy Grail, and of the Nibel-
ungen were being put into deathless literary form.
It was the century of Thomas Aquinas, of Louis IX
of France, and of Dante.   It was, in fact, a century
when some of the classic achievements of mankind
were going rapidly forward in a score of ways; but
government, justice, liberty, lagged far behind.   This
was due, no doubt, to the harsh grip, and in some degree to the attractiveness, of the feudal system, which
Professor Vinogradoff defines as "an arrangement of
society on local lines under the guidance of a land-
owning aristocracy." [1]   Nothing could oppose a stouter
obstacle to the progress of liberty than a system such
as this.   Each local lord was a despot, and his despotism was based upon the tenure of land.   Nothing
but an all-powerful absolute king or a world-shaking
revolution could overturn a system like that.   The
all-powerful absolute king came first, and the world-
shaking revolution followed in due course.   It seems
odd for a modern democrat to speak of the absolute
monarchy as an instrument in the development of
popular liberty, but such it undoubtedly was.   The
tyrannical and despotic power over the plain people
that was ruthlessly exercised wherever the feudal
system reached, was divided among countless local
magnates.   Each one was a despot strengthening and
enriching himself at the expense of his feudatories and

[1] *English Society in the Eleventh Century* (Oxford, 1908), p. 208.

waging constant war against those of similar rank who assumed to be his equal. If the feudal system was primarily a system of land tenure, it was secondarily and only in slightly less degree a system of organized warfare. In any case, the gainers were the feudal lords; the losers and the sufferers were the people. The first step toward destroying absolutism was to gather it together in one place where it could be dealt with and where, if worse came to worst, its head could be cut off with a single blow of the axe. This explains why Charles Stuart lost his head at Whitehall in 1649, and why Louis Capet lost his outside the Tuileries Gardens in 1793. Both Charles and Louis paid the extreme penalty, not for their own personal misdeeds, not for their own acts of omission and commission, but because the people of England and of France, finding that all despotic and tyrannical power had finally been gathered in the person of one absolute king, determined to destroy it, not merely to punish the individual monarch but to symbolize the end of an era and a régime. So it happens that the progress toward liberty is by the tortuous and stony path that leads from an absolutism, divided and dissipated among a host of feudal lords, up through the absolute monarchy into which all despotic power is gathered, on to its overthrow—we say it with profound sadness —when necessary, by violence.

Lord Acton left us a striking, if unfinished, essay on the history of freedom.[1]  Next to religion, he tells us, liberty has been both the motive of good deeds

---

[1] *History of Freedom and Other Essays* (London, 1907).

and the common pretext of crime, from the sowing of the seed at Athens two thousand five hundred years ago until the ripened harvest was gathered by men of our own race.  He calls liberty the delicate fruit of a mature civilization, and takes note of the fact that in every age its progress has been beset by its natural enemies, by ignorance and by superstition, by lust of conquest and by love of ease, by the strong man's craving for power and by the poor man's craving for food.  At every stage of human history the sincere and unselfish friends of freedom have been unfortunately rare.  The triumphs of liberty have been due to minorities, who have, in season and out of season, kept the meaning of liberty before the minds of men.  The rule of the tyrant is tyranny, whether he have one head or many.  The principle of absolute majority rule is as profoundly immoral and as profoundly undemocratic as is the principle of the divine right of kings.  Majority rule is a practical device for the working of free institutions, and not a principle without limits or bounds upon which free institutions may be based.  Liberty is something more than the right to agree with the beliefs and practices of another, whether that other be a monarch or a majority. Tyranny is none the less odious when it doffs the royal ermine and dons the garb of the people.

Lord Acton defines liberty as satisfactorily as it has been defined by any one.  He says that liberty is the assurance that every man shall be protected in doing what he believes his duty against the influence of authority and majorities, custom and opinion. Individual liberty is the corner-stone of the free state, and the assurances of Magna Carta were given seven hundred years ago to the free men of England and their heirs forever. Into that noble inheritance we have entered.

In celebrating the seven hundredth anniversary of Magna Carta we celebrate one of the most notable happenings in the history of the American people. Magna Carta, the Petition of Right, the Charter of Liberties and Privileges for the inhabitants of New York and its dependencies, the Bill of Rights, the Declaration of Independence, the Constitution of the United States, and the Emancipation Proclamation of Abraham Lincoln are chapters in one long serial story. The story traces the movement of the English-speaking race, from the old island home to the far-flung settlements round about the globe, whether colonial or independent, toward securing the liberty of the individual and the political institutions that are based upon it. There is a constant ebb and flow of the tide of authority that is easy to be measured against the rising structure of liberty. In the ancient world the state assumed authority not properly its own and severely limited personal freedom. In the mediæval period government possessed too little authority, and it suffered other and alien forces to intrude upon it. In our modern days states fall first into one of these classes and then into the other. They are for a time engaged in invading the proper domain of liberty and then for a time they are engaged in neglecting its protection. The surest test by which we may judge whether a people is really free is the amount of security enjoyed by minorities. Where the individual is as secure in his opinion and his lawful practices as the majority are in theirs, although without the authority of the majority to determine policies and to choose courses of practical action, there true liberty exists. Therefore, it is in pursuance of a sound political philosophy and in accord with the teachings of history that the Constitution of the State of New York first defines and assures the sphere of individual liberty, and then erects and limits a government to carry on the business of the State, to care for the common concerns of the people, and to see to it that no man is so great or so powerful as to be able to invade the liberty of any other man, however humble or however weak.

There is then a most real and vital relationship between that striking, half-barbaric scene at Runnymede, hundreds of years before the name of America was known, and this convention of revisers of the fundamental law, assembled in the Capitol of the State of New York. Imagination inspires this relationship with reality and gives it genuine power. Look back across the tumbling ocean and over the troubled and blood-stained centuries, and take courage from the steady, if slow, progress of liberty among men. Order had first to be established by whatever means were at hand; killing was once as natural as rising with the morning sun. When order was established, then opportunity was offered for men to exert their powers, to express themselves, to achieve, and to possess; and the history of Western civilization is the story of what happened. Under the rule of order came the struggle for liberty. It was a struggle against false philosophies, against vanity, selfishness, and greed, against the grasping for power and the fortifying of privilege, against the tyranny of the one and against the greater tyranny of the many. The mile-stones that mark its path are far apart, and one mile is often many, many times longer than another. The road is narrow and steep and rough, and it leads sometimes to the edge of precipices and by the side of impassable morasses. Nevertheless, the road is there, and the progress along it is plain and easily marked through the ages. To define, to secure, and to protect liberty is the first and highest aim of the fundamental law. If Magna Carta was, as has been sometimes said, a reactionary document, it was reactionary only in that it revived and confirmed liberties that had been forgotten and that had been invaded by royal power. These liberties are part of man's nature and an attribute of human personality. To deny them, to hamper them, to invade them, is to install tyranny in the land. To take note of them, to build upon them, and to appeal to them, is to open the door to that constructive progress whose limits are set only by the spiritual aspiration, the intellectual power, and the moral earnestness of man.

XV

# THE MAKING OF A WRITTEN CONSTITUTION

An address delivered before the Constitutional Convention of the State of Massachusetts, in the State House, Boston, Massachusetts, August 23, 1917

# THE MAKING OF A WRITTEN CONSTITUTION

Surely this is an inspiring moment in the history of democracy! When those principles upon which this ancient commonwealth was founded and upon which our nation has risen to its place in the world are struggling for their very existence on the field of battle, you are here engaged in restudying and perhaps in remodelling some of their foundations. To a lover of democracy, and to one who is optimistic enough to believe that whatever be the immediate signs of the moment its permanent triumph and extension are secure, there can be nothing more striking than the task upon which you are engaged. You have been summoned by the citizens of Massachusetts to restudy not the superstructure, not the ornamentation, not the minor details, but to restudy the very foundation of her form of government; to see how far ancient principles still maintain themselves, how far men of an open mind may suggest their readjustment to meet new needs and new conditions, and to take account of the changing social and economic order that confronts us all around the world. For nothing is more certain than that in this very war democracy is experiencing a new birth. It is coming to have a new and clearer understanding of what its principles are, and of how those principles are to be applied, and it is going to spread its beneficent opportunity over millions and tens of millions of human beings who have never known it before.

We all know the history of our Federal Constitutional Convention. We know the history of the Convention and the National Assembly of France. We have seen the making and the remaking of constitutions in more than twoscore of our sister States, and we have watched constitutions made not by, but for, the peoples of several European nations. May it not be said that those of us who are convinced democrats and believers in constitutional government have come to a substantial agreement upon three great points, and that these three points will shortly be included almost beyond peradventure in the document which is to issue from the forthcoming Constitutional Convention of the new democracy of Russia?

In the first place, it is the essence of a sound constitution that the method for its amendment shall be such as to put within the reach of the people opportunity, after adequate consideration and discussion, to readjust it from time to time to new needs and for the solution of new problems. We are sometimes apt to overlook the formula for constitutional amendment, but I think on reflection we should all agree that it goes to the very essence of a constitution that is to be a document of advance and of progress and of life, and not merely a fixed formula for a given year and a given generation.

And then, second, are we not agreed that there must be in the constitution, if it is to last and if the people are to be really free, an adequate organization of liberty which is based on our familiar Bills of Rights, and which marks off the sphere in which the individual, either alone or in company with his fellows, may freely undertake those various activities which give him opportunity for development, for self-expression, for gaining an honest competence, and for its enjoyment free from the interference or arbitrary act of government? And do we not know that in that organization of liberty and sphere of free action has been the great contribution of our American nation to the world? It is because we marked off a field of liberty which may not be invaded either by executive or by legislature, and put it under the protection of an independent judiciary, that we have been able to build up the nation that confronts and surrounds us. That organization of liberty, sufficiently definite to meet the needs of the people, sufficiently elastic to keep its limits from solidifying into harmful boundaries—that organization of liberty is the essence surely of a sound constitution, whether it be for nation or for commonwealth.

And then there is the organization of government itself. Curious enough, this is the only aspect of constitution-making that has attracted the attention of certain of the European nations. If I am not mistaken, the Constitution of France and the Constitution of Italy, at this moment, are simply organizations of

government and nothing more.  They set up a frame
of government, but they do not set it up as over against
a field of liberty, nor do they attempt to protect the
one from the other.  Therefore they leave the individual citizen in his undertaking, in his employment,
in his activity, at the mercy of a passing phase of
opinion or a temporary majority, or perhaps even of
a prejudice that will pass away.  There is no great
constitution but our own and that of the German
Empire in which any reference is made to the organization of liberty—no written constitution; and in the
Constitution of the German Empire, left as it is without judicial protection and under the mercy of an
autocratic form of government, this becomes little
more than a mere formula or recital of words.

You are concerned at this moment, I take it, very
largely with studying the organization and framework of government.  It is mere every-day knowledge
to say that the framework of our government has come
down to us over a hundred and forty or fifty years,
that it has done reasonably well, but that here and
there it has shown defects of working which men everywhere are sincerely trying to improve by this device
or by that.  I suppose that, taking the nations of the
world at large, the political experience of modern man
would tell us that one of our greatest mistakes has
been the too sharp separation of the executive and the
legislative branches of the government.  We are constantly trying, now by following a device familiar in
this country, now by following a device familiar in

another, now by throwing out some new idea of our own, to overcome such practical difficulties as the history of the last century has developed in that regard. We are aiming to bring about a relationship between executive and legislature, now by the suggestion of an executive budget, now by giving cabinet ministers seats in the legislative houses, now by this device and now by that, through which one of the weak points—or one of the weaker points, shall I say? —that history has disclosed in the framework of our government may be overcome.

It is fortunate that about all this there is no suspicion of partisanship or party advantage or party feeling. I know from the printed records of the Convention that you are here as loyal, patriotic, high-minded citizens of an ancient commonwealth, determined on studying and solving the problems of the moment in the light of patriotic duty, the wisdom of experience, and the needs of to-day and to-morrow. That the outcome of your deliberations and your suggestions will be fortunate to Massachusetts, of advantage to the nation, and useful to democracy everywhere, I am perfectly certain.

# XVI

## ALEXANDER HAMILTON

### NATION-BUILDER

An address delivered at the Hamilton Club of Brooklyn, New York,
January 11, 1913

# ALEXANDER HAMILTON
## NATION-BUILDER

You have summoned me to a grateful and an honorable task. To a lover of Hamilton nothing could be more pleasing than to be asked to speak of him on the anniversary of his birth, to a company of gentlemen assembled in a club which bears his name, in the borough on whose soil he received his baptism of fire in the War of Independence, and now part of a city so devoted to his personality and his political opinions that it was called by his enemies Hamiltonopolis. But it is not possible for me to say anything new about Alexander Hamilton. Every American who knows his country's history, every American who has penetrated beneath the surface of our political life to an understanding of its making and its fundamental principles, knows full well that Alexander Hamilton has joined the company of the immortals.

You need not expect from me a severely critical estimate of the man, of his service to our American life, or of his place in history. I love him too well. I am too much under the spell of his personality, of his eloquence, and too profound and convinced a believer in the doctrines of liberty and of government that he taught and made to live in institutions on this soil, to speak of him in words of cautious and hesitant criticism. You will have to accept from me the reflections of a convinced believer in Hamilton as the one supremely great intellect yet produced in the Western world; as the only man whose writings on political theory and political science bear comparison with the classic work on politics by the philosopher Aristotle. I am prepared to defend the thesis that the two great epoch-making works in the whole literature of political science are, for the ancient world, the *Politics* of Aristotle, and, for the modern world, those contributions known as *The Federalist* and the various letters and speeches which taken together represent Hamilton's exposition of the American Constitution and the American form of government.

There is nothing that I can say about Hamilton which will be novel to members of a club that bears his name. Yet after the passage of all these years, what a splendid memory that personality suggests, what a romance that life was, what a revelation of human power and of human service his contributions to mankind and to the progress of civilization!

I like to think of the strands that entered into the making of that personality and that character. There was the high-purposed, rugged determination of the Scot, together with the almost fanatical devotion and enthusiasm of the Huguenot; these strands not meeting and intertwining under ordinary circumstances or under a gray and unfriendly sky, but under the bright sun of the West Indies on a little point of rich volcanic land, representing, perhaps, the ambition of mother earth to thrust herself up through the blue waters of the tropical ocean in order to make a fit birthplace for a political genius. I like to think of the youthful beginnings of his boyish life, of the admiration of his mother for her brilliant child, who, in infancy, had the maturity of an experienced philosopher; a boy who, at nine, was writing letters worthy of a sage, and at thirteen was managing an important business for a distant client in the province of New York. I like to remember that when that dying mother felt the hand of death upon her at the early age of thirty-two, she summoned the little boy to her bedside and said to him: "My son, never aim at the second best. It is not worthy of you. Your powers are in harmony with the everlasting principles of the universe." Was ever a child, an orphan child, sent out from an island home to seek his fortune in a new and strange and troubled land with higher prophecy or with more beneficent benediction?

And then the boy crosses the sea to the province of New York. He casts about for an opportunity of obtaining an education. He is thirsting for information. He had read a few great books, books far beyond the capacity of an ordinary boy of his age. He was seeking direction, instruction, opportunity, and he presented himself to President Witherspoon of Princeton College. He said that he wanted to become a student there; that he had no time to devote four years to the very moderate course of instruction of that day, but that if he were allowed to pursue the course in less time and to complete it earlier he would be glad to enter his name.  The president told him—after the fashion of college presidents—that there were rules that could not be broken and that his proposal was impossible.  Did the boy enter himself at Princeton for four years?  Not in the least.  He moved on to New York and appeared before Myles Cooper, the scholarly Tory who was president of King's College, and made the same proposal to him.  Myles Cooper, trained at Oxford and more a man of the world, said that it could be arranged, and it was.  So Alexander Hamilton became a pupil in King's College over yonder, on the King's farm, just beyond where Trinity Church now stands and not far from the churchyard where his ashes lie.

It was well that he did so, because within a year the angry mob of New York rebels, stirred to anger by the actions of the British Government and by reports from across the sea, as well as by the Tory president's pamphlets in defense of British policy, appeared at the college doors and demanded the punishment of President Myles Cooper.  This stripling of eighteen stood on the college steps and held them at bay with his eloquence while the president of the college escaped by the rear gate, and was taken off by a boat to a British ship lying in the Hudson.  If Alexander Hamilton had gone to Princeton, Myles Cooper would have been lynched.

And then I like to think of him at that early age, a boy, a mere child, putting down in the note-books which have been preserved for us the list of things he was interested in and the books that he read. In them you come upon this item: "Read particularly Aristotle's *Politics*, chapter 9, Definition of Money." You begin to see the shadow of the first Secretary of the Treasury, of the author of the Report on Manufactures, of the author of the Report of the National Bank, and of the man of whom it was truly said afterward by Webster that he struck a blow on the rock of the national resources, and revenue gushed forth for the people of the United States. At seventeen, then, Hamilton was reading the greatest work of antiquity on the science and art of government among men.

I like to think of him strolling on the Common yonder, at the head of what we now call Bowling Green, with the youth of his time, eager and enthusiastic; then writing pamphlets in defense of the rebel position, that attracted the attention of the whole country in answer to the Westchester Farmer, one of the learned men in the Colonies, the boy concealing his own identity. In two short years after coming from his West Indian home, so completely had he entered into the feelings and aspirations and hopes of the Colonists, so thoroughly had he mastered the problems before them, that even before they knew his name or his age, they were hailing the writer of those pamphlets as their deliverer from the oppression of Great Britain. I submit that in the whole history of government there is nothing to be found like this. We have seen great and precocious genius in literature, as, for example, in Chatterton; we have seen great and precocious genius in music, as, for example, in Mozart; but where in the affairs of men, where in those large matters that have to do with the organization of liberty, the establishment of government, and the perpetuation of everlasting standards of right among human beings —where from the dawn of history have we before seen a youth of nineteen leading the thought of a people and laying the foundations of a nation ?

Then I like to think of his part in the army during the War of Independence, of his close association with Washington and of his admiration for him, and of Washington's dependence upon the younger man. I like to think of his eager and exultant defense, by voice and by pen, of every act of the new people, and of his part in shaping the slowly forming government that the thirteen colonies were feeling their way, tentatively, toward building into a visible and permanent form.  I like to think that at no single step in the process did Hamilton fail to take a most conspicuous part.  At no time did he fail to strike the heaviest blow.  Never was he found anywhere but among the leaders, the real leaders, of political opinion in the American colonies.  Whether it was in New York, in Massachusetts, in Virginia, or in South Carolina, the American people of that day doffed their hats to Alexander Hamilton as the one supreme genius in intellectual leadership and in exposition that they had among them.

As soon as the war was over he found his place at

the bar and in the Congress of the Confederation. He
warmly defended the treaty with Great Britain. He
insisted that it must be lived up to even though unpopular; that even a young nation could not afford
to be false to its pledged word. He insisted that our
people never would be free and never would be safe
until they had formed a real government with real
powers, and had made themselves, not a loose federation of independent units, but an integral, independent, self-respecting, self-supporting, self-defending
nation. That was Hamilton's task. He had to com-
pete with men otherwise minded, to overcome prejudices, and to answer reasonable as well as unreasonable
objections. He had to meet all these; and then he had
to combat the selfish and the self-seeking as well. He
was tireless, this stripling only then in the twenties
and early thirties; tireless with voice and with pen in
making men understand what the United States
might be and what America ought to be.

Finally, almost by a subterfuge, he got a constitutional convention. In those days you could not easily
persuade the several colonies to come together in conference for any purpose, lest they might, in some way,
as a result of conferring, sacrifice a measure of their independence and their sturdy separateness. He persuaded some of them, however, to convene at An-
napolis to settle questions relating to the navigation
and use of Chesapeake Bay. Having brought them
into conference, he persuaded them to call a constitutional convention. He did not quite call it by that

name—had he done so it might never have been held —but he persuaded them to call another conference to devise a more adequate plan of government. He went back to Albany and got himself elected as one of the three delegates from New York; the other two, being convinced opponents of the whole undertaking, outvoted him in the convention, so long as they remained in it. At the psychological moment Alexander Hamilton took the floor in the convention. Was he in doubt about the making of a constitution? Not in the least. He had a constitution all ready; he proposed it. For five hours, as Madison tells in his journal, he held spellbound this convention of the ablest men ever gathered together in one room for a like purpose, while he explained the principles on which the nation's government should be organized. The fundamental principles of that plan of government are contained in the Constitution of the United States in this year of grace. Other plans were proposed and many of their features adopted; long debates ensued, but that genius, that patience, that persistence, that skill of exposition never failed. His two colleagues from New York left the convention in disgust when they saw that the Constitution was going to be made; but he remained and signed it as the sole representative of what is now the Empire State. Had it not been for Alexander Hamilton the name of the State of New York would not have been included among the members of the constitutional convention, who accepted and recommended for adoption the great instrument and the form of government that were the result of their deliberations. The ardor and the cogency of Hamilton's exposition in *The Federalist* of the meaning and value of the new Constitution are more convincing evidence than any draft plans or written records could possibly be that the Constitution as adopted by the convention was in harmony with Hamilton's own fundamental convictions as to political policy and political practice.

Then came the heaviest task of all—how to get this Constitution ratified by the people of the several States. It was provided, as you know, in the instrument itself that it should become operative when ratified by nine States, but no one knew better than Alexander Hamilton that nine States would not do. He knew that that provision was a mere device, and that every State must ratify if the Constitution was to become effective and the supreme law of the land.

There followed what I venture to think is, perhaps, the greatest forensic triumph of modern times. The Convention of the State of New York met at Poughkeepsie. There were sixty-five delegates from the various counties of the State. Nineteen of them, including Hamilton and the other delegates from New York, Kings, and Westchester, were committed to the Constitution. The remainder were followers and friends of George Clinton, who bitterly opposed it. Chancellor Kent has told us what happened. Long after, nearly half a century after, Chancellor Kent wrote his recollection of what took place. He went to

Poughkeepsie and sat in the gallery of the convention and listened to every word of the debates for six weeks. He has told us what Hamilton said, what Jay and Livingston said, what was said in reply, and how obdurate and stubborn and insistent was the opposition to the ratification of the Constitution. Hamilton sent a runner out to the east so that he might report at the earliest moment the news whether or not New Hampshire had ratified. He sent a runner out to the south to report at the earliest possible moment the news from Madison as to whether Virginia had ratified. Finally, by sheer force of intellect, by the display of political genius of the first and most enduring order, Hamilton wore away all opposition and the Poughkeepsie convention ratified the Constitution on behalf of the State of New York by a majority of three. That was before the days of bosses; it was a time when men had to be won over from one side of a proposition to the other by force of argument and by intellect, and Hamilton wore down the powerful and determined opposition by no other instruments than those.

The Constitution was made. What was the government? Where were its resources, and what scheme of taxation was it to employ? How was it to differentiate its scheme of taxation from that which supported the several colonies, now States? How was this new national unity to develop? How was it to make itself real? Obviously, the centre point of the fighting-line was the Department of the Treasury, and to that department Alexander Hamilton went at George Washington's call. There he sat for the six most fateful years of the history of the government of the United States. One great report after another was poured in upon the Congress. It consisted of clever and intelligent men, but they were almost stupefied by the wealth of information, the rush of argument, the appeals that were made to them to formulate a system of taxation, to charter a bank, to raise revenue, to organize a treasury system, and to call the latent forces of a nation into action for purposes of national support and for national administration. No one doubts—no one can—that Hamilton did every atom of work in connection with all this. The Congress had hardly anything before it of great magnitude but his proposals. It had nothing to do but to accept, to amend, or to reject them; you may read the history of those Congresses for yourselves. They accepted in principle, and almost in detail, every great fundamental recommendation that he made, and that is how the government of the United States was built. There was no use in making a government that was a framework of bones and skin alone; these bones must be covered with flesh; these arteries and veins must be filled with blood; there must be food to assimilate, power to gain nourishment, ability to act. Hamilton saw to it that all this was done. Read the history of the first three Congresses. Read the communications made to them; read their debates, their votes; read the history of Washington's administration, and tell me whether Alexander Hamilton did not make the government of the United States in body and in spirit, just as truly as he had planned and constructed it in form.

Hamilton withdrew from the service of the government at thirty-eight. At thirty-eight this great epoch-making work was done. At an age when most men, even those of talent, of power, of training, are just ready for the active and constructive work of life, Alexander Hamilton was through as the builder of the greatest government of any people that the world has ever seen. He withdrew to the practice of the law. He lived over across the river in Wall Street at No. 58, in a little house almost opposite the great building which was formerly the Custom-House, well known to all of us. It was in passing that house that no less a person than Talleyrand, on his visit to New York, said, when he saw the light burning in Hamilton's study window at midnight: "I have seen the eighth wonder of the world. I have seen a man laboring at midnight for the support of his family who has made the fortune of a nation."

Hamilton's career at the bar was without an equal. As an advocate and in exposition, particularly in defense of fundamental principles of justice and equity and human liberty, the testimony is that he was a marvel of lucidity and of power. Long afterward— in 1832, I think it was—Chancellor Kent wrote a striking letter to Mrs. Hamilton. Hamilton had then been dead twenty-eight years and Mrs. Hamilton was an old lady. She wrote to Chancellor Kent and asked him whether he would not put on record some of his reminiscences of her husband; whether he would not tell her what he, Kent, thought about Hamilton's relations to the making of the Constitution; what he, Kent, thought about his work at Poughkeepsie where Kent had watched him, and what he, Kent, thought about his work at the American bar. Kent wrote in reply one of the most beautiful and charming analytical eulogies that one human being could write of another. Remember that Kent was, with Marshall, the greatest of American jurists; remember that Hamilton had been dead and gone for twenty-eight years; remember that the shadow of the great contest as to slavery was already projecting itself over the land; remember that new men and new issues were in the places of prominence, and that there was nothing due to Hamilton but the dispassionate, fair, and honorable judgment of history. Kent rendered this judgment in one of the most memorable documents of our American literature. I commend it to every student of American politics and American literature. It tells us what James Kent, that maker and interpreter of American law, thought about Alexander Hamilton as the guide, philosopher, and friend of the government, the bench, and the bar of his day.

I have wondered sometimes whether Kent must not have overheard one of Hamilton's most charming sayings, many years before, when they were on circuit together—as I remember it, in Orange County in this

State—Kent as judge, Hamilton as barrister. They found themselves spending the night in an uncomfortable and ill-furnished tavern in a country town. Hamilton awakened in the night, shivering because of the insufficiency of his covering; he got up from his bed and with his covering in his arms carried it into the room where Kent was sleeping, and quietly and softly spread it over him, saying: "Sleep well, sleep warm, little judge; we cannot afford to have harm come to you." I have often wondered whether Kent in his sleep did not hear these affectionate words, and whether he did not fifty years afterward reflect, in his judgment to the stricken widow, something of the feeling of affection and regard which the great barrister, the great constructive statesman, felt for him.

Then came Hamilton's end; that tragic, fateful end, to be ascribed, as we look back on it now, to the false sense of honor that prevailed a century ago, which made men think that it was necessary for them to kill each other in order to avenge a fancied or a real insult. In this connection, too, I recall now another interesting story of Kent. Kent had been a friend of Aaron Burr, but the devoted admirer of Hamilton. He never saw Burr for years after this terrible calamity until one day when Kent was walking up Nassau Street, in New York, he saw Burr coming down on the other side. The little Chancellor crossed the pavement and went over to Burr and said: "Mr. Burr, you are a damned scoundrel. Sir, you are a damned scoundrel!" Burr looked steadily at him, took off his hat, and replied with mock politeness: "Mr. Chancellor, your judgments are always entitled to be received with respect."

It is not possible for us—even for those of us who remember the taking off of Lincoln, the killing of Garfield, or the murder of McKinley—to picture the feeling of this country—then a mere strip on the seaboard to be sure, without telegraphs, without telephones or rapid post—when it was learned that Hamilton was dead. It did not seem possible to the people of the United States of that day that this very symbol of power and vitality, this centre of the constructive force of the nation, who seemed able by his charm and persuasiveness and potency to ride down every obstacle, to conquer enemies, and to bring the great mass of the population to the support of his specific projects— it did not seem possible that at forty-seven Alexander Hamilton had passed from earth. And yet he had.

Before venturing to speak to you on this subject, I have been reading over again the records of that time, in order to get back into the atmosphere of the period, to catch something of its feeling, and to refresh my memory as to some of the men and events of those years. In doing so I came upon the funeral oration delivered two weeks after Hamilton's death by the Henry Ward Beecher of that day, by Dr. Mason, senior minister of the Collegiate Dutch Church in New York, who was the favorite pulpit orator of this part of the United States. He had been selected to deliver the funeral oration on Hamilton before the Society of the Cincinnati at a great meeting called in New York, and I ask the privilege of reading a few paragraphs from that oration in order to take you back with me into the atmosphere of July, 1804, when it was known that Hamilton was really dead.

After describing Hamilton's career, what was then so fresh, so new, so full of suggestion, and after tracing the whole history of the making of the Constitution, Dr. Mason concluded his oration with these words:

The result is in your hands. It is in your national existence. Not such, indeed, as Hamilton wished, but such as he could obtain, and as the States would ratify, is the Federal Constitution. His ideas of a government which should elevate the character, preserve the unity, and perpetuate the liberties of America, went beyond the provisions of that instrument. Accustomed to view men as they are, and to judge of what they will be, from what they ever have been, he distrusted any political order which admits the baneful charity of supposing them to be what they ought to be. He knew how averse they are from even wholesome restraint; how obsequious to flattery; how easily deceived by misrepresentation; how partial, how vehement, how capricious. He knew that vanity, the love of distinction, is inseparable from man; that if it be not turned into a channel useful to the government, it will force a channel for itself, and if cut off from other egress, will issue in the most corrupt of all aristocracies—the aristocracy of money. He knew that an extensive territory, a progressive population, an expanding commerce, diversified climate and soil and manners and interest, must generate faction; must interfere with foreign views, and present emergencies requiring, in the general organization, much tone and promptitude. A strong government, therefore; that is, a government stable and vigorous, adequate to all the forms of national exigency, and furnished with the principles of self-preservation, was undoubtedly his preference, and he preferred it because he conscientiously believed it to be necessary. A system which he would have entirely approved would probably keep in their places those little men who aspire to be great; would withdraw much fuel from the passions of the multitude; would diminish the materials which the worthless employ for their own aggrandizement; would crown peace at home with respectability abroad; but would never infringe the liberty of an honest man. From his profound acquaintance with mankind, and his devotion to all that good society holds dear, sprang his apprehensions for the existing Constitution. Convinced that the natural tendency of things is to an encroachment by the States on the Union; that their encroachments will be formidable as they augment their wealth and population; and, consequently, that the vigor of the general government will be impaired in a very near proportion with the increase of its difficulties; he anticipated the day when it should perish in the conflict of local interest and of local pride. The divine mercy grant that his prediction may not be verified!

He was born to be great. Whoever was second, Hamilton must be first. To his stupendous and versatile mind no investigation was difficult—no subject presented which he did not illuminate. Superiority, in some particular, belongs to thousands. Pre-eminence, in whatever he chose to undertake, was the prerogative of Hamilton. No fixed criterion could be applied to his talents. Often has their display been supposed to have reached the limit of human effort, and the judgment stood firm till set aside by himself. When a cause of new magnitude required new exertion, he rose, he towered, he soared; surpassing himself, as he surpassed others. Then was nature tributary to his eloquence! Then was felt his despotism over the heart! Touching, at his pleasure, every string of pity or terror, of indignation or grief; he melted, he soothed, he roused, he agitated; alternately gentle as the dews, and awful as the thunder. Yet, great as he was in the eyes of the world, he was greater in the eyes of those with whom he was most conversant. The greatness of most men, like objects seen through a mist, diminishes with the distance; but Hamilton, like a tower seen afar off under a clear sky, rose in grandeur and sublimity with every step of approach. Familiarity with him was the parent of veneration. Over these matchless talents Probity threw her brightest lustre. Frankness, suavity, tenderness, benevolence, breathed through their exercise. And to his family—but he is gone. That noble heart beats no more; that eye of fire is dimmed; and sealed are those oracular lips. Americans, the serenest beam of your glory is extinguished in the tomb!

That is the contemporary judgment; spoken, to be sure, under stress of great feeling and deep sorrow, the contemporary judgment of one of the greatest orators of his day, voicing the opinion of men of intelligence, high spirit, and good-will everywhere as to the man who was killed by Burr's bullet on the shelf of the Palisades.

I said a few moments ago that I could tell you nothing new about Hamilton. This is all a twice-told tale. This is part of the warp and woof of our American history; this is part of the very fabric out of which we are made and of the institutions under which we live. And yet, who would have supposed that after the lapse of a hundred short years the work of Alexander Hamilton must be done all over again? That is the condition which confronts the American people in these opening years of the twentieth century. What Alexander Hamilton taught of civil liberty, of freedom, and of order; what he taught of effective, responsible government, of its purpose, its organs, its instruments, has become so familiar, so built into our daily life and into the fabric of our business, that we have for-

gotten, many of us, that it is essential to our welfare
and to the perpetuity of our government. Yet to-day,
from one voice and another, meeting a fair measure of
approval all over the land, come attacks upon these
very fundamental principles of our government, until
many of us cry aloud for the spirit of Hamilton to
come back to us and lead this great empire of ours
still farther forward in the fight for the permanent upbuilding of civil liberty!

When the Constitution of these United States was
framed, our fathers staked out clearly two great fields
of activity and conduct. On the one hand, they
formulated a plan of government. They constituted
it of an executive, a legislative, and a judicial branch,
and they ascribed to these their several functions.
Then they marked out just as clearly the field of civil
liberty. They forbade the government to invade it,
and they erected great courts of justice to see to it
that it was not invaded. Never before in the history
of mankind, and never since, has that been done. In
no ancient state, in no mediæval state, in no modern
state but ours, is civil liberty a part of the fundamental
law of the land. The nearest approach to it is in the
Constitution of the German Empire; that Constitution written after the war with France, in 1871, under
the guidance of Bismarck. Neither the Constitution
of France nor the unwritten Constitution of Great
Britain—none of these modern constitutions of which
you read, not one of them—defines and protects the field
of civil liberty as our fathers did one hundred and

twenty-five years ago. To-day it is proposed to us as an advance, as a step forward, that we should unite to throw away the only thing which distinguishes us from the other nations of the world; to put civil liberty into the melting-pot; to make it subject to any majority, however temporary, however fickle, whether at the polls or in the legislature, and to make it possible to strip a man of his property, his liberty, and freedom; and that, if you please, by any mere rush of tumultuous passion!

Never has a more preposterous, never has a more ignorant, proposal been made by anybody. In absolute defiance of history, in utter ignorance of the history of Europe, in ignorance even of the history of the United States, without any appreciation of what we have been doing these one hundred and twenty-five years, we are now asked to strip ourselves of the one great fundamental protection which the fathers won for us, and to which the enlightened peoples of the world have been looking for a century and a quarter as the greatest evidence of political progress that mankind has ever seen!

I submit that it requires not only a large measure of ignorance, but a total lack of the sense of humor, to propose such a programme in the name of advance. This new programme may be a wise one, but then put upon it the name that belongs to it—reaction! Say frankly that we have gone ahead too fast; that we have staked out territory that man is still incompetent to occupy; that we are not ready for liberty; that we should go back to the days of Francis I and Henry IV and Henry VIII, and, substituting the many for the one, turn over our civil liberty to the tender mercies of a tyrant. That is what is seriously proposed to the American people to-day.

This is not a party question; it rises far above faction or names or personalities or political parties. I beg you to believe that I should not speak of this matter in this presence, on an occasion such as this, did I not believe that it goes to the very roots of our American life, and that those things with which the great names of Hamilton and Jefferson and Washington and Madison and Marshall and Webster and Lincoln are associated are at stake. They are all at stake in the issues that are being debated before the American people to-day.

You may, if you choose, solace yourselves with the optimistic thought that everything will come out well. Hamilton never did. He saw to it that it came out well. He addressed himself to the Constitutional Convention lest error be made. He later addressed himself to the New York convention at Poughkeepsie lest the Constitution be rejected. He addressed himself to the Congress of the United States lest we have no adequate financial system, no national income, and no properly ordered system of taxation. He was never content to let matters drift. He saw to it—trusting as he did, and as every American must, in the good faith, the honor, and the intelligence of the American people—he saw to it that the facts were laid before them with such clearness, the arguments adduced with such cogency, the objections answered with such overwhelming force, that they were led to walk in the strait and narrow path of national safety.

The building of this nation has been a long, a solemn, and a sacred task. It is the work of four generations of men who have conceived lofty ideals, and who, without regard to party, religious faith, or section, whether up in the pine-forests of Maine or over across the continent in the orange-fields of California or down on the plantations of the sunny South, have wrought for freedom, for liberty, for stability, for justice. The American people have, in a singular sense, regarded themselves as the instruments of Providence in the working out of a great government and a mighty civilization. Almost alone among the governments of the world, they have been in the habit, from the beginning, of invoking the Divine blessing upon the deliberations of their legislative bodies, and they have seen to it that religion has been represented on every great occasion of national festivity or rejoicing. They have felt that here in this Western world, with an endowment by Nature the like of which history has never recorded, the opportunity has been given to try on a huge scale, opening their arms to all who would come, the fateful experiment of self-government. Many men of all types and kinds, soldiers and sailors, jurists and teachers, legislators and executives, philosophers and popular leaders, have contributed to that great end. But out of them all I name six men who stand forever in the American Pantheon as supremely important among those who have builded the nation's government. I do not speak now of those who have made other and important contributions; I have not in mind those who have led great parties, who have accomplished important acts, or have set in motion great and fine and lasting currents of thought; but I speak of six men who, one after another, have struck the blows that were necessary to the construction of our great American ship of state—the nation's builders.

The first is George Washington. Without his calm and even temper, without his serene and unruffled mind, which was as influential because of what he refrained from doing as because of what he did, the existence of this American nation is unthinkable. His is, beyond all comparison, the great self-sacrificing character in political history. Washington, through his personality, drew the people of these colonies together, made them feel loyalty to a single person, and, through that person, to the idea which he represented, and then he deftly withdrew his personality and left them to worship the new and beautiful ideal that he had given them.

By his side and with him was Hamilton, the supreme constructive genius in political philosophy and in statesmanship. He showed what to do and how to do it; how the executive and the legislature could be adjusted to each other; how the nation's business could be carried on, and how the various departments of government should be organized. He taught the great mass

of the American people what the fundamental principles were which underlay this new and fateful project.

Next comes John Marshall, who, from his great
place as Chief Justice of the United States, gave to the
new Constitution that interpretation—at a time when
two interpretations were possible—which welded the
nation together in unity and gave to it supreme power
and legal control over its several parts.  But Marshall's
work was challenged.  Thomas Jefferson petulantly
put obstacles in his way, and no less a man than
Andrew Jackson said: "John Marshall has made the
decision, now let him execute it."  The people of the
United States had to be taught that when the nation
spoke—whether by voice of the President, the Congress, or the Supreme Court—when a constitutional interpretation was made, it was to be obeyed, even if it
took the whole of the nation's power to compel obedience.

That great act of public education was performed
by this same rugged Andrew Jackson of Tennessee in
his great proclamation to the nullifiers of South Carolina.  When the distinguished gentlemen of South
Carolina said they would not enforce the tariff act,
that they did not approve of it, that they would not
accept it for their State, Andrew Jackson—speaking
perhaps by the pen of the great jurist Edward Livingston of Louisiana—made a famous proclamation to
the nullifiers in which was conveyed the substance of
his reported personal message to John C. Calhoun,
one of the greatest of all American statesmen and

political philosophers. This was that if one drop of blood was shed in defiance of the laws of the United States, he, Andrew Jackson, would hang the first nullifier he could lay his hands on to the first tree he could find. And so the laws of the United States were not nullified in South Carolina. There was a compromise? Perhaps, but there was also no nullification. The decisions of the Supreme Court were undisputed thereafter, and this nation took a long step forward toward real nationality.

Then came the eloquent voice of Daniel Webster, who, for thirty years at the bar, on the platform, and in the Senate of the United States, educated public opinion to a point where resistance to the secession movement that had to come was both natural and necessary. We need not blink the fact that without Daniel Webster the Civil War could not have been fought to a successful conclusion. It was not possible to rest our national contention in that war upon a purely legal basis, even upon legal propositions so clear and firm; for they were cold and rational only. Daniel Webster had for thirty years made them live. He burned into the hearts of the American people the idea of nationality. Whether you take one great speech at Plymouth, another at Boston, another in New York, or the great and conclusive reply to Hayne in the Senate, it makes no difference; they are all part of one great going to school by the people of the United States to Daniel Webster. He taught them not alone in terms of constitutional law and of legal definitions, but in terms of every-day thought and feeling and action, that this nation was one. It was he who prepared the way for what followed.

Daniel Webster made it possible for Abraham Lincoln—that sad, patient, long-suffering man—to carry this nation through the final crisis of its birth throes; because he had put under him and behind him the great body of opinion which believed that this nation was one, was to be kept one, was to live as one, and was to live as a free people.

These six men are both the symbols and the moving forces of the constructive nation-building of the American people. They are drawn from all parts of the United States, from different classes of society, with varying political views, touching the people with different interests and at different points. These six men are the most prominent in the galaxy of our nation-building heroes. Each one of them would be affrighted could he know from his place in high heaven that at this late day it is seriously proposed in the name of greater justice, of more effective advance, to undermine and to break down the very foundations on which this government and the civilization of this people rest.

And so, as we mark this anniversary of Hamilton's birth and pay to him the highest tribute, we can give him his most just and well-earned recognition only if we remember not alone what he was, not alone what he did, but what bearing all that has upon the America of to-day; what lessons his career and his teachings have in relation to the great problems of politics, of economics, and of the development of civil liberty that are to be solved in the future. There is no safe guide for the future but the experience of the past. When we know what has happened under certain conditions we may with some assurance predict what will happen when those conditions are repeated. When we see out of what a morass of mediævalism, out of what a morass of injustice and ignorance and squalor, the people of the United States and their ancestors have come; to what heights they have mounted under their Constitution and their laws, their civil institutions, their liberty and their freedom, it is to me inconceivable that as these people come to know what the issue of the moment really is, they will turn their backs on Washington and Hamilton and Marshall and Jackson and Webster and Lincoln, and tear their governmental structure down just to see what will happen.

# XVII

# THEODORE ROOSEVELT
AMERICAN

A minute presented to the Chamber of Commerce of the
State of New York, February 6, 1919

# THEODORE ROOSEVELT
## AMERICAN

With the suddenness of a thunderbolt forged in a sky that had but just begun to darken, the life of Theodore Roosevelt ended, without suffering or struggle, at his home at Oyster Bay, on the early morning of Monday, January 6, 1919.

The Chamber of Commerce of the State of New York, whose roll of honorary membership was adorned by his name and in whose halls he was a familiar friend, halts the onward march of its business to pay sorrowful and affectionate tribute of respect for his memory and of admiration for his life and character.

Theodore Roosevelt was a native son of New York, and in his training, his private life, his public service, and his countless intellectual interests, represented and reflected the life of the great metropolis to which he was always proud to belong. He knew and loved the New York of the early Knickerbockers, of the English colonists, of the nation-builders, and of the long series of splendid men who in church and state and trade and commerce have made the name of this city honored the whole world round. He knew and loved the New York of vision, of constructive sagacity and foresight, and of warm and generous sympathy for just causes, for suffering peoples, and for stricken lands. He knew

and loved the New York which holds aloft the torch of
liberty at the nation's gateway, and which feels every
heart-throb in the life of a people whose homes stretch
from pine to palm and from the waters of the Atlantic
to the long rolling waves of the Pacific Ocean.  He
knew and loved the New York which is proud to be
called the Empire State, since it is an empire of freemen bent on keeping freemen free.

Theodore Roosevelt was called, while his young
manhood was yet in the making, to the service of his
city, his State, and his nation.  At each successive
post of duty his alert human interest, his restless zeal
for action, and his quick appreciation of the thing that
needed immediately to be done, marked him in his
youth as a notable leader of Americans, and as a personality of quite unmatched attractiveness.  Within
a few days of his fortieth birthday he was chosen to be
Governor of New York, and for two years filled with
distinction and high acceptance the post which had
been adorned by George Clinton, by John Jay, by
DeWitt Clinton, by Martin Van Buren, by William
L. Marcy, by William H. Seward, by Silas Wright, by
Hamilton Fish, by Edwin D. Morgan, by Samuel J.
Tilden, and by Grover Cleveland.

Elected at forty-two to be Vice-President of the
United States, Theodore Roosevelt ascended the steps
of the White House shortly thereafter under circumstances of tragic sorrow and amid a nation's mourning
for its murdered Chief Magistrate.  Of native-born
New Yorkers only Martin Van Buren had before him

reached the chief magistracy of the republic, despite
the rich contribution of New York for a full century
and a quarter to the intellectual and moral leadership
of the nation. He found a rich and rapidly expanding
people forced to undertake the solution of new and
difficult problems that went to the very roots of their
economic and social life. He attacked these problems
with the ardent eagerness of a crusader. He had an
abiding faith in the American people and supreme
confidence in their right judgments, if only they could
be brought to see the facts, all the facts, and nothing
but the facts, precisely as they were. His administration accompanied an era of large and rapid readjustment in the public and the business life of America,
and at no instant was his firm grip upon the wheel
that steered the ship of state in any degree relaxed.
Not the voices of those who personally knew and loved
him, but the calm, clear voice of history, will appraise
the permanent value of his public service. Suffice it
to say that for us it is a landmark in the history of our
nation.

Theodore Roosevelt's ruling passion was love for
America, belief in America, and joyful purpose to serve
America to the utmost of his powers. Singularly en-
dowed with intellectual alertness, vital force, and rich
and deep emotions, he blended these attributes together in a personality dynamic both in its generating
power and in its popular attractiveness.

Theodore Roosevelt had keenest joy in combat.
The sense of conflict, of overcoming difficulties and re-

moving obstacles, of beating down stupidity and malice, gave him gladdest satisfaction. Into a combat he carried every power of his being and for the battle he used every resource in the great armory of argument and cunning and skill. He hated a sneak, a coward, or a trimmer, and he had no concern for him who, knowing the truth, dared not maintain it.

In sixty quick years he lived the space of a Methuselah's life. So packed were those years with incident and activity and accomplishment that each one of them seems a decade. Yet sixty years are the years not of old age, but of maturity. Theodore Roosevelt did not live to grow old. His maturest years were spent in contact with great questions that racked the best brains of the world and taxed the stoutest hearts. He saw clearly and true the underlying, and at first hidden, significance of the Great War. He seized quickly upon the moral issues involved and loudly called upon his countrymen to play the part of men when the world was in flames. He lived to see one of the two great enemies of freedom broken and vanquished on the field of battle and its representatives and title-bearers in flight from home and country. He died while the other great enemy of freedom was hissing and raising its head to strike. Who can doubt that, had his life been spared, he would have been in the front rank of those who fight to beat down anarchy and the forces of unreason and destruction, as he was ready to go into the front rank of those who fought to beat back autocracy ?

Theodore Roosevelt's passionate love of humankind

was accompanied with an equally passionate love of nature and all that nature had to offer for the pleasure and the satisfaction of man. The animals of the household and the farm were his friends and constant companions. He spoke to them with the familiar affection of a father talking to his children. The habits and characteristics of the wild beasts and the history of the animal dwellers in the distant and dangerous places of the earth were well understood by him. The flowers of the garden and the roadside he tended with his own hand and the birds of the air he called each by its familiar name and note.

With all this many-sided interest, and with all his zest for constant action, Theodore Roosevelt was withal a man of books and letters. He feasted alike upon prose and poetry, upon travel and adventure, upon history and fiction, and upon all that described and revealed the world's humbler folk and children. From his wide reading he drew an astonishingly rich and varied vocabulary and he has given currency to many striking and forceful phrases, bearing the stamp sterling, that will continue in circulation for generations to come wherever the English language is used as coin. In the Bible and in *Pilgrim's Progress* he found more than one word or phrase that his ingenuity as an artificer made directly to apply to conditions and happenings of the moment.

Fully to comprehend the interests and affections of Theodore Roosevelt, one must extend the scope of the famous line of the Roman poet and say that he was truly a living being, and that nothing which had life was outside the range of his interest and his affection.

It is not yet possible to think of America with this busy life ended and this ardent spirit gone from the arena of combat and strife to its everlasting rest. In the darkness of the early morning, while the dawn was still awaiting its call to daily service, Theodore Roosevelt set his feet in the path of silence that leads to those golden gardens of memory where rich and ripening spirits love constantly to dwell.

May the Light Everlasting shine upon him!

XVIII

THE WORLD'S DEBT TO ENGLAND

Introductory remarks at the Fifteenth Anniversary Banquet
of the Pilgrims of the United States, at the Waldorf-
Astoria, New York, March 5, 1918

# THE WORLD'S DEBT TO ENGLAND

To mark the high significance of this night no words of mine are needed. For fifteen years the Pilgrims have been privileged to assemble to greet notable men from all parts of the British Empire who have come bearing eminence and fame. To-night we mark our anniversary with unprecedented distinction by welcoming at one and the same time two of the most notable representatives of English public life, high dignitaries of the English Church and of the English State. What memories, what images, what visions are called up by the names of their great posts! The Archbishop of York and the Lord Chief Justice of England carry us back to those early morning hours in the history of free, Christian government when the dawn was breaking that was to drive before it the darkness of an outworn world and of a pagan worship. As the dawn grew into day the light of liberty in church and state steadily spread itself in ever-widening circles, until to-day the whole free world is in arms for freedom against the last lingering obstacle to its extension everywhere.

During that long bright day of liberty's life there has been a great procession of Englishmen and men of English blood, the like of which the history of no other

nation can record. Search the story of Greece and
there are not so many. Call the roll of ancient Rome
and it still falls short of this great galaxy. There are
Alfred the Great and Edward the Confessor, the second
Henry and the first Edward, Simon de Montfort and
Wyclif and Burghley, Hampden and Pym and Crom-
well and Milton, Chatham and Burke and Fox and
Canning and Gladstone; and their cousins-American,
Washington and Franklin, Hamilton and Jefferson,
Marshall and Webster, and last of all, marching alone,
Abraham Lincoln. Where else can the history of
liberty be so well read as in the story of the lives
of these heroes of English and American history?
What other peoples have pursued liberty longer,
more earnestly, more steadfastly, and with greater
success?

The British Empire is itself a marvellous model of a
community of free states. An empire, as Burke once
said, is an aggregate of many states under a common
head, and there is about the name no necessary im-
plication of either arbitrary or autocratic government,
or of any particular form of external policy. An empire
may be free and liberty-loving and world-wide, like that
of Britain, or it may be autocratic, severely disciplined,
and highly concentrated, like that of our Teuton
enemies. After the present war had begun to run its
course, a celebrated German historian announced that
the world would be healed by being Germanized. We
think not. Great Britain and America have already

stood witnesses of two notable triumphs of the militaristic spirit and policy, and they are resolved that there shall not be a third. They saw militarism triumph with Metternich as a denial of the hopes and aspirations of liberalism, and later they saw militarism triumph with Bismarck in a positive victory over liberalism and its ideals. In this present conflict it is their stern and steady resolve that militarism shall not conquer.

This fight and this stupendous sacrifice for an idea are the answer of a new-born world of the spirit to those sciolists who see in history nothing but a cunning contest for material gain, and who weigh all effort and all achievement in the scales of accumulated wealth and of control over others. The power of the spirit, armed with new and potent strength, has accepted the great challenge issued to it by the power of material interest and of brute force in human affairs. The end may yet be distant, but it is secure.

Our two eminent guests are in their persons the representatives of Faith and of Justice, the two great pillars of all civilization and of all progress. It is Faith that lights the fires of the spirit and lifts man's gaze to those high places where the real victories of life, and the victory of life over death itself, are won. Under the guidance of Faith, it is Justice which makes liberty possible, which reveals opportunity, and which protects the weak in his sincere effort to live side by side with the strong. It is just these achievements

of Faith and of Justice which constitute Liberty; and
in Shelley's fine lines

> "Yet were life a charnel, where
> Hope lay coffined with Despair;
> Yet were Truth a sacred lie,
> . . . If Liberty
> Lent not life its soul of light."

In the earliest hours of August, 1914, the government of Great Britain was called upon to make a momentous decision. Belgium had been wantonly attacked and its neutrality violated. Great Britain's
name was on the bond which pledged to Belgium protection and security. Britain was at peace and absorbed in grave problems of internal policy. Should
she turn aside from commerce, from industry, from the
examination of insistent domestic questions and stake
not only her prosperity but her very existence on
her plighted word? History records the answer and
eternity will applaud it. There was only so much
hesitation as was required fully to ascertain the facts
and to make sure that there was no other alternative
than faithlessness or war. Great Britain chose to
preserve her faith and to accept the gage of battle.
With that act a world-wide contest for right against
might and for freedom against despotism was begun.
Great Britain's national and imperial achievements
since that decision was taken stagger the imagination.
Huge armies have been raised and trained and carried
not only overseas but to remote provinces and to dis-

tant continents. Canada, Australia, New Zealand, India, and South Africa have hastened to England's side with their bravest and their best. Ceaselessly and sleeplessly the British Navy has done its epoch-making work. Vast sums of money have been provided not only for the emergencies of war but for loans and supplies to allied peoples. Old customs have been overthrown and long-established habits of life and work have been quickly set aside. As a result, Great Britain stands to-day, both on land and sea, in the very front line of Liberty's defenders wherever the contest is being waged. There are no words that can adequately portray this colossal effort, and no appreciation which can completely convey the extent of a world's obligation. The age that is dying finds in Great Britain, in France, and in the American Republic its overmastering conquerors, and the age that is coming to birth finds in them its natural leaders and protectors.

So to-night the Pilgrims celebrate, with all the honors, the presence at their board not only of these two eminent and honored personalities, but of two chief representatives and spokesmen of that England which for a thousand years has been the faithful guardian at the gate of the house of Liberty.

# XIX

# FAITH AND THE WAR

An address delivered at the War Dinner in honor of the Archbishop of York and the Members of the House of Bishops
given by the Church Club of New York, at the Waldorf-
Astoria, April 10, 1918

# FAITH AND THE WAR

A kindly fate has made it possible for me to have the pleasure of that friendship which Homer described. It was given to me in this great hall some five weeks ago to share in welcoming the coming guest, and it is now given to me to-night in this same hall to help speed his parting.

These have been memorable weeks for us, and I trust that they will be remembered weeks for the Archbishop of York. Much has been crowded into them. He has asked the blessing of Almighty God upon the Senate of the United States. He has addressed great audiences in halls and public places in twoscore or more of cities. He has preached before vast congregations in cathedrals and churches. If it be the fact that but ninety or one hundred thousand Americans have come within reach of his voice, I speak nothing but the truth when I say that millions have come within reach of his influence.

The Presiding Bishop has ventured an allusion to old York and to New York. Your Grace, it was at New York that you fittingly landed, it is from New York that you will set sail. I could spend a much longer time than would be becoming in talking to you about this very interesting and unique and attractive city. Very few persons understand New York, and many persons are moved to speak unkindly of it. But it is a curious fact that in its more than two hundred and fifty years of history, New York has maintained a singleness of character which the historians have noted. In turning over the pages of our scholarly and accomplished historian Mrs. Schuyler Van Rensselaer, I found a fine characterization of New Amsterdam. She describes New Amsterdam in this striking paragraph:

> Liveliness was one of the few things it never lacked, torpidity one of the moods of mind it could not encourage, peaceful sloth one of the careers for which it offered no chance.

I submit that those words, written of the New Amsterdam that was passing at the hands of Governor Nichols and his corporal's guard into New York, remain true after two and one-half centuries of this metropolitan community in which Your Grace has won so permanent and so endeared a place.

But I have been thinking, as the Archbishop has gone about the country, and as word has come to us of the great impression made upon those addressed— now by this sermon, now by that public appearance— of what it is that has really happened, not only to make his visit possible, but to make his visit so splendid in its results.

Do you remember that five years ago we were all busily engaged in preparing to celebrate, in fitting fashion, one hundred years of peace between the nations of the English-speaking world? Leaders of

opinion in Great Britain and America, eminent ecclesi-
astics, statesmen, men of affairs, were all taking part
in the formulation of plans that would fittingly mark
that great happening in the history of modern man,
when suddenly we were interrupted by this stupendous
cataclysm. And what followed? That very happening, so awful in itself, has not only celebrated one hundred years of peace in the English-speaking world,
but it has made the English-speaking world an intellectual and moral and spiritual unit for all time to
come!

I need not say to you what that means, and is to
mean, in the history of the race, and in the history of
those great causes for which the free world is now
fighting. My friends, as we sit here to-night, over
yonder, across three thousand miles of dangerous
ocean, there is a battle-line of freemen bending backward and forward under the thrust of hundreds of
thousands of armed men, who are carrying every resource that modern science can develop to aid their
purpose. Over there is a little thin battle-line, waver-
ing backward and forward, holding precious soil,
defending still more precious ideals, waiting for you
and me. And as for the moment the issue seems
doubtful, I recall that there is a famous incident in
American naval history which one likes to think of at
a time like this. You remember that when John Paul
Jones, sorely stricken and apparently overpowered,
received the message asking whether he was ready to
surrender, he sent back his answer, quick as a flash:

"I have not yet begun to fight." Those who think that there is about this great contest any weakening or compromise in the hearts of the American people, do not understand them. They have been as a people slow, too slow for some of us, fully to understand and appreciate; but that understanding and that appreciation have come to them, and that understanding and that appreciation will not be let go.

We hear much, and rightly, of the conservation of our material resources, of coal, of food, of labor; but should we not, and more especially in a great country like this, take some note of the need to conserve our spiritual resources? Are we not at a time in the world's history where we may perhaps be suffering from intellectual, moral, and spiritual exhaustion? Where are the world's great poets? What voice is singing the song of idealism to the world as it was sung fifty years ago? Where are our great idealistic philosophers? Who are they who are guiding the world as it was guided not so long ago in paths of intellectual and moral and spiritual construction? May it not be that in fastening our attention upon the satisfactions of life, we have turned our attention away from its purposes? May it not be that in our eagerness to weigh and to measure and to count, we have turned our faces away from the true standards of value? And may it not be that behind all this immeasurable suffering, this incalculable loss, this perfectly appalling sacrifice, there is some good concealed? May it not be that out of it all our world—your world and mine

—is going to learn new lessons and see more clearly than for a generation past, the enduring standards and the full significance of the moral and spiritual forces? This contest has restored to the whole world the practical power of Faith. We are fighting because we have faith in a principle, in a tradition, in an ideal. Suddenly all our zeal for material gain cools and slackens. All our accumulations are mobilized and hastened to the post where they will best serve. All our customary occupations are left behind, and we move with rapid feet to that point where we can most effectively sustain Faith—faith in the everlasting principles of liberty and justice and right, which are themselves founded upon eternal Christian truths. There is no escape from the meaning of this. There is no escape from the lesson that he who runs may read in the lives of men and women as they hurry to do what they can for this great contest. That makes me not only hopeful, but absolutely confident, of the end.

I came the other day upon a most extraordinary letter of Lord Acton. It is a letter written of one of the most famous and most admirable of contemporary Englishmen. After describing this man's extraordinary traits and characteristics and accomplishments and powers, Lord Acton ended his striking portrait with the unforgettable sentiment that his subject was capable of all but the highest things since he had no faith.

It is just this that it is possible to learn from our participation, from Britain's participation, from

France's participation and sacrifice in this struggle.
Those nations are capable of the highest because they
have this faith, and as they grimly turn all their power
and all their resources to this tremendous task, it is
nothing but faith in those principles that could by any
possibility sustain them. Who cares whether German
Imperialism rules the world or not if there are no
principles in which we believe? Why should not the
autocratic power of a German empire extend itself
from pole to pole and all around the world? It would
give order; it would give peace. You remember what
Tacitus made an ancient Briton say of the Romans:
"They made a desert and called it peace." The German imperial power can do that. Why should we not
accept this lordly and benevolent and efficient rule?
And why should we not subject ourselves to this German peace? There is only one reason—because we
have faith, because we have convictions, because we
have beliefs, no one of which we will surrender. It is
just that, just that and nothing more, which stands
between us and the world-power of German Imperialism. Those armies, those navies, are sent by Faith
to fight for Faith. There is no other enemy that Germany has to-day that could stand against its might
for a moment except Faith; and therefore this whole
world is, through this insight, through this new grasp
upon realities, through this new and amazing revelation of the true significance of things, receiving an education in Faith and its power the like of which no
prophet would have dared to predict.

I remember so well the impression made upon students of my generation when we read the first paper in the famous *Essays and Reviews*. That book was published in 1860, and twenty years later, when some of us were in college, it was part of the usual reading of serious-minded students. The first chapter of that book, as many of you will recall, is an illuminating paper by Dr. Temple of Rugby, afterward Archbishop of Canterbury, entitled "The Education of the World." To the young student who, for the first time, read in these clearly-stated pages what was the meaning of the events that followed after each other in such extraordinary succession—the eastern world and Greece and Rome and the Middle Ages and modern Christendom—the whole of these happenings seemed to take on form and reason and persuasiveness, and the youth seemed to understand the real meaning of the point at which he stood, and how that point had been prepared for him by what had gone before. We are now in another stage of the education of the world. It had pleased Providence so to order events that this tremendous happening has taken place, and those who read history as a movement of intellectual and moral and spiritual force and power toward ends, see in this another great step onward in the education of mankind. We see in it an education of mankind in Faith, for Faith, and to a new appreciation of Faith.

It is not easy, I admit, to stand in your presence at a moment like this and speak of anything which might be considered a brighter aspect of the war. One would not, if he could, lessen the demand upon us for stern resolution and unbending energy; but are we not right to try to seek an explanation of the power which is ours, to try to seek an explanation of the purposes which we profess, in terms of those higher values which are civilization? It may be that there is a long story yet to come. It may be that there are many pages of this book yet to be turned. But one thing seems to me certain, and that is that Great Britain and America will never loosen this new and splendid bond of inter-relationship. It seems to me certain that these English-speaking peoples will more consciously than before accept their joint responsibility for their share in freedom, for their splendid place in the history of liberty, and that they will not treat it as something which can be left to care for itself, and be subjected to the buffeting of tide and current, of time and circumstance, of enmity and jealousy and envy. We Americans shall have a new purpose and a new determination in the protection of our ideals, and we shall have a new sense of companionship with the liberty-loving peoples across the sea.

It is impossible, Your Grace, to let you go home from this American visit without some attempt, however imperfect, to express to you in public presence what your personality, your speech, and your teaching have done among us. We shall have to try by what we do, and by what those whom we can influence may do, to testify not by words, but by acts and deeds over years, to our sincere appreciation of the sacrifice you have made in coming to us, as well as to our affection for your person and our profound admiration for the people and the cause that you have so eloquently and so tenderly represented among us.

## XX

## IS AMERICAN HIGHER EDUCATION
## IMPROVING?

An article written for the *Youth's Companion*, Boston,
Massachusetts, June 21, 1917

# IS AMERICAN HIGHER EDUCATION
## IMPROVING?

We can say that higher education is improving only if the quality of its product is being steadily heightened and if it is constantly adapting itself to the newer needs of the community. We must at once admit that American higher education lacks some of the very useful and helpful characteristics that it had a generation ago. It lacks, for example, the admirable discipline that a student gets from close occupation, under strict surveillance, with a few difficult subjects of study. No educational instruments have yet been found that, in disciplinary value and in capacity to train a powerful and subtle mind, are equal to Greek, Latin, and mathematics. The descriptive and the experimental sciences cannot do it—or at least they have not done it—and the same is true of the newer subjects of study that are humorously, if roughly, classified together as the "unnatural sciences"— economics, sociology, and the like.

Through long centuries of educational use Greek, Latin, and mathematics have acquired an educational form that gives them the qualities of a highly tempered and highly polished tool. It may be that the descriptive and the experimental sciences, and the so-called " unnatural sciences " as well, will one day ac-

quire the same attributes. It suffices for the present
argument to take note of the fact that as yet they
have not done so.

The use of Greek, Latin, and mathematics in the
higher education of America is declining. In a few
years it will be as rare for a student to know Greek
as to-day it is for him to know Hebrew; and it may
not take more than a generation or two for Latin to
follow the same course. How long the higher reaches
of mathematics—those noble and inviting reaches in
which philosophy, poetry, and imagination combine
to play with the intricacies of space and the notations
of time—will continue to find extensive educational use
is also a question.

The belief that mathematics will always be pursued
for its practical value is groundless. The modern
architect, and even the modern engineer, hires his
mathematician and no longer deigns to know the
subject himself. Counting machines and various similar mechanisms are invading the province of the four
fundamental rules. It is plain that some stronger
reason than practicality will have to be found for the
general study of mathematics a generation hence.

It becomes, therefore, a very serious question what
the educational instrumentalities shall be that are to
provide the next generation or two with the sort of
discipline and training that Greek, Latin, and mathematics provided for our fathers and for many of us.
The vague discussion of what are called social questions will not discipline or train anyone. If history

be regarded as something quite independent of chronology and as recording merely the results of the operation of economic law, then it, too, will become of little or no educational value. Those who empty out of philosophy its ancient and honorable content, and try to substitute for it a sort of checkered pavement of the sciences, are engaged in agile exercise, but they are not accomplishing any good either for philosophy or for education.

It must be said, therefore, that the higher education of the United States is at present in a condition where it may readily drop backward rather than improve. The college student of to-day, and in some cases even the university student, is permitted to sprawl over so large and so varied an area of intellectual interest that he loses the discipline in concentration, in hard work, and in the mastery of some relatively small field that comes from pursuing a better and older method. There is just now, however, a marked tendency among the better colleges to aid and to guide the student toward concentrating his interests and his energies upon a small group of subjects that have some common centre of interest and some well-marked relationship. This movement is a sound and hopeful one, and should be encouraged and aided. The student should follow the group of subjects that he chooses far enough to carry him beyond their mere elements. No mind can be called really trained or educated that has never got beyond the elements of anything. It is necessary for many of us to remain satisfied with a knowledge of the elements of most things, but there should be some small part of the field of knowledge in which we have gone far past the elements and have gained some notion of what the higher reaches of the subject contain.

It may be said that, from the standpoint of the quality of its product, higher education in the United States is improving wherever sound and satisfactory progress is making to put into the place of the disappearing Greek, Latin, and mathematics some educational material that is sufficiently well organized and long enough pursued to give training in concentration, in application, and in genuine knowledge.

There is marked improvement, too, in the manner in which our higher education is adapting itself to the needs and aspirations of the people. The colleges, and particularly the universities, are outgrowing the worship of some of their ancient fetishes. All sorts of subjects that were once frowned upon are now found worthy of study and of investigation. Moreover, an institution of higher education no longer considers it to be proper to lock up its buildings, its libraries, and its laboratories from June until September. The summer session, which began as an exotic, has been academically acclimated, and is now that part of the academic year in which, at more institutions than one, the very best work is done.

The same is true of what is known as Extension Teaching, which began as a system of more or less popular lectures to untrained audiences, and in some places still remains so. Where extension teaching is best developed, however, it means something quite different. In such cases it is genuine work of the same quality and quantity as that given in the so-called regular classes, but carried on at such hours and in such places that those who have to earn their living can attend. Wherever the same standards of admission and examination are required, extension teaching is just as good as any other kind of teaching, and will be merged sooner or later in the so-called regular work.

The problem of vocational training is not so hard in the field of higher education as it is in that of secondary education. In higher education it is easy to indicate what the aim and the standard of vocational training should be. The best universities agree that not less than two years of work in a college of liberal arts and sciences is the minimum that will give the maturity and accomplishment necessary for admission to a really first-class school of law, medicine, engineering, architecture, or teaching. If the student is able to pursue an even longer college course, so much the better, provided he makes thoroughly good use of his rare advantage and opportunity.

In training in law, in medicine, in engineering, in architecture, and in teaching, higher education in the United States is improving by leaps and bounds. That is the case not only because the best professional schools have enforced a higher standard of admission, but because there has grown up in the United States a competent body of trained scholars in the various professions who are distinct from the successful practitioners.

Practical knowledge and experience are, of course, of great value to a teacher in a vocational or professional school; but mere practical knowledge and experience, without scholarship, originality, power to conduct and to stimulate research, and without skill in teaching, will no longer suffice. A young American who knows how to choose and who takes full advantage of his choice can now obtain at least as good a professional education in the United States as he can anywhere else in the world, and in some subjects a better one than he can get anywhere else.

The two or three best American schools of law have no equals in Europe. Our best schools of medicine have no superiors in Europe, although there are three or four European cities that have better chances for clinical observation and study than any cities in this country. Our three or four best schools of engineering, if not so good as the best in France, Germany, and Italy, certainly press them very hard indeed. The best American schools of architecture, although organized on a sounder and broader basis than any of the European schools, cannot yet rival in prestige and in influence the *École des Beaux Arts* in Paris. The best American school of education is in a class quite by itself, and at a half dozen universities schools of similar type are rapidly coming forward to take places in the front rank.

There is a mistaken notion that scholarly research is more esteemed and more eagerly pursued on the continent of Europe than in the United States. That was true until a decade or two ago. At present, however, the scholarly investigation going forward in America equals in amount and in quality that which is going forward in any other country.

The quality of the American college and university professor is in some respects not so good as it was a generation ago, but in other respects it is much better. Forty years ago you could count on the fingers of one hand those Americans who had made an international reputation of any sort for scholarly endeavor; to-day the number of such Americans is very considerable. The price that has been paid for that gain, calculated in terms of personality, of breadth of view, of deep human sympathy, and of genuine wisdom, has been rather high. It is my own hope that this phenomenon is, however, only temporary.

Too many American college and university teachers of to-day are proselyters for some particular philosophy of life. They are not content to teach, but feel under the obligation to preach as well. To the discriminating student such preaching of social and political doctrine does little harm, because he takes it only at its proper value. The less discriminating student, however, and particularly the women students of to-day, are sadly imposed upon by lecture-room talk of that sort. The good teacher understands the distinction between what he himself knows and believes and what it is wise and proper for him to teach the young and immature student. The poor teacher, on the other hand, mixes all these things up together.

Moreover, the college and university teacher suffers from lack of criticism and supervision. I do not mean that sort of criticism and supervision which would be appropriate in a factory or in a counting-house, but that criticism and supervision which, particularly at the outset of an academic career, can do so much to guide, to strengthen, and to develop a teacher's powers and effectiveness. Our public school systems abound in illustrations of the supervision that I have in mind, but in the colleges and universities nothing of the kind exists. A more or less vague notion prevails that Mr. So-and-So is a good teacher or a poor teacher, as the case may be, and that notion is based largely on what his students say about him. His own immediate colleagues base their judgment of him, not upon what he does in the class-room, for they have no knowledge of that, but upon his personal characteristics, his published work, and his general reputation for scholarship. It is for those reasons that a man may be a most admirable scholar, and yet a wretched teacher of the young, without that fact being pointed out to him or even discovered through a long academic career.

It may fairly be said, therefore, that, in spite of the obvious grounds of criticism, higher education is improving in the United States. The fact is, we expect more of higher education than ever before in the history of the world. Our American democracy is impatient to meet its needs, and to meet them quickly is no easy matter. The problem before those who are charged with the care and oversight of American higher education is to preserve its standards and its ideals while meeting to the full the demands of a new and increasingly complicated economic and social life.

# XXI

# THE COLLEGES AND THE NATION

An address delivered on the occasion of the installation of
Dr. Richard Eddy Sykes as president of St. Lawrence
University, Canton, New York, June 7, 1919

# THE COLLEGES AND THE NATION

## I

We are gathered to-day at one of the power houses of American character and American life.  It is from this centre, and from scores of others like it scattered over our hills and valleys from Maine to California and through our cities and towns from Canada to the Gulf, that there go out year by year those streams of influence and of instruction that have contributed so powerfully to make the American people what they are.  Each one of these institutions is an act of faith. Each one of them has come into being because there have been men and women of vision with the spirit of generous sacrifice, who have believed that mankind could reach still greater heights of accomplishment and achievement, still higher measures of satisfaction and happiness, and still larger capacities for unselfishness and service.  The American college is not built upon knowledge;  it is built upon faith. Knowledge is its instrument, but faith is its motive power.

To-day we hail a new captain in the Army of Faith in the republic, as he takes his appointed place and sets his hand to the grave tasks of to-morrow.  These captains in the Army of Faith in the republic are a characteristic product of American life and of American opportunity. Europe, although many centuries older than we in educational endeavor and in educational experience, is still searching for ways and means to train and to make use of such officers. Government officials cannot occupy quite the same place as do these captains, chosen by their fellows and associates to the difficult and delicate task of leadership in a nation of free men. Rules and formulas cannot be devised to produce them. They must themselves be the offspring of our intellectual life and our intellectual endeavor, and they must stand or fall by their individual capacity, their individual competence, and their individual achievement. The history of American higher education for well-nigh a century is written largely in terms of the personalities, the strivings, and the accomplishments of these captains. Strike from our record the names of Wayland of Brown, Mark Hopkins of Williams, Seelye of Amherst, Tappan and Angell of Michigan, Anderson of Rochester, White of Cornell, Barnard of Columbia, McCosh of Princeton, Gilman of Johns Hopkins, Eliot of Harvard, and Harper of Chicago, and the history of American higher education would be meaningless.

The post to which you, sir, have been chosen is one of leadership but not of command. You will not be able, and if able you would not wish, to impose your own will upon your associates. You will, on the other hand, be the centre point for consultations and for the free meeting of sincere minds, in order that policies may be worked out and plans adopted to represent in fullest fashion the life and the purpose of this university.   Your task is an institutional one, not a personal one.   It is to give vitality and force and, when opportunity serves, to give voice to the hopes and the ideals of St. Lawrence University.   If my own years of experience in an office of similar character may serve as guide, I should say, using the language of the political life of Great Britain, that your duties would be those of a Prime Minister holding the portfolios of finance and of foreign affairs.   You will have to guide and to counsel both the teaching staff and the governing body of the corporation in adjusting means to ends, and you will have to oversee and largely to undertake the representation of the university and the extension of its influence beyond the limits of its home town.

I recall a striking story told by Mr. Gladstone which illustrates the sort of sagacity which gives to institutions, built by the life of the spirit, both permanence and force.   Shortly before the meeting of the Vatican Council, Mr. Gladstone, then a powerful figure in the life of England, was received in audience of Pope Pius IX.   In the course of the conversation between these two great men Mr. Gladstone asked His Holiness to what human agency or policy, if any, he attributed the permanence and the vitality of the Roman Catholic Church, which had seen the rise and fall of nations, the upbuilding and the overturning of dynasties, the discovery and settlement of new continents, and literally stupendous changes in the mental and moral life of men. Amidst all this the Roman Catholic Church had maintained its continuous life through many centuries, and Mr. Gladstone earnestly pressed his question as to how this had been possible. The answer of Pope Pius IX was this: The Roman Catholic Church owes its permanence and its vitality amidst all these striking changes to three things: the first of these is consultation; the second is consultation; the third is consultation.

This story teaches a highly practical lesson to everyone charged with the oversight and the care of an institution which springs from the life of the spirit. Its acts and its policies must be truly institutional and not merely individual if they are to continue in power and in influence. So it is the task of each captain in the Army of Faith in the republic to make use of consultation as a method and an instrument in the formulation of policies and in the expression of the institution's life. Through consultation lies the path of safety and of wisdom in the life of a university as in that of a church or a state.

## II

For what purpose is our Army of Faith in the republic recruited? Why do we so eagerly hail its marching battalions, cheer its flags, and honor its heroes? The answers to these questions reveal the stirrings and the strivings in our American life.

He is blind indeed who cannot see the unrest and

the dissatisfaction that are abroad in the land. In the face of the epoch-marking achievements of the American people since they became a nation, in the face of the increasing acceptance by other peoples of the principles upon which the American Republic is built, there are voices too numerous and too strident to be unheard or neglected who cry out in protest against America and in dissatisfaction with American principles and American ideals. These unhappy persons are constantly casting about for some new weapon of destruction with which to break down American accomplishment, in order to substitute for it some old and usually some mad form of political and social experimentation. Men and women who are so minded are usually mentally unbalanced, but whether mentally unbalanced or not they are so consumed by egotism and vanity as to fancy that a poor product of their own emotional life can take the place of the whole of human experience and the whole of human endeavor. What has really happened to these people is that they have lost their faith and they are once more striving in the impossible attempt to make the very limited knowledge of an individual do duty for the faith of a race. These persons are not willing to learn by experience, but perhaps the familiar story of St. Augustine might temper the ardor of their self-assurance. It is related of St. Augustine that while walking one day upon the shore at Ostia, meditating upon the intellectual doubts that withheld him from embracing Christianity, he suddenly perceived a child that with a shell was ladling the waters of the sea into a hole in the sand. "What are you doing, my child?" asked the saint. "I am emptying the ocean," was the reply, "into this hole." "That is impossible." "Not more impossible than for you to pour the universe into your intellect," said the child and vanished.

For civilization to continue and to advance, the knowledge of the individual must rest upon the experience and the faith of the race. This experience and this faith point with convincing clearness to individual liberty and the right of individual self-determination as the essential elements in a really advancing and constructive political, social, and industrial life. For liberty there is no possible substitute. Of opportunity there can be no successful imitation. Each human being, the seat of an immortal soul, has his own place in the world and is entitled to his own chance to make the most of himself. What he justly gains and saves is rightly his own, and private property, which alone makes possible industry, trade, commerce, and finance as we know them, is a part of liberty itself. The attempt to destroy the institution of private property is as reactionary an undertaking as can well be imagined. It is nothing less than a proposal to go back to the very beginnings of all civilization, and to try to compel the race to climb up again the hills and the mountains over which the procession of progress has been so painfully passing for centuries. What we need is more, and more widely distributed, property rather than less. The aim of a free state is to make every citizen a capitalist in the sense that it will give every citizen an opportunity to work, to save, and to employ his savings as he will. This is what we mean by liberty under law. This is the finest and highest ideal of government. To overthrow it, to weaken it, or to cast discredit upon it, is not progress but backward revolution.

### III

Colleges and universities are places where youth are assembled for training and for instruction in the truth and in high standards of appreciation and of action. The truth is not, as some academic wit has said, any lie that works, but something which is apprehended and comprehended by those who are able to draw a distinction between the right and the wrong, the true and the false. Those for whom there is no distinction between right and wrong but expediency, naturally can find no fixed distinction between truth and falsehood. Such are not safe or helpful teachers and guides. They have themselves something yet to learn before they may undertake to instruct others.

Open-mindedness is characteristic of the cultivated man, but by open-mindedness is not meant a mind that is open at both ends. All happenings are not matters of indifference, and all acts are not equally important or equally valuable. There are some things which rational and cultivated men exclude from discussion as long since definitely determined.  The individual's right to self-determination, for example, is not held to extend to the right to commit suicide.  So is it with the state.  Policies and methods of government are fit subject for discussion and for difference of opinion, but the question as to whether there shall be a government to maintain order, to protect liberty, and to assure justice between man and man, is no more debatable than is the right of the individual to commit suicide.

It is well to fix some of these fundamental facts in our minds, and when this is done we can better understand the importance of the great Army of Faith in the republic and the place which the captains in that army are called to occupy in the nation's life.  These captains are not appointed to tear down but to build up.  They are not selected to turn back the course of progress but to aid in pointing the way for new advance.

The American people have a faith in education that is both sublime and pathetic.  It is sublime because it reveals so fine a spirit and so noble a purpose.  It is pathetic in that it depends upon frail and feeble human instruments for its accomplishment.  If the schools and colleges of the country were so to conduct themselves as to shake the nation's faith in them and in education, the resulting crash would be heard all round the world.  Cynicism would displace confidence, faith would give way to despair.  But the schools and colleges will not fail. They have their points of weakness and they have had their unfortunate representatives and spokesmen. But, on the whole, and in overwhelming majority, they have been firm in the faith and worthy of the confidence which the American people have so richly bestowed upon them.

# XXII

# EDUCATION AFTER THE WAR

An address delivered before the Association of Colleges and
Preparatory Schools of the Middle States and Maryland
at Princeton, New Jersey, November 29, 1918

# EDUCATION AFTER THE WAR

The name of Lord Melbourne is not to be found in any of the histories of philosophy, but he was a good deal of a philosopher none the less. It was Lord Melbourne who said that it is tiresome to discuss education, tiresome to educate, and tiresome to be educated. Even one whose enthusiasm is not dampened after nearly forty years spent in the work of teaching and its oversight may smile in appreciative understanding of Lord Melbourne's cynicism. Whether to discuss education be tiresome or not, it is something which must just now be done, and something for which fatigue, if anticipated, must be endured.

Any one of imitative instincts and some acquaintance with letters might well hesitate at the rich choice of models offered him for procedure in discussing many aspects of the education of to-day. He might, for example, undertake to impale some present-day schoolroom theories and practices on a spear made in the shape of one of Dr. Johnson's crushing retorts; or he might attempt the wit and sarcasm of Dean Swift, or the self-satisfied and highly amusing, if painfully inconsequent, argumentation of Mr. Bernard Shaw. Then there is the vehement and intolerant endlessness of Mr. H. G. Wells, whose zeal for the lengthy discus-

369

sion of education appears to be in inverse ratio to his understanding of its chief purpose. Aristophanes, provided that his name, date, and place in literature have not wholly escaped attention, might suggest a yet different and most satisfactory method of presenting to an amused and interested world the foibles and follies of much that wears education's mask. Such a treatment as that, however, would call for a high type of genius and literary skill. No modern Aristophanes has as yet revealed himself.

The war has distinctly helped us. It has killed other things than human beings, and it has burnt up other things than towns, libraries, and churches. It has laid to rest some rather wide-spread illusions, and it has burnt up many sources and causes of intellectual, moral, and social waste. It has shortened by many years, perhaps by a generation, the path of progress to clearer, sounder, and more constructive thinking as to education, its processes, and its aims, than that which has occupied the centre of the stage for some dozen years past. We have been living in an era of reaction that has masqueraded as progress, and we have been witnessing energetic acts of destruction whose agents sang the songs and spoke the language of those who build. Chatter about education has been so prevalent that one has often had to wonder whether interest in real education and capacity for clear thinking concerning it had not entirely surrendered the field to the poisonous fumes of an irritant gas.

Part of what we have been living through and putting up with as best we could, has been due to a false psychology and part to a crude economics. The moral and spiritual values have been ground between the upper and nether millstones of a psychology without a soul and an economics with no vision beyond material gain. Most of the old and exploded fallacies of bygone centuries have been solemnly paraded before us in the trappings of new and highly important discoveries. We have been asked to doff our hats in salute to illusions of one sort or another that the world of intelligence found good reason to class as such long ago. Discipline was solemnly pronounced to be not only unnecessary, but impossible, although a hundred little disciplines are right enough. A general education or training—which goes back to the time when Socrates pointed out to Hippocrates the distinction between ἐπὶ Παιδείᾳ and ἐπὶ Τέχνῃ—has been shouldered aside, not because it has not been justified by centuries of experience but because it is not deemed sufficiently materialistic or gain-producing to be recognized as part of an educational theory that is strictly up to date. According to this newest philosophy, no such admirable virtue as thrift, for example, could be taught, but only the saving of ten-cent pieces or of dollar bills, or possibly of Liberty Bonds, as separate arts or vocations! Industry, honesty, loyalty, charity, and truthfulness have been ingenuously referred to as vague notions or catch-words that are very apt to delude the unwary—the unwary being probably the

unselfish. A sense of humor or a flash of common
sense, had either been present, might have saved us
from being obliged to listen to all this and to contem-
plate the ideal world as made up of highly competent
apple-polishers and pencil-sharpeners early trained
to their engrossing tasks, and vocationally guided to
be loyal and charitable to themselves alone.

What a sense of humor or a flash of common sense
did not intervene to accomplish, the war has done.
At a critical moment for the history of education in
the United States the German people found occasion
to reveal themselves to an astonished world as the
apostles and representatives of just this type of philosophy of education and of life. Psychology without
a soul has been a favorite German industry for a long
time, and organization for material gain has been the
ruling thought of the German people for quite thirty
years. On this form of psychology and on this form
of economics as a foundation the Germans erected
their superstructure of military autocracy, of insolent
aggression, and of lust for world domination. With
these they instantly challenged the rest of the world
to combat for its mastery. For months, even for years,
the issue hung uncertainly in the balance; but at last
the nations that had not surrendered their souls, the
nations that had not cast aside their moral and spiritual
ideals to bow down before the idol of material gain,
the nations that had not put efficiency above freedom,
brought down this proud and boasting Teutonic structure in the dust. Nothing in history that aimed so

high has ever fallen so low, and the effect upon the world's education ought to be, must be, instant and overwhelming. We ought now to be spared, at least for a time, the vexing spectacle of men in places of authority in education and in letters who spend their time standing in front of the convex mirror of egotism thinking that what they see reflected in it is a real world and their own exact relation to it.

The war has taught the lesson that the proper place of efficiency is as the servant of a moral ideal, and that efficiency apart from a moral ideal is an evil and a wicked instrument which in the end can accomplish only disaster. Belgium and Serbia, measured by Teutonic standards, were inefficient; France was not only inefficient but decadent; Great Britain was not only inefficient but on the point of disruption; and America was not only inefficient but hopelessly given over to pleasure and to gain. True it is that no one of these nations had kept its ideals as clear and as sharply defined as it should have done; but the ideals were there none the less. Long experience of freedom had made safe and well-protected resting-places for those aims and purposes and convictions which have always shaped, and will always shape, the upward movement of men. Therefore it was that when the attack was made these ideals sprang from their hiding-places and took command of the apparently unorganized and inefficient nations. Meanwhile, organized efficiency, immoral and brutal, was hammering at their doors. The free nations held the enemy until their ideals could call their own efficiency and power of organization into play as servants, and when that had been accomplished the end was in sight. That end has now come with a suddenness and a completeness that no one would have dared foretell.

When we turn from the war to its lessons for education, we not only miss the point entirely but we make a criminal blunder if we infer that the war teaches us to imitate Germany in any particular. On the contrary, the war teaches us to avoid Germany and to cling to those principles and purposes that have made France and Great Britain and the United States. Our American common sense had protected us from many of the ill effects that would have followed the more general adoption of he philosophy of education which was being urged upon us, and which had found many votaries wherever teachers are trained or discuss their training. It is time now to consider how we can best move forward to the re-establishment of truer values and sounder processes in American education.

The first step is to ask again, and in terms of present-day experience, what may be the meaning of education, and what knowledge is of most worth. If we would hearken to those who have just now been urgently asking to guide us, we should have to say that education is apparently the art of conducting the human mind from an infantile void to an adolescent vacuum, emphasis being laid upon self-interest while the transition is going on. Perhaps, however, we should do better to insist that education is a process of body-building, spirit-building, and institution-building, in which process skilful and well-interpreted use is made of the recorded experience of the human race, of the capacities, tastes, and ambitions of the individual, and of the problems and circumstances of the world in which he at the moment lives. The purpose of this body-building, spirit-building, and institution-building is not simply to strengthen and perpetuate what others have found to be useful and good, but rather by building upon that to carry both the individual and the race farther forward in their progress toward fuller self-expression and more complete self-realization. To attempt to turn education into a merely mechanical process, with a purely gainful end, is nothing short of treason to the highest, most uplifting, and most enduring human interests.

So soon as we fix clearly in our own minds the meaning of education, and not until then, we are in position to answer the question as to what knowledge is of most worth. We can then see that that knowledge is of most worth which best furnishes and disciplines the human spirit, which best nourishes and strengthens the human body, and which best contributes to an understanding and improvement of human institutions. Given these standards, the process of applying them becomes one of good judgment and practical sagacity.

Regarding man in his capacity as a self-directing

individual, there are three fundamental aspects of civilization that have continuing and permanent significance. To each of these three aspects massive contributions were made by the ancient Greeks, who were the first to distinguish and to recognize them, as well as to give them their names, and massive contributions have been made by all that vast human experience which lies between the time of the Greeks and our own time. These fundamental aspects are Ethics, the doctrine of conduct and service; Economics, the doctrine of gainful occupation; and Politics, the doctrine of reconciliation between the two and of living together in harmony and helpfulness.

These are the three subjects which must lie at the heart of an effective education which has learned the lessons of the war. To these all other forms of instruction are either introductory and ancillary, or complementary and interpretative. Literature, history, art, and philosophy will continue to preside over them all, and to offer the largest and most inviting opportunity for the rarest and best-furnished spirits unforgetably to serve their kind. One Shakespeare, one Gibbon, one Michael Angelo, one Aristotle, are worth a thousand years of human waiting and human travail.

The doctrine of conduct and service will include the study of both personal and social ideals, as well as the discipline and the precepts that will promote their accomplishment. The doctrine of conduct cannot be one of selfishness, of greed, or of exploitation if it be constantly combined with the doctrine of service.

Those very qualities and characteristics which we have lately been told cannot be inculcated, such as loyalty, charity, truthfulness, are to be unceasingly enjoined, taught, and exemplified. The individual is to be made more self-regarding only that he may have more to give in service. His individual personality is to be kept before him as something very precious, but as something not complete until it is enriched by his relationships and interdependences with others.

The doctrine of gainful occupation will include both the means and the end of activity for self-support and self-dependence. It will, when a stage of adequate maturity is reached, add to the general knowledge and general discipline of the individual that special knowledge and special discipline which will enable him to relate himself to the productive activity of the world at some specific and useful point in some definite and useful way; but the steps toward the achievement of this aim will be constantly interpreted in the light of a far higher purpose than that of mere gain or accumulation. The close relationship between the doctrine of conduct and service and the doctrine of gainful occupation, will be steadily emphasized and illustrated.

The doctrine of reconciliation between Ethics and Economics will include the study of how men have attempted to find ways and means of living together in harmony and helpfulness, how far they have succeeded, in what respects and to what extent they have failed, and how they may carry forward the great experiment of their own time to still more fortunate results by making Ethics, Economics, and Politics not three distinct and mutually exclusive or contradictory disciplines, but rather three aspects of one and the same discipline, which is that of human life, its highest achievement and its ripest fruit. The study of education from this view-point will put behind it the German-made psychology without a soul, and the German-made economics with nothing higher than gain as its end.

The care and protection of the public health will hereafter assume new importance. Preventive medicine, which has made great strides in recent years, is only at the beginning of its history. The physician and the nurse will shortly be looked upon as educational factors quite as important as the teacher himself. Care for the public health will not content itself with the mere inspection of children and youth in school and college, or with the care and cure of definite disease. It will establish a relationship between home conditions, school conditions, and work conditions. It will have helpful advice to give, both general and specific, as to diet and exercise, and it will insist that neither at home, in school, nor at work shall children and adolescent youth be subjected to conditions that impair their bodies as well as starve their souls.

There will be much more attention paid to the determination of individual differences of taste and capacity, and to making provision for them. This is a

point at which a sound psychology can render greatly
increased service to educational practice. The object
of this determination is to prevent waste of effort, the
loss of opportunity, and the blunting of talent by trying to sharpen it upon the wrong whetstone. The
different tastes and capacities of children often reveal
themselves with great plainness through their different reactions to one and the same study or occupation.
A danger to guard against is lest waste be not diminished but increased through trying to determine definitely upon these individual differences too soon, and
before the youth has been brought in contact with
some forms of intellectual interest and employment
which might well touch unsuspected springs hidden
in his nature.

Despite the vast expenditure of the past fifty years
for equipment and teaching in the natural sciences, the
people at large, including those secondary school and
college graduates who have studied one or more natural
sciences for a longer or shorter time, are in practical
ignorance of them. We have succeeded in training
some eminent chemists, physicists, and biologists, but
we have not made chemistry, physics, and biology part
of the mental furniture of persons who are called educated, largely because we have insisted upon going the
wrong way about it. The popular American text-
books in chemistry and in physics are almost without
exception examples of how those subjects should not
be taught, while the popular text-books in biological
subjects are only a little better. The best text-books

in geology and astronomy are more wisely made. The teachers of all these sciences have almost uniformly proceeded as if every student who came under their influence was to become a specialist in their particular science. They have mistaken the training of scientists for the teaching of science. They have insisted upon confounding the logical with the psychological order in the presentation of new material to the youthful mind, and they have assumed that in order to gain a knowledge of one of these sciences the individual must travel over again the road taken by preceding generations but in somewhat symbolic and highly concentrated form. If these sciences are ever really to form part of the mental furniture of our people, they must be taught not through compelling every student to follow painfully their experimental processes and determinations, but through demonstrating and interpreting established facts, thus bringing the student to realize why they are true and how they were proved, through associating great discoveries and advances with the names and personalities of those who have made them, and through putting emphasis upon the human interest, the human relationship of that theoretical and practical knowledge which is included in the term natural science. The academic teachers of these subjects are, however, usually so wedded to their idols that there does not appear to be much likelihood of a quick reform and the establishment of better methods of teaching. These must wait upon a more general appreciation of the difference between the method of discovery and the method of exposition. For admirable and persuasive examples of the method of exposition one need look no further than Professor Huxley's lecture to the workingmen of Norwich on a piece of chalk or Professor Tyndall's lecture on magnetism to the teachers of the primary schools of London.

Substantially the same thing may be said about instruction in foreign language. Greek and Latin have been in large degree asphyxiated by wholly wrong-headed methods of teaching, and French and German are a sad spectacle to look upon. Intelligent youths who have spent three, four, and five years on the study of one or both of these languages, can neither speak them easily nor understand them readily nor write them correctly. Here, too, as in the case of the natural sciences, the reason is to be found in wrong methods of teaching. It is a sorry commentary as to what is going on in our secondary schools and colleges in this respect to learn on the best authority that there are now in France at least two hundred thousand American young men, who, after six months of military activity in France and three or four hours of instruction a week in the French language, can carry on a comfortable conversation under ordinary conditions and circumstances with the mastery of a vocabulary of at least a thousand words. On the other hand, many an American college graduate who has studied French for years is as awkward and as nonplussed in a Paris drawing-room as he would be in the driver's seat of an airplane. There will hereafter be marked impatience with the notion that one may spend an indefinite amount of time upon a foreign language without hoping or expecting either to speak it easily or to understand it comfortably. The notion that boys and girls are to study a foreign language as an end in itself or with a view to becoming grammarians or philologists must be given up. The purpose in studying a foreign language is to gain sufficient practical mastery of it for use in daily intercourse, and so to obtain some comprehension of the life, the institutions, and the modes of thought of the people whose language it is. French is not only the universal language of diplomacy but it is the common link between educated men and women the world over. It is of the first importance that American schools and colleges should teach French, teach it practically and in the spirit and for the purpose that have just been described. The teaching of Spanish, of Italian, and of German will naturally be for similar purposes and on similar lines.

For nearly a generation past American education has laid the greatest emphasis upon the study of the English language and literature, and this is as it should be. In one important respect, however, damage has been and is being done, and again the cause is to be found in a wrong method of teaching. The idea is prevalent that the best way to improve the written English of students is to compel them to write constantly and on all sorts of topics. This is a fallacy.

The inventor of the daily theme did an almost incalculable amount of damage when he started a movement that rapidly spread all over the United States. The one best way in which to teach students to write good English is to teach them to read good English. He who constantly reads the best English and also the best French, the best Latin, and the best Greek, and who writes occasionally and when he has something to say, will have a far better written style than he who pours out a few hundred words five times a week on diverse topics as to most of which he has no knowledge and little interest. The waste of time through excessive devotion to English composition is very great and is not likely to be patiently borne much longer. The daily writing is obnoxious to the student and the inspection and correction of their work is drudgery for the teacher uncompensated by any adequate result. That those who write daily themes and whose written work is carefully corrected, make technical improvements in their written style goes without saying, but the fact remains that the method is a wasteful and inefficient one and that the path to good writing leads through good reading. If there is to be such a thing as good reading, proposals such as that the English of the Bible should be turned into what is called the vernacular must be given short shrift. To hear the English of the Bible spoken of as "a beautiful and unfamiliar dialect which was spoken three centuries ago," because it happens to be beyond the immediate comprehension of some ignoramus who reads a writer or a book called Nick Carter and the newspapers, is sufficient to upset the equanimity of a saint. We shall probably next be told that it is found desirable to supply the plays of Shakespeare with descriptive and enticing headlines after the fashion of the last editions of the metropolitan evening papers. There would appear to be no limit to human folly.

There has been for some time past a considerable amount of time and energy devoted to the study of government and politics in secondary schools and colleges. Unfortunately, however, most of this time and energy have been given over to the study of the machinery and the details of government rather than to a comprehension of the principles upon which good government and republican institutions rest. The responsibilities of citizenship increase day by day and have been multiplied by the effects and results of the war. There is double need, therefore, of training the youth of to-day who are to be the men and women of to-morrow in the fundamental principles of good citizenship and in a knowledge of those rights, duties, and opportunities, national and international, which constitute the elements of the world's organized life. How many members of Congress there may be, what their terms and what their compensation, are facts of slight importance compared with an understanding of the reasons for the existence of a Congress, of its powers and duties, and of the ways in which and the purposes for which its functions have been fulfilled for one hundred and forty years. As has already been suggested, a true theory of politics will supplement and unite a good understanding of both ethics and economics.

The swing of the pendulum away from interest in the ancient classics has plainly come to its end. There are many signs that a deeper insight and a wider sympathy are manifesting themselves, and that during the next generation the classical languages and literatures will be more earnestly pursued and better taught than they have been in the recent past. It is not practicable to use the classics directly in any plan of wide-spread popular elementary and secondary education, but it is entirely practicable for that education to be carried on with full appreciation of the importance of the classics and with full understanding of the lessons which they teach and of the standards which they set up. The classics remain the unexhausted and inexhaustible fountains of excellence in all that pertains to letters, to art, and to the intellectual life. The secondary schools and the colleges must make adequate provision for their study and their proper teaching. Those in whose keeping the classics are placed must fix their minds much more on matters of human interest, human conduct, and human feeling, and much less on matters of technical linguistic accuracy and skill.

It is worth remembering that the educational ideals of modern France are drawn from the classical tradition and are shaped under classical influence, and that the French are probably the best-educated people in the world. Only recently the French minister of public instruction and of fine arts told in a public address an anecdote of a student in the University of Montpellier, who overheard one evening in the trenches the conversation of his men: "I," said one, "am fighting for my fields of grain;" "I," said another, "am fighting for my wife and children;" and "I," said the third, "am fighting for my mountains." Then the young officer said gravely, "I am fighting for La Fontaine and Molière; La Fontaine the immortal heir of Æsop and of Phædrus; Molière the immortal heir of Plautus and of Terence, and still farther of Aristophanes and of Menander." This young lieutenant knew well both how to live and how to die, for the beauty of the world and of man's achievement in it had seized hold of his soul.

In an industrial age like that in which we are living and are likely to continue to live, it is little short of monstrous that there is so slight a direct relationship between formal education and industry. Fully thirty years ago a well-organized and clearly defined movement was undertaken in the United States to bring the fundamental and elementary industrial processes into use as general educational instrumentalities. Largely as a result of the Russian exhibit at the Centennial Exposition of 1876 in Philadelphia and at the Paris Exposition of 1878, the attention of American teachers was drawn to a practical method of using the elementary principles of the mechanical arts as subjects of school instruction and training. Sound physiological, psychological, and economic arguments were urged for this step and some headway was made toward accomplishing the end which the reformers of that day had in view. Despite some distinct successes here and there and despite the soundness of the principles on which the movement was based, it failed to establish itself generally for a variety of reasons which need not here be detailed. For one thing, the movement was somewhat in advance of the public opinion of the moment and to be in advance of public opinion is quite as fatal to any new departure as to be behind public opinion. There is every reason now why this subject should be taken up anew and why those general educational instrumentalities that have done such yeoman's work for generations should be supplemented by new instrumentalities designed particularly to train the hand, the eye, the power of co-ordinating the two, and the constructive capacity of youth in ways that will eventually add to the economic usefulness of the individual and to the economic advantage of the community. It is specially important, by linking handwork with capacity, artistry, and understanding, to restore that joy in the job with its resulting satisfactions both individual and social which mass-work and highly specialized industry have combined as largely to destroy. It is not likely that the importance of education to creative industry and the importance of creative industry to education will longer be disregarded.

On the other hand, the elementary school must be brought back to its proper business, neglect of which has been general and much remarked for years past. The elementary school, being well organized and universal, has been seized upon by faddists and enthusiasts of every type as an instrumentality not for better education but for accomplishing their own particular ends. The simple business of training young children in good habits of exercise and in good habits of conduct, of teaching them the elementary facts of the nature which surrounds them, and of giving them ability to read understandingly, to write legibly, and to perform quickly and with accuracy the fundamental operations with numbers, has been rudely pushed into the background by all sorts of enterprises from lectures on the alleged evil effects of alcohol and tobacco to the sale of War Savings Stamps. It may be necessary one of these days to organize a society for the protection of the elementary school in order that that indispensable institution may have an opportunity to mind its own proper business.

Vigorous steps must be taken promptly to make the teaching profession more attractive to men of high competence and ambition. While administrative officers are still frequently more or less dependent upon political or other conditions which should not be permitted to influence educational organization and work, teachers as a body, whether in school or in college, are so secure in their tenure as to constitute a highly privileged class. The politician and the intriguer must be taught not to concern himself with the office of superintendent of schools or with the organization and direction of educational work. Mere security of tenure does not, however, attract the highest type of person to any branch of public service. What must be added to a tenure whose security is absolute so long as competence accompanies it, is opportunity for individual initiative and enterprise and an adequate wage. Not only must the wages of teachers be very greatly increased, but the prizes of the profession, those conspicuous, influential, and well-paid posts that are freely open to talent, must be multiplied both in number and in importance. The ambitious and high-spirited man will be drawn to education as a career, and held in it, so soon as he finds that it offers him an opportunity for reputation and for usefulness that is commensurate with his ambition and his capacity.

By the mere force of inertia there will be a tendency for schoolmasters to lapse back into old habits, old routine, and old methods when the present emotional stimulus is withdrawn. In the name and in the hope of true progress and of learning the lessons of experience, this tendency must be avoided and combated. The new world into which we are so rapidly moving will be built upon the old world which it displaces, and it will gather into itself all of the lessons of that old world's experience while resolutely throwing away its dross. Unless all signs fail it will be a world of vigorous individual activity, of large opportunity for

initiative and accomplishment, and of constantly increasing co-operation for high purposes between individuals, between groups, and between nations. After
all that may be said in sharp criticism of American
school and college education in the past two decades,
it remains true that the American people, and particularly the American soldiers, have shown themselves
capable of the most striking accomplishments in the
shortest time through the possession of almost unequalled initiative, resourcefulness, and zeal for service. What may not be expected of such a people,
and, if the need ever come again, of such soldiers, if
their theory and practice of education are all that they
should be? One's imagination hesitates to attempt
to measure the capacity of one hundred millions of
thoroughly well-educated, well-trained, and well-dis-
ciplined American men and women. Yet nothing
short of this should be the aim of American educational
policy. That policy as it steadily advances to newer
and higher levels of ambition and accomplishment
must not fall a victim to the temptations of that egotism which regards the affairs of the passing moment
as of such importance to the world's history and of
such significance for the world's future as to justify
contempt for all that has gone before. That policy
will succeed if it remains steadfast in its republican
faith and if it continues to prefer the solid foundations
and noble ideals of the American republic to the
crude and undemocratic devices that are urged in
its stead.

# INDEX

# INDEX

393